# Walking Between Worlds

# Belonging to None

By Ann Andrews

Walking Between Worlds, Belonging to None by Ann Andrews
Copyright© 2007 by Reality Press
All rights reserved.

Reality Press
An imprint of Reality Entertainment, Inc.

For information contact:

REALITY ENTERTAINMENT
P.O. Box 91
Foresthill, CA 95631

ph: 530-367-5389, fx: 530-367-3024

www.reality-entertainment.com

ISBN: 0-9791750-3-8

# DEDICATION

FOR ALL THE CHILDREN
WHO ARE HERE TO TEACH, ASSIST
AND GUIDE US INTO A NEW REALITY.

# CONTENTS

# INTRODUCTION

My name is Ann Andrews. I am happily married to Paul and have been for the past 29 years. We have two grown up sons; Daniel, who is now 27, and Jason, 23. I grew up in South East London and had a very normal and ordinary upbringing. Ordinary is how I would describe myself - except that I have had to learn to cope with extraordinary situations and events over the years, which all started when Jason was born.

We now know without a shadow of a doubt that our youngest son, Jason, is a multiple alien abductee and a 'Star Child', or 'Indigo'. This wasn't something we readily accepted, and we looked for answers elsewhere for the strange things that were happening to him and to our family.

We have taken Jason to see psychiatrists, psychologists, child behaviourists, and many other doctors searching for a rational explanation for everything. Jason has been in and out of hospitals and clinics; undergone tests for sleep epilepsy, brain malfunction, etc., and all tests proved negative. We put a lot of faith in the medical profession; we wanted someone to come up with the problem and the cure. All we ever got was confirmation that there is absolutely nothing wrong with him - either physically or mentally. We still have the letter from the psychiatrist stating that our son is not psychotic; therefore, his accounts of what happens to him and his story - which has not altered since he was first able to talk - is the truth. We were, eventually, grudgingly forced to accept the real truth of our still ongoing situation.

My greatest regret in all of this is the fact that it took me 12 years to finally accept what was happening to our son. As parents, we were always there for him in the way that most parents are - to hold him when he would run screaming about his "nightmares," but I couldn't believe what he was telling me - my social upbringing would not allow me to believe such things, even though I had no other explanation.

At this writing, Jason is now 23 years old, yet whenever he is asked if he has one memory in all of this which stands out, he will always answer "the day my Mum and Dad said that they did believe me.

To write any book referring to UFOs and aliens is always difficult for the topic always seems to get categorized with science fiction - general headings which sometimes encompass flaky and unbelievable topics. The UFO subject is guilty by association. Becoming serious about the alien presence requires a long, careful process, and it is underway.

A slow, steady stream of documentaries have aired on television. The now-familiar figure of the alien "grey" has become integrated into our terrestrial television advertisements - albeit tongue in cheek - but it is there, and books on the subject are much more abundant. The truth is trickling out there as it is meant to do. There has been no panic, just acceptance that maybe there is life "out there" after all and that maybe it is benevolent.

However, the powers that be here on Earth have moved to stop this peaceful UFO concept - block-busting films were released that portrayed aliens as the enemy ("Independence Day" springs readily to mind). Television programs soon followed suit, and, even when portrayed as human-looking beings, the aliens were always hostile and hell bent on destroying the human race so that they could take over the planet.

The powers that be got the response that they wanted from the public in general - the UFO/alien issue is again something to fear. The reason is simply that if the general public is afraid of something, then they will look to their governments to guide them - to lead them - to tell them what to do - and to give away their personal power so that their leaders will protect them. Governments need to keep up the fear so that they will always be seen by their constituents "to be in complete control." One of the major unwritten rules of top politicians is to firstly, create the situation, then get the public up in arms about said situation, then finally, offer the solution. Result? Overwhelming appreciation from the public, who will have no hesitation in voting said politician into office as he "gets things done." Simple and effective.

So, now consider what would happen to the powers that be if aliens and UFOs were discovered to be friendly and trying to help this planet. In effect, governments would become powerless. People would flock to the visitors - the governments would have no control - and there would be no need for military domination, because there would be no enemy. This scenario would never be allowed to become reality. Then another question poses itself: why then do the visitors not just land en masse on the White House lawn and announce their good intent? Because not everyone on the planet would be able to cope with that. While it's true that a lot of people today are becoming psychically aware and open to such things existing, there are still many millions throughout the world who aren't. Maybe the shock would be too much for them - panic would take over, and violence would probably ensue. No, the slow release of information on the existence of benign beings from another world is the key and is working quite well.

So, how does any of this involve us?

Like a lot of other people, we know without a doubt what is going on regarding the alien agenda. Things happen around this issue almost on a daily basis. Its first intrusion into our lives was met with a lot of skepticism then as it became more apparent, confusion set in, then gradually came a grudging acceptance. We didn't embrace this bizarre disruption to our lives, but rather accepted it because we had no other choice.

We had no idea where all this was leading us and how our youngest son, Jason, would develop - with "their" help - to become what he is now - a powerful psychic with amazing healing abilities. He has been allowed to travel astrally through time and space to this planet and many others. The spiritual world has been laid bare to him, as have various dimensions of our own planet, and therefore, he has much knowledge of this world and of others. He has - in his own words - now been "awakened" by "them" to the truth of who he really is - to the fact that he - Jason - is of ET origin.

Our hope is that this book can help others going through similar traumas of becoming a multidimensional family. The earlier the acceptance comes, the easier and more peaceful life becomes. The more parents can really accept their children's capabilities, experiences and most importantly - what they have to teach us - the faster this planet will evolve to its inevitable union with the greater galactic benevolence that has cradled us for centuries. It is time for us to begin.

# ONE
## THE BIRTHDAY PARTY

It was almost the end of a hot, sticky day in July, 1987, when Jason finally collapsed into sleep on the couch in the living room. It had been an exhausting and
exciting day for our youngest son; his first proper birthday party. Hours earlier,
our little farm cottage in Kent had been filled with excited, chattering children
all there to celebrate Jason's fourth birthday. Now, my husband Paul, Mum, and
I relished a few moments of peace and tranquility whilst we relaxed and sipped
our well-earned cups of tea. A storm was threatening outside, and Mum commented that we could do with the rain, as she draped her coat over her grandson in case he was chilly. Suddenly, there was a loud banging on our front door
- urgent and insistent. We all looked at each other, puzzled as to who it could be
- after all, it was quite late at night. The banging continued and Paul rose to answer it. However, as soon as his hands touched the door, the banging ceased. He
opened the door, but there was no one there. He peered up and down the lane,
which led only to our cottage. The gathering storm made the evening appear
even darker than usual, but Paul could see no sign of anyone about. He closed
the door and stepped back into the living room when there was a great crack of
thunder, louder than we had ever heard before. It was swiftly followed by distant
rumblings, which built into swelling crescendos that sounded as if each roll were
breaking right over our cottage. The noise was so great that for a moment we
forgot all about the knocking at the door.

The intensity of the storm had awakened Daniel, our older son, who had been
asleep in his bedroom. He appeared at the foot of the stairs sleepily rubbing his
eyes and climbed onto his grandmother's lap. Jason slept on, oblivious to the
storm.

Again there was a flash of lightning so fierce in intensity that even Paul, a big,
unflappable man, jumped. Then, as if on cue, Jason sat bolt upright, sending

5

Mum's coat sliding to the floor. Both the big Pyrenean Mountain dogs whined and cowered together under the dining table. Jason was staring, eyes open but oblivious to the room and the people in it. He opened his mouth and started to talk, pouring out an incredible stream of numbers - fantastic numbers, huge numbers, strange algebraic configurations, mathematical terms like "pi" and "binary codes" all spewed out of the mouth of this four-year-old boy who normally struggled to count up to ten.

The loud banging at the door began again. Then it seemed to come from the window, then all the windows and doors at the same time, and the whole cottage seemed to shake to its very foundations.

Paul grabbed the phone to dial 999 (emergency 911 in England). Nothing happened. He had the dialling tone but the emergency digits would not register. He tried again, and after a third attempt he threw the phone down in fear and temper. Mum and I looked to Paul and, sensing that he should be in control, he began to stride toward the door. However, just as suddenly as he had started, Jason stopped talking. At exactly the same moment, the banging ceased. Then Jason slid from the couch and, still in a trancelike state, walked towards the door. Paul put his hands on Jason's shoulders, gently restraining him. "Where are you going, boy?" Paul asked. "It's pouring down outside. You'll get soaked."

Jason looked up at his dad and replied in a strange, emotionless voice: "They're waiting for me. I have to go."

As soon as he spoke, the violent knocking began again. Mum was crying uncontrollably. Terrified, I grabbed hold of Daniel and held him tight to me - a talisman of normality. Jason meanwhile had pulled free of Paul's light hold and was heading towards the door again. In desperation, Paul whisked him up into his arms and began shaking him gently but forcefully, commanding him to "snap out of it." At first, Jason fought harder to get down, and the knocking grew louder and stronger, reverberating throughout the house. Then, Jason blinked his eyes, and Paul, sensing the turn in the tide, gently slapped him, talking to him all the time.

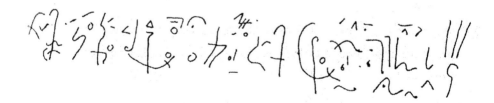

**Jason wrote pages of these symbols when he was young.**

Gradually, Jason woke up, and as he did so, the knocking receded, dying out completely when Jason looked at his dad and innocently asked if he could watch television. Within minutes, the two boys, in matching Batman pajamas, were in their favorite positions, lying in front of the television set, as if nothing had happened. Mum went into the kitchen to put the kettle on for more tea - her way of coping with all eventualities. The two dogs emerged from their hiding place and patrolled the room, enormous tails wagging, before settling down next to the boys. No one said anything; I just looked at Paul. He reached for the phone again, and this time was able to get through to the police. He told them about the knocking, and they promised to get a car round as soon as possible. As Paul was trying to explain events to them, he was overwhelmed by the impossibility of making sense of it all.

The police arrived a few minutes later, and Paul went through what had happened - without mentioning Jason's part in it. The two officers and Paul went outside with a flashlight to look for signs of damage to the doors and windows or disturbance to the garden. "It's the oddest thing," said the older of the two policemen as he stood framed in the doorway so as not to walk mud onto the carpets, "but there's no sign of anyone being about - not one single footprint in the mud. With all this rain, you'd think there would be footprints."

This was not the first event of this kind. Strange and inexplicable events have surrounded Jason since he was born on July 2nd, 1983, but it took 12 years before we had any lead on what was happening to our family - and to Jason especially. At first, it was an explanation that we could not accept: it was so far fetched, so incredible, so outside anything we had ever considered that Paul and I refused to believe it. However, the more we found out, both about Jason's experiences and those of others in similar situations, the more we realized that our son's problems exactly fit this theory.

Jason was born in Queen Mary's Hospital in Sidcup, Kent. Throughout the pregnancy, my doctor was extremely worried about me. When our older son Daniel was born, everything went perfectly, so there was no reason to think that having a second child wouldn't be the same. Although there were no real problems as such with this second baby, I found that I was being advised to take a lot of bed rest and expend very little exertion when I was allowed to be upright! Then, the expected date of the birth arrived and passed, and we soon found that the baby was well overdue. Finally they decided to take me into the hospital and help it along. I wasn't too worried, as Daniel had been two weeks late and, as Paul always jokes, throughout my life I have rarely been early or on time for anything; I was even late for my own wedding!

The labor didn't go at all well, and I was put on a drip and hooked up to a fetal monitor to check on the unborn baby's heartbeat. From then on, things got worse. The staff seemed to erupt into panic calling for a doctor as it became clear that the machine, which had been picking up a weak heartbeat, was no longer picking up any heartbeat. Although I was oblivious to this at the time, our baby was expected to be born with serious problems - if not stillborn. Paul had asked the nursing staff not to mention anything to me. He felt that I had enough to contend with, and any further upset at that stage was unnecessary.

I was rushed to another room with a doctor attending and an incubator ready. I was given so many drugs that I wasn't even sure what day it was, let alone know what was happening. The cries of "push" and "no, stop pushing" faded into the background, and even though I was managing to follow their instructions, it was more or less as if I were in some sort of dream state. However, the panicked staff where soon all delighted - and very surprised - when Jason arrived. He had jet-black hair and an exceptionally strong cry. They wrapped him in a blanket and laid him next to me. Two of the nurses were discussing how beautiful he looked - for a boy - and that he was a miracle baby, as he needed no further assistance from the vast assortment of machinery on standby. Paul was delighted with the new addition to our young family, but Daniel expressed his feelings - that he would have preferred another puppy to a baby brother! My parents were delighted, too though from then on my dad would always refer to Jason as his "little papoose" because he always said that Jason looked so dark - especially with his beautiful black hair - that he reminded him of a Native American baby.

In our elation, we had all forgotten about the fetal monitor, but when we saw a maintenance man wheeling it away, we assumed that it was broken or faulty. It wouldn't be until many years later that we would find out what really happened that day.

A few weeks after Jason was born we put him in his own cot in his own bedroom, and that is when mysterious things started to happen. When he cried, I would go into his room to find him either at the wrong end of his cot or underneath it. On a few occasions, I found him elsewhere in the room - under a chair, or behind the door. Paul and I supposed that Daniel was the culprit and that it might have been a little bit of jealousy for his new baby brother. Although only four years old at the time, we assumed that if he stood on a chair and really stretched, then yes, it was possible for Daniel to pick up the baby. Even though our oldest son strongly denied that he would do anything like that, our social upbringing forbade us to look at any other possibility as that would mean looking into paranormal reasons, and we would never allow ourselves to do that. There were even at least a couple of times when Daniel was at Mum's house for the day, yet Jason would still be moved from his cot. I pondered over this and tried to discuss it with Paul when he got home from work, but Paul with his Newtonian view of the world, refused to discuss it, telling me that I must have made some kind of mistake. Strange things did not and would not be allowed to invade our normal lives. Even the incident that happened at Jason's birthday party four years later would be rationalized to suit Paul's way of thinking: The knocking had been nothing more than thunder; the intense lights were just lightning; and Jason was just dreaming and then sleepwalking. That was all there would be to that incident. It would never be open for discussion.

Try as I might to rationalize these strange events with the baby being moved, I found that I never could. However, after a few months; this stopped happening, and I went back to convincing myself that indeed it must have been Daniel and that he had just grown tired of his game.

All was quiet after that - except for the fact of Daniel having his "imaginary friend" around late at night. He even described him to me one day. "He was taller than Daddy, with light blonde hair, big blue eyes and was dressed in a white, but sometimes shiny, all in one space suit." There were some nights when I would hear Daniel giggling and chatting in his bedroom, but he would always stop as I entered and then greet me with the words "Aw, mum, you've frightened Junus away - again."

After the strange events of the fourth birthday party, we began to notice that the house seemed to change. We would hear strange noises during the night; furniture would be moved around by the next morning; electrical equipment had a mind of its own, and strange lights would appear in and around the house. There were also strange smells - something like burnt sugar. Added to all of this were Jason's nightmares. This time there was no denying the activity, but I found it easy to accept - and explain. When I was a child, my dad always said that we had a friendly ghost who lived in our house as, there too, things would go bump in the night and objects would be moved around. So, to make him seem less frightening, Dad had nicknamed the "friendly" ghost from my own childhood Charley. Charley, I remembered, had been up to the same sort of mischief as our "ghost." To me this was acceptable, as again, our social upbringing made it okay for us to believe in ghosts and spirits, so we accepted that all the paranormal behavior was the work of our own ghost, and it seemed appropriate to name him Charley, too. After all, our house was more than a hundred years old, so why shouldn't it have its share of spirits from the past? Daniel readily accepted Charley's antics and boasted of him to his friends. Jason was always terrified.

Jason's nightmares continued on and off over the next eight years. Sometimes he would have these nightmares for weeks at a time - sometimes months. Then we would all savor the quiet periods when he would be free of these terrible "dreams" for several months at a time. The only constant in all of this was that they would always return and the scenario was always the same - small "people" would instantly appear in his room, followed by a taller "person," sometimes a couple of them. Jason's next recollection was of being in a hospital awaiting surgery on a big, high table in the middle of the room. He would always feel cold and would find that he was unable to move at all - except for his eyes, which would record the whole terrifying incident.

Jason was 12 years old when we were finally given our first real clue as to the possible truth behind our son's nighttime misery.

The revelation about Jason's nightmares came to us one evening when we were watching television. It was one of those debate programs where the audience had a contribution to make. It was a debate about the use of hypnosis - as entertainment, or as a tool to help people overcome addictions such as smoking or to help conquer real but unfounded fears, like the fear of flying or of spiders. The audience joined in with the experts and voiced their opinions, which were as varied as the subjects. Finally, they began to discuss the use of hypnosis to re-cover hidden memories. A man in his forties explained how he had been driving his normal route home from work one evening, a journey of 35 minutes, but on this particular occasion, it took three hours and 20 minutes. He had no explana-tion for what had happened in the extra two hours and 45 minutes, but since the mysterious time loss, he had developed inexplicable mood swings, depressions and an irrational fear of the dark. In the end, he had visited a hypnotherapist in order to recover his memories of the lost time. The program was just beginning to explore what happened at his hypnotherapy sessions when, without warning, Jason leapt to his feet and launched a china ornament at the television set. He missed but the ornament exploded on impact with the video recorder, shattering into a thousand pieces.

Paul angrily demanded to know what was going on, and as Jason turned to face him, tears were coursing down his face. His breath caught between sobs. "That man on there is so stupid, so stupid! He should be glad he can't remember. He should leave it like that because I can remember. I remember everything. I'm scared. They won't leave me alone. Why can't they leave me alone?" And with that, he fled the room.

We sat there stunned, trying to make sense of what had just happened. It was Daniel who spoke first, "Do you still not understand?" He spoke with barely disguised contempt for us. "This guy on the telly was abducted - by aliens. Don't you both get it yet?" At 16, Daniel was four years older than Jason and rarely got involved with any family issues. In fact, it was noteworthy that he was sitting in the same room watching television with us!

My mind was racing. The strange behavior that the man on the television de-scribed was just like Jason's: He had talked about scars appearing and disap-pearing on his body; he suffered a sudden and terrible fear of the dark; he had a need to be with someone at night; he felt unexplained fatigue even after long hours in bed; his mood swings were beyond his control; and he carried an over-whelming sense of panic.

Surely this was just a coincidence? Surely this man's retrieved memories of being taken against his will to an alien spacecraft were those of an overactive imagination?

I had seen stories from time to time in newspapers about people claiming such things, but I scarcely bothered to read them. I just assumed that the world was full of cranks and weirdos. As for Paul, if he couldn't touch it, then it didn't exist.

Daniel continued. "Mum, remember me telling you about my soldier guy who sat on my bed when I was little? You thought that I had imagined him? Do you remember how upset I was when he said he wouldn't be coming to see me for a while, as I wasn't the one he should be working with?" I vaguely remembered Daniel telling me through his tears all those years ago that his soldier friend he talked about so often had gone away. I remembered how I had humored him, never once believing that he was anything other than an imaginary friend. Lots of children have imaginary playfriends.
"I know that my soldier guy was real.
I've always known he was real."

Paul grunted his disbelief and disap-pointment at his older son.

"See Mum?" Daniel continued, "That's why I've not said anything because I know what you and Dad think of all this. Besides, I thought that the shrink that you are taking Jason to would have gotten the truth out of him by now, so I wouldn't have to say anything. My soldier guy told me that Jason has an original soul - whatever that means - and I know that they won't really hurt him, but he needs help, Mum. He can't cope with all this. It's really screwing him up, and he's terrified."

I know Daniel well enough to know when he is sincere, and this time he was. Paul was the first to get up and placed his hand on Daniel's shoulder.

**One of the "helper" Greys
that would often appear.**

11

Then he walked out to the kitchen where Jason was still sobbing. I followed, and we sat at the table with Jason, in silence at first. Then, through his sobs, Jason began recounting his experiences: "It's always the light that comes first. It wakes me up. Then I see the tall one rise at the foot of the bed. Then all at once, there's lots of little ones everywhere. They're fuzzy and indistinct, and they can move very fast. I can't move or speak, but I'm awake and I can see and hear and feel. I want to scream and run, but the sound doesn't come, and my body doesn't move. Sometimes, I think I am screaming - I can hear myself screaming - but it never wakes you, you never come to help me. I hate them! I hate them! I hate you for not coming when I need you!"

Jason sat up and stared accusingly at Paul and me. "Why do you let them take me? I have to go with them. They take me to an operating theatre - like at the hospital. It's all white and shiny. Sometimes it's a round room with a metal floor, and it's always cold. I want to go home, I hate it there. They're there, and the big one touches me, but I don't feel it, like I've had an anesthetic. I hate it! I hate it..."

I put my arms around him and pulled him close. I had heard what he said and, though I told him that we believed him and would try to find a way to help him, I knew that I was lying to myself. I believed wholeheartedly that Jason believed that this was the truth of what was happening to him and it was purely this belief of his that I resolved to help him with.

Paul and I decided that the best way to help our son was by looking into this crazy subject of UFOs and aliens for ourselves so the following day, we combed the book shops looking for relevant reading matter.

However, all this is jumping ahead a little. Before I continue, I feel I need to delve into our past a little more before explaining how we came to realize what was really happening to our youngest son.

# TWO
# HAWKSNEST FARM

Animals have always played an important role in our lives. We are never without at least two dogs in the house, numerous cats, assorted caged birds and often livestock and a snowy owl!

I remember when we still lived at Sweetbriar cottage. Daniel would have been about seven and Jason three years old. One evening I went into Daniel's room to collect his washing, and I was stunned to see an enormous white shape perched on the outside window ledge. It was already late in the year, so the afternoons were quite dark, which made its white shape look quite menacing. Daniel told me not to be afraid - that it was only Barney, his friend. The shape shuffled, and I could see that it was a snowy owl - a beautiful large bird with huge orange eyes. Daniel stated that Barney often flew up to his room, and sometimes, when he opened the window, the bird would fly into the room and perch quite happily on the back of a chair. I was no longer afraid, and I accepted the owl, although I did find its huge eyes sometimes intimidating. Daniel relished the times Barney would visit, and I assumed that the bird had perhaps been brought up by humans and released back into the wild, which is why it wasn't afraid of us. It was only years later that I found out that such a bird is extremely rare to our country, let alone in my son's bedroom! I also found out that sometimes the ETs create "screen memories" - especially for children - so that their true look doesn't frighten them. I believe that this was the case with Barney, although Jason remained terrified of it.

Barney visited sporadically for six months, sometimes coming three or four times a week, but sometimes not for days. Then it stopped coming for several weeks, and then made one last appearance in which it sat gazing at Daniel. After this, it never came again and Daniel was okay with that. It was almost as if it had returned that last time in order to say good-bye to him.

Things weren't going well for our family. Paul was having problems at work. He was getting up at 6:00 A.M. in order to make the long train journey into the center of London, where he worked as a gold refiner. Since Jason's nightmares had begun, he was spending most of the night in our bed, and Paul was frustrated that we never seemed to get any time to ourselves. In addition, Jason was clingy all the time, even crying outside the bathroom when I was inside, as he didn't want to be left alone. On one occasion, when the two boys and I were driving back late one evening from my mother's, Jason managed to unbuckle his child seat. He launched himself at me, clung so tightly as I struggled to drive, and repeated through sobs that he didn't ever want to be left alone again - ever.

Like any good father, Paul was sympathetic to his child's needs, but the frustration he felt of always having Jason there coupled with his frustration at the antics of the new management at work proved to be too much. I had seen the anxiety building in him, and when he returned from work early one afternoon announcing that he couldn't take any more, I felt a strange relief. Paul had worked for the same company since leaving school and had worked his way up to assistant manager. He had been there 14 years, yet he was relieved to have had his say about the new running of the company - just before they fired him.

Over the coming months it was great having Paul at home, and he worked relentlessly on the house, although he dreaded the day when he had to go into town to collect his social-security payment. He befriended the old farmer whose cows grazed the fields next to our garden and soon learned everything he could from him about keeping livestock. The old man said that Paul was a natural herdsman.

Our financial crunch got worse, and nine months after Paul lost his job, the building society informed us that our house was about to be re-possessed. We pleaded with them because we loved our Sweetbriar cottage, but they were insistent. The only concession they granted us was to give us three months in which to find a buyer ourselves, as that way we would be able to come out of it with some money. We agreed, although it was a bitter sweet moment when we found a buyer who fell in love with the cottage the same way that we had.

When everything was finished, we had 30,000 pounds sitting in our bank - and no home. We had a touring caravan (trailer) and stayed on sites near the coast for awhile, until we decided that since Paul was good with livestock, we should try our hand at farming. We didn't have enough money to do it in a big way, but maybe a small holding would support us and all our needs. With the decision made, we set about looking for the right place, and we found it near Sevenoaks in Kent.

Hawksnest Farm was beautiful - just ten acres of flat grassland surrounded on all sides by thick woodland. There was a vehicle track that led from the road up through wheat fields and woodland, terminating at our gate. We paid cash for the land and had enough left over to purchase an enormous mobile home and some livestock - including our first four calves.

We soon settled into our new lives, and within weeks we were able to send for Craven, the horse my dad had promised me since I was six years old, a promise he kept just three weeks before he died. Craven is still very much a part of our family, and at 23 years young, I'm watching him in the paddock now as I write this. He means the world to me because he reminds me of my dad - and a promise kept to a six year old.

Things were going well for us, and more importantly, Jason's nightmares seemed to have stopped. Paul would always call on Jason to help him with the stock, as he seemed to have a natural ability with all animals. Within months, our calves were well grown, and we were able to sell them for top price at the market. We decided that we should continue raising calves until they're about six months old, then sell them to local farmers who don't have the time or resources to look after babies. Calves need feeding four times a day and their living quarters must be kept spotlessly clean. Big farms don't have time for this but are often interested in purchasing older animals that are about six months old. So, armed with the glowing market report, we were able to get our bank to agree to give us a loan of 20,000 pounds for new buildings, bedding, feed and stock, and we were doing well.

We had bought another horse, Shannon, only because he had been cruelly treated, and we wanted to give him a good life. We also justified this extravagance by saying that he would be a companion to Craven, who would often alleviate his boredom by chasing the sheep around. However, one morning in August, 1989, Shannon didn't come to me when I called him. He was standing quite still in the middle of the field. Paul and I walked down to see what was wrong, and we were both shocked to see that a large square flap had been cut into his shoulder, and the skin was just hanging. The wound was very fresh and beginning to weep a little, although there was no blood anywhere to be seen. Paul and I were astounded as to what could possibly approach a horse and take such a large piece of flesh without it running away? We called the vet who arrived a couple of hours later. The vet confirmed that the wound had been inflicted deliberately, as the edges were perfectly straight and also that several layers of tissue had been removed. It would have been possible for someone to have come through the woods in the night, but surely we would have heard something. The vet also remarked that the horse was exceptionally calm, and he didn't require any anesthetic.

On September 13th that same year, we lost our first young steer. This happens on occasion - cattle deaths can occur through a number of illnesses - but this felt different somehow, particularly as the animal had been completely healthy the night before. We called in the vet, who was totally puzzled as to the cause of the death, and he decided to send the carcass to the Ministry of Agriculture for a post mortem. The next day three more steers were dead. Over the course of two weeks, we lost 24 seemingly healthy animals. We got the report back from the Ministry which stated that the first animal had died of a rare form of salmonella known as salmonella typhimurium 204C. We also had a visit from Ministry vets who proclaimed that our premises were beyond reproach, and that the animals had not contracted the disease from anything we had done or not done. We were told to burn the carcasses, but then the following day we received a phone call from the Ministry telling us not to. We were informed that we must leave the carcasses together away from the buildings. We were never given a reason, but, as the call was from the Ministry, we complied with the request.

A few days later, a van turned up with six men dressed from head to foot in white space-type coverall suits. The one in charge solemnly announced that they were from the Ministry. The only other thing he said was that they would be investigating Sevenoaks livestock market, where we bought the stock.

They moved as a group around the farm, and some of them had what ap-peared to be Geiger counters. Shortly afterwards, a large lorry lumbered up the track and stopped in the yard. The six men then wrapped each carcass in plastic sheeting and loaded it carefully into the back of the lorry. Each time Paul approached, he was turned away by the shake of a hand and the "go away" mo-tion. Then, cargo loaded, and without another word, the small convoy made its way back along the track. Daniel and Jason had been dropped off at the end of the lane after school, and they appeared at the gate moments later, yet neither of them had seen the convoy. Although we pre-warned the proprietors of the market that they would encounter a visit from Ministry officials, they never did hear anything more about the incident - nor did any officials ever turn up. For years we assumed that the Ministry, was the Ministry of Agriculture. Looking back, we see we may have been very misled.

Several years later while conducting research for this work, I spoke to the officer in charge of notifiable diseases at the Ministry of Agriculture. He confirmed that he was in charge of this department in 1989, yet he had no recollection or re-cords of this particular salmonella outbreak. He asked me to forward him a copy of the report, which we had been given at the time of the Ministry's inspection so that he could look into it. He rang me a few days later and confirmed that he could find absolutely no records pertaining to this incident, and he assured me that he would continue to delve into it. When I heard nothing for several weeks, I rang the Ministry and was told that this particular officer no longer was located there. Apparently, he had been moved to Wales, and although I tried calling there, I was told that they had no idea what I was talking about and I must have gotten the name wrong. To this day I have never heard from this man, but I did get a call from the Ministry again asking me to send them the original report I had - not a copy and they would then look into this matter further. I did not comply with this request - despite three further reminders - and never heard from anyone at the Ministry again.

It was also about this time that a neighbor living near the farm came to see me. She and her husband are quite high up the ladder in their social standing, and she told me that the previous evening they had attended a big dinner party at the Manor House. Amongst the guests were some high-ranking army personnel who served on the Mereworth Army Base, which was just a mile from Hawksnest. The entrance to the base was from the road, but then the thick woodland seemed to encroach on the rest of it so it couldn't be well seen from any vantage point. Our neighbor Caroline told me that she was talking to a major, and the conversation turned to the mysterious deaths of our cattle. At this point, the major - who was already very much the worse for drink - laughed. Caroline chastised him, saying it wasn't a laughing matter, but the major went on to explain - in a rather slurred fashion - that the deaths were caused by an experiment that had gone badly wrong. He claims that using "other" technology (he wouldn't elaborate on this), they had been experimenting with some sort of microwave energy, which had killed the cattle. He explained to her that a huge cover-up then ensued, which included convincing us that a rare type of salmonella was responsible for their deaths. He also admitted that they had pulled the strings of the local authority, pressuring them into forcing us to leave the farm. The local council had turned up the day after the lorries had collected the carcasses, and politely informed us that as we had lost all our stock and, basically, our living, we therefore forfeited the right to live on our own land. We were told that we would be housed - temporarily - in the village until we had built up stock levels again, at which time we could apply to the authority for permission to move back to the land. It was merely a formality. We believed them. We were moved to a council house within weeks - even though the waiting list was incredibly long - and we would spend the next nine years fighting for the right to live on our land and work it once again.

We never succeeded. We finally admitted defeat in 1998 which is when we moved to South Lincolnshire, but, I digress. I thanked Caroline for this information, but later that night she called me to say that when she returned home after visiting me, the major in question was waiting on her doorstep. She said that he was in a dreadful state, and told her that if he had said anything to her the night before - anything at all - about the situation with the Andrews farm and cattle, then she must swear to him that she would never repeat it. She said that she told him that he hadn't said very much, and pretended to ask what it was all about, at which point the major seemed to breathe a sigh of relief. He reiterated his remarks, making her subsequently promise faithfully that she would never talk about their conversation on this subject to anyone.

Even though we were no longer allowed to live on our property after this strange incident, we did try again to keep cattle there about 12 months later. This time though, we opted for older stock, but all we could afford at that time were four fully grown and expectant Charolais cows. They are a big, sturdy French breed - white to cream in color - and reputed to calve easily without much fuss or assistance from a vet.

We bought them from a farm in Sussex, and all four animals were guaranteed healthy and in calf to a Hereford bull. We understood that they would calve in late September to possibly early November (unless artificially inseminated, the `natural' way can not be accurately predicted). We bought them in late June, and already we could feel the unborn calves moving inside their mothers.

Jason was over the moon with his new charges and, incredibly, they allowed him to approach them and stroke and cuddle them whenever he wanted to. With the rest of the family, they would predictably be wary (as most cows are with humans). Jason delighted in placing his hands on their ripening stomachs and telling us excitedly how he could feel the babies moving about.

September came and went and then October, without any sign of any of the four giving birth. In fact, they all looked thinner and less pregnant. By mid November, there was still no sign of them calving, and, despite the fact that they were all in healthy condition, Paul was uneasy and rang the vet.

The vet was due to visit on Thursday, November 21st, and on Wednesday we went up to the farm as usual. I got out of the car to open the gate and was astonished to see, in the mud, deep cow-hoof prints. It had rained heavily the night before, so the prints were obviously fresh and easy to distinguish.

I was amazed by the prints. They appeared to go around in circles yet led nowhere, nor did they come from any direction - they were just there - dozens of them by the gate. Paul got out of the car to join me, obviously puzzled by my delay in opening the gate. He too, was amazed by the prints. Then suddenly I spotted another print on the edge of the group. It was that of a boot - a very large boot. Paul put his foot beside it in order to gauge the size, and his print was dwarfed beside it.

We both made our way towards the gate and were relieved to discover that the padlock had not been tampered with and was still in place. We then went immediately to the barn to check on the cows. They were all there, but clearly they were very disturbed, snorting nervously, and backing away when we approached them.

The vet arrived bright and early the next morning and the cattle were all very calm - very different from their state the previous day. After spending more than an hour with the cows, the vet astounded Paul and I with his findings. He told us that only were two of the cows pregnant - but they were only four to five months pregnant. Yet, how was this possible? We had watched them grow; we had felt the new lives moving in their stomachs; their births were imminent. There was absolutely no way that the farmer from whom we had bought them could have made a mistake - we had seen the evidence ourselves. Even the vet was lost for words. He could offer no explanation. The timing of these pregnancies meant that the two cows would have to have been inseminated when they were already at Hawksnest! And what had happened to the nearly complete fetuses they each carried just days before?

We waited until the two cows calved - one on a cold wet morning in late March and the other in mid-April. They were both good strong bull calves, and we duly sold all four adults and the youngsters to another farmer in Kent. Jason was devastated to see them go, but for Paul and me, it was yet another chilling lesson that nothing was ever going to be completely safe on the farm. After that, we never had another bovine creature on our property. We couldn't take the chance.

# THREE
# THE BREAKTHROUGH

Being in a normal house in the village was also good - particularly for the boys. They loved the idea of flicking on lights without first having to start the generator (we had no electricity on the farm). While we made our house comfortable, we wouldn't get into too much decorating, as we were convinced that the authorities would keep their word and we would soon be living back on our own land. In the meantime, 12-year-old Jason, who had been free of his nightmares now for a few years, started behaving very badly at school. He was rude to the teachers and generally uncooperative, which wasn't in his character at all. We tried to talk to him to find out what was troubling him, but we found that we were getting the same reaction as his teachers. The situation was getting out of control. Then, just before the start of the school summer holidays, he was suspended from school, and we were informed that they would only take him back next term if we agreed to take him to see a psychiatrist. Reluctantly, we agreed.

His doctor, Pauline Stevenson, was a very quiet, gentle woman in her early fifties. She was very stereotypical of most English people's idea of a psychiatrist - slimly built with short, cropped hair and glasses attached to a neck chain. She wore tweed skirts with twin-set jumpers and cardigans and flat, sensible shoes. She worked for the local authority and had many children with behavioral problems referred on to her because she was good with them. She started seeing Jason on a fortnightly basis, but she insisted on interviewing me and Paul and Daniel to look for any signs of verbal or physical abuse that might account for his drastic change in behavior. I was quietly pleased, as it seemed that we would at last make some progress and have some answers, and I didn't mind being interviewed. After all, I had nothing to hide. Paul on the other hand, resented the fact that someone could even think that he would hurt his own son - mentally or physically - but he agreed to be interviewed, if only to allay any suspicions. Needless to say, none of us were found guilty of anything beyond loving and being concerned for Jason, but we weren't getting anywhere either. I was very surprised to learn that Jason had told the doctor about a miscarriage I had had in 1989, stating that he knew the baby was a boy. We hadn't mentioned this to anyone. Even my own mother didn't know anything about this for many years. The doctor told us that she knew he was holding something back - something that he couldn't bring himself to talk about to anyone. Her only advice was to be tolerant and above all, be patient with him.

At home, Jason was once again terrified of his nightmares, which had returned with a vengeance. Then something very weird began to happen - in the mornings we would find Jason deeply asleep somewhere else in the house. Sometimes he was on the floor at the foot of his bed - just as we had found him on the floor at the foot of his cot when he was a baby. Sometimes he was on the floor in the living room and once he was stretched out, fast asleep, on top of a hard kitchen worktop. Paul put it down to sleepwalking, but even he became very alarmed when one morning he went to the bathroom and, on impulse, stuck his head round Jason's door to see if he was all right. His bed was empty. This was about 3 A.M. He checked all the rooms in the house, and when there was still no sign of Jason, Paul woke me. In panic, I double checked the house - even kitchen cupboards where it would be impossible for a large 12-year-old to hide. I was desperate.

Our hearts were racing, and even though the house was securely locked from the inside, and the dogs had given us no indication of movement, Paul decided to check outside in case Jason had been sleepwalking. Then I remembered that we hadn't checked the shed at the bottom of the garden, and I asked Paul to help me. Like the rest of the doors, the back door was locked and bolted, as was the shed door. Paul kept electric tools in there, and didn't want to risk them being stolen, so he had put a bolt and padlock on the heavy wooden door. The locks were undisturbed, and Paul said that he couldn't possibly be inside, but he opened the door anyway at my insistence. As the light from the moon poured in, there in the corner was the huddled shape of a young boy dressed only in pajamas. He was in such a deep sleep that he didn't even wake when Paul picked him up and carried him inside.

Safely back in his bed, Paul and I puzzled over how he could have gotten into the shed. It was impossible to lock it from the inside and the only window didn't open. Then there was also the issue of getting firstly through a locked and still-bolted back door. We went around in circles, but we could find no logical explanation.

The following day, Jason's behavior was so bad that a violent argument ensued between him and his father. Jason was defiant and shouted back at Paul. Finally the tears started to run down Jason's face, and Paul's' attitude changed to one of sympathy and caring. He then begged his youngest son to tell him what was wrong.

Jason calmed down and the three of us sat at the table. Paul and I waited for Jason to catch his breath, hoping that he would finally confide in us. He did.

"It's the dreams, Dad." He began, "I'm getting the dreams again like I did when I was little." This time Paul had an answer. If it was the dreams that were bothering him, then he must be encouraged to talk to the psychiatrist about them at his next appointment. Jason agreed.

We explained to Dr. Stevenson that our son was having horrendous nightmares, and she gently probed him about them. Reluctantly, Jason explained:

"The first memory I have is of the hands," he whispered. "I was crying for some reason - I've no idea why - and I can clearly see long fingers reaching down into the cot to pick me up. They were very different from Mum's hands. These fingers were much longer - at least twice as long with large joints at the knuckles. They were dark in color, not black or brown, not even grey. I've never seen a color like it, like a dark dolphin color. I don't know what happened after they picked me up.

"The next memory I have is when I was a bit older, able to walk. Again, I remember the hands lifting me. I was old enough to know about fairies and elves and demons - Mum read stories to me every night - and I thought I was being taken away by elves.

"Another time I saw what I thought was a soldier on the landing. The house where we lived was near an old ruined castle, and I thought that this little person - he was only about 2'6" tall, the same height as me - was the ghost of a soldier who had died there. All I can remember is seeing him. I don't know what happened next."

Jason had other confused memories of those early years when we all lived at Sweetbriar Cottage, but almost all of his memories involved hands reaching out for him and little people in his room. He remembers the terror he felt when they would appear from nowhere, but each memory stops when they made contact with him. As he got older, the memories naturally became clearer and more cohesive.

"I can remember being terrified one night and running to Mum shouting, "They're coming to get me!" By then I knew what was happening. I knew I was being taken away - and I never wanted to go. I couldn't remember where I went, or what they did to me, but I know I hated it, and all Mum would say was that it's a dream. She would cuddle me and comfort me, but it made me so mad because she wouldn't believe me that it wasn't a dream. I kept on trying to think of ways to make her believe me, but I realized it was no good. I remember the horrible feeling I had when they - Mum and Dad - would never believe me. I felt so lonely and miserable.

"There was one time when I felt a sharp pain in my side and went in to show Mum. She lifted my pajama top and saw a deep red mark and although it hurt, I was pleased that there was something, as she would now have to believe me. She was very worried about it, but eventually got me back to sleep, and in the morning the mark had gone. Mum then said that it must have been where I was lying on my side, but I knew it wasn't, and I felt angry again.

"There is a pattern to the bad nights," he continued. "The nights when things happen to me I settle down to sleep and have a very good sight of the alarm clock, which always stops around 3 A.M. That's the time it happens. I lie in bed awake though I don't know what wakes me, and the dogs are always growling. Then suddenly the dogs shut up, which is unusual for our dogs. I always then try to go back to sleep in the hope that nothing will happen, but then I see something at the end of the bed, almost out of the corner of my eye. It rises up through the floor. It's the big one. It's about 5'4" tall, just a bit shorter than me. The head is large, with big black eyes on a slant, which go around the side of the head, and it has a very small nose and mouth. It's thin and has long dark fingers that I remember from my baby days. That's all I notice, really - the fingers more than the face. It's not always the same one, although I don't know how I know that because they look the same. Once, one had a strange zig-zag shape to the top of his head as if a lump had been chopped out. It never came again. Then, once I've seen the big one rising up, I'm aware of the little ones. I never see where they come from - they're just there. They are similar to the big one, gray in color, but smaller, and they busily scuttle about. There are usually about half a dozen of them. Sometimes they bring other creatures with them. I call them Koalas because they are small and furry, like little bears. They don't seem to have a distinct shape - they're fuzzy at the edge. And they don't seem to do much - as if they are pets for the others. Mum used to have a collection of teddy bears with a couple of Koala bears amongst them, and I can remember even when I was tiny that I wouldn't touch the Koalas because they reminded me of these creatures.

"I see them in my bedroom, and I see the big one stretching out its long fingers just as it did when I was little. Then I never remember what happens next. Sometimes I don't have any more memories of that night - except that when I wake in the morning I am very tired, and my alarm clock is two hours slow. But sometimes I wake up somewhere else - somewhere cold. I can't move my body at all - only my eyes, and I can't speak. I'm lying on something smooth and cold. It feels like marble, but I don't think it is. It doesn't have corners - everything is rounded and smooth. The room is dark, but there is a light coming from somewhere that I can't see. Sometimes, all I can remember is being there, but other times they are with me. I can remember seeing a big one holding something about 8" long, like a metal ruler. Sometimes I can see the big one touching me, but I can never feel anything, as if my body is paralyzed. I'm always terrified.

"I used to lose my temper and scream at Mum, `You must believe me!' I think she and Dad just thought that I was very badly behaved. At school I used to get frightened. I hated sitting by the window because I was sure that they could see me there and could come and get me. Once, when there was a lot of lightning, I locked myself in a cupboard. I'm not frightened of thunder and lightning, but the lightning reminds me of the beams of light I sometimes see when I am with them.

"I don't see the point of being nice to anyone, because nobody believes me. People treat me like some kind of idiot who doesn't know the difference between dreams and things that really happen."

Dr. Stevenson sat back in her chair and looked at Jason. She appeared to be very open-minded and did not dismiss what he was telling her out of hand. Jason was encouraged - at last he felt that he had somebody to talk to.

Within days of opening up to the psychiatrist, another breakthrough occurred. He watched the television program on hypnosis, which finally gave a name to his experiences - abduction.

After he tried to smash the television set, Paul and I listened to him. We had already been pondering on his words spoken to the psychiatrist, but now this phenomenon had a name. Even if it was all in his head, it meant that other people were also suffering from this, and if this was the case, then it could be cured. For Jason, it was the first time in his life that we weren't fobbing him off with the words - dreams and nightmares and sleepwalking. Paul and I were on the threshold of accepting that something very real - and very strange - was happening to our son.

# FOUR
# OUR LIFELINE

There were no books on this bizarre subject of "alien abduction" at the library. In fact, I remember that the librarian looked at me as if I were totally mad. However, Paul managed to track down four UFO books that did briefly cover this subject. We began flicking through them - idly at first - but then we began to be amazed by the similarities between what Jason was telling us and the accounts from other people. Since the age of four, Jason's story had remained the same. It never altered, so I know that he could not possibly have made any of it up. To our son this was real, and it was happening to him. By now we had conceded that something very strange was happening that was certainly beyond rational explanation, but we still doubted the idea of all this being the work of some sort of other worldly creatures! However, the more we read, the more the doubts crept in, and somewhere in the back of my mind I began to consider that it was a possibility.

In the appendix of one of the books was a short list of useful telephone numbers, and I decided that I should ring one of them. I figured that if I could speak to someone who was knowledgeable in this area, then at least I could ask questions. The number for Quest International in England looked impressive, and I geared myself up one afternoon when the house was quiet, and I dialed the number. I got through straight away, but I found myself stuttering for a moment. I still couldn't quite believe what I was doing! However, I took a deep breath and asked the man if he could help us. I half expected a derisory laugh or insistence that I see a doctor, but instead the man took it all in stride and suggested another number for me to call. I thanked him for his time and immediately rang the number he had given me. Again, I explained to them what my son believed was happening to him, and again I was met with understanding, and I was so amazed that what I was saying to him wasn't unfamiliar. He asked for my number, saying that he would pass it on to one of their investigators, but I panicked and put down the telephone. I didn't want to leave my number - what if this man passed it around saying it was from a mad woman who believed in aliens? I told Paul later, but he persuaded me to ring back, saying that if it all went pear shaped, we could always say it was a joke. I rang the man again and apologized for my rudeness, but he was very understanding. This time, I left my number and later that evening I received a call from the person who helped us all make sense of our lives, a man whom we have all come to refer to as our lifeline - Tony Dodd.

At that time, Tony was the Director of Investigations for Quest International, an organization devoted to the subject of ufology. He first became involved in the subject in 1978 when he was a serving police sergeant. He spent 25 years in the force, leaving with an exemplary service record. He has the cynical, hard bitten attitude common among officers who spend their lives involved directly with people's crises.

For Tony it all started with an astonishing incident as he was on night patrol across the Yorkshire Moors. He was with another officer and, by coincidence, another patrol car was approaching his position from the opposite direction. It was 2:30 A.M., and as Tony's car rounded a bend, both he and his colleague saw a large, bright object moving slowly across the road. He estimated that it was about 100' across in diameter and about 100' from his position. No sound came from it - in fact the whole area was eerily silent. Then Tony's car engine died. A glow of light surrounded the object, which was moving slowly - no more than 10 to 15 m.p.h. - away from the road. The two officers watched it until all they could see was a faint ball of light in the distance.

Tony had served in the Royal Air Force before becoming a police officer, so he was very familiar with the shape and dimensions of aircraft. He knew this was not a plane. The object clung to the contours of the hills as it moved away, yet it was too far off the ground to be any sort of hovercraft.

As soon as the two men recovered from the shock of what they had seen, Tony tried to radio the station but got only static. He kept trying until eventually the radio set burst into life again and he was able to re-start the car. He reported his sighting. Later, back at the station, he learned that the officer who had been driving towards them had also witnessed this craft, and his report tallied exactly with that of Tony and his colleagues. Baffled but intrigued, Tony was determined to get to the bottom of it, expecting a rational explanation, but gradually his search for an explanation took over his life. He retired from the force in 1988 and now works full time on UFO research. He has since had many sightings of strange craft on the moor, but he also knows for certain that he too, is an abductee.

We got to know Tony extremely well over the years since that first telephone call, and he has always been there for us. For Jason, it was the realization that he is not the only one that this happens to, and that was such a relief. Jason found that he could confide in Tony, and talk honestly and openly about his experiences, knowing that he would understand and help him through it. We could ring him anytime - day or night - and no matter what the emergency was, he would always tell me to calm down in his deep, authoritative Yorkshire accent and state that nothing is ever that bad.

In America, it is quite possible to get help from psychiatrists, psychologists, scientists and many other professional people who accept abduction and can provide strategies for coping with it. However, in England, there are no such groups so we consider ourselves incredibly fortunate that we found Tony Dodd.

**Jason at 14 with a new puppy.**

The relief of being able to talk openly made a huge difference to Jason, and for a few weeks after the first contact with Tony, he slept better at night and school went well. Then, the experiences began again.

I remember well one morning waking him for his appointment with the psychiatrist, but he was in a lot of pain. He showed me a mark on his side. It was a perfect 2" triangle, deep red in color with angry, inflamed skin around it. Jason said that the pain was easing bit by bit, so I decided to take him to his appointment and lost no time in showing the doctor the mark.

She didn't know what to make of it - nor could she explain how it had been done. Carefully, she placed her glasses across the bridge of her nose and gently prodded the inflamed skin. She called other colleagues into the room, and they all stood around Jason gently poking and prodding but no one could offer an explanation. The mark began to fade in front of their eyes. With such a room full of eminent medical persons, the only comments heard over and over were ones of amazement and wonder. Each of them gradually left the room after taking a final good look at the mark, which had faded even more. As they departed each of them was visibly stunned by something that they were at a loss to explain.

Dr. Stevenson wrote to our family doctor on several occasions, once stating, "The patch on his tummy was triangular with (approximately) 2" sides and slightly brownish, but having no raised component or edge.... Jason has shown me marks on his left side stating that this is where the `creatures' cut into him. I do not know what to make of them. I have never seen anything like this before."

However, it was clear by now that the psychiatrist was not giving him the help he needed and he wasn't getting anywhere. So, after eight months, Dr. Stevenson decided that she could not help Jason and could not refer him, as she had no idea who to refer him to! She was clear, however, that Jason was not mentally ill - she wrote to his doctor in November 1995 stating that, in her opinion, Jason is not psychotic. [See letter on page 31] This unambiguous endorsement of his sanity echoed what she had already confirmed to me - that Jason was not hallucinating - this was real.

Jason's experiences continued, but Paul came up with a solution: He planned to sit up all night in Jason's room, armed with a baseball bat. As Paul now worked as a taxi driver on the night shift, he was accustomed to staying awake at night. Jason always knew when an abduction was about to happen because he would get a tingling sensation at the front of his head. All these years later, this is still the case. He warned his Dad that something would happen one particular night, and, armed with a flask of hot coffee and the bat, Paul sat up in Jason's room. However, he was rudely shaken awake in the morning by Jason, who was upset that he had again been taken - and his father had been sound asleep the whole time!

We have since realized over the years that for Paul, falling asleep almost immediately whenever the subject of aliens or abductions are discussed, is inevitable.

Chairman Brian Oatley
Chief Executive Jon Wilkes

MAIDSTONE TRUST
...escent Service

priority care

N H S   T R U S T

Child & Adolescent Services
Brunswick House
Buckland Hill
Maidstone
Kent ME16 0SB
Tel. (01622) 756534
Fax. (01622) 671202

Our ref: PS/BC
Your ref:

Confidential

12th October 1995

Dr.K.Parkes
Borough Green Medical Practice
Quarry Hill Road
Borough Green,
Kent. T15 8BE

Dear Dr.Parkes,

re: **JASON ANDREWS dob 2.7.83, 66 Fairfield Rd.Borough Green TN15 8DR**

The above named attended for an appointment on 10.10.95 for individual/family/follow up therapy. The main problems/issues were -

1. Jason is still having this "alien" experiences

2. There have been various other experiences which they consider para normal (electrical upsets, animals, spooked, etc.)

3. Jason has been talking to Mr.Dodds of Quest International whom he finds helpful. Jason has been suspended from school for one day.

Mother says that he gets wound up and loses his temper at school on occasion. Jason thinks he is trying harder and improving.

The following management plan is suggested -

1. Continue the Amitriptyline 25 mg.nocte.

2. We talked as to how to live with his experiences. These do not appear to be psychotic.

His mother and maternal grandfather are said to have had similar experiences at a less severe level.

The date of the next appointment is 24.10.95. Please let me know if further information is required, or if you wish to disucss the above. A further letter will follow with our findings.

Yours sincerely,

Pauline Stevenson.

DT

**Letter from Dr. Stevenson, October 1995, stating that Jason's experiences "Do not appear to be psychotic."**

It isn't that he isn't interested in the subject - he is! But for some strange reason, the immediate sleep seems to be some sort of protection mechanism for him. In other words, perhaps he isn't supposed to be involved in this subject. It has been further suggested that it is Paul's job to keep our feet on the ground - to be an anchor for the rest of us - and maybe he couldn't do this job if he were as involved in the whole situation as the rest of us.

On the night of Tuesday, October 3rd, there was a huge thunderstorm over Kent. Paul and I were preparing to go to bed when a huge clap of thunder and fierce lightning invaded the house. Abruptly, Jason was at the foot of the stairs. He walked past us, totally oblivious to our presence, and sat on the edge of the couch with his back very straight. Then, just like after his fourth birthday party, he began to spew out incredible numbers again, just as if he were reading them from an invisible screen. This went on for a few minutes, and when he finally stopped talking, his head dropped forward and his body slumped back against the couch. He sleepily rubbed his eyes, was released from where ever he was, and asked how he had gotten there. I told him that he had come downstairs to see if the dogs were okay and had fallen asleep. He accepted this.

With Tony's help, what we had read, and the evidence of our own eyes, Paul and I came to a grudging acceptance of the truth of alien abductions. We still couldn't do much to help, but at least this time we knew what was happening and could be there to help Jason cope with it. Then something occurred that changed everything.

I was awakened in the night by the sound of Jason screaming. I leapt out of bed and rushed into his room to find him standing in the middle of the room. He was still screaming. I remember thinking "no, not again," and held out my arms to him. At least I could cuddle and comfort him, but then, realizing that I was there, Jason stopped screaming and calmly put out his hand to stop me.

"Don't touch me," he commanded, "You mustn't touch me." Puzzled, I asked why, but he simply repeated it. I have never felt so helpless and, tearful, I turned to leave the room when he spoke again. His tone was softer this time, gentle. "Mum, they're making me feel and see what they feel and see. I will be all right."

I smiled at him as I left the room but I was deeply worried. Even on the occasions when he had been physically taken from his bed - and there were a lot of times like that - I was always upset, but I took heart in Tony's promise that abductees are always returned and that Jason was always back in the morning. But this was something else - something different. I spoke to Tony about this incident the next day, and he told me that it wasn't unusual and that I shouldn't worry. He told me that Jason was always in control and that he would only let them share his feelings if he wanted to. He felt that it is possible that as he feels more of the pain that "they" feel, he will allow them to experience more of his inner feelings. Tony also thought that this might be a positive sign - perhaps Jason was coming to terms with his abductions and was listening and learning from his experience rather than fighting it. What Tony said made sense, so I tried to put it out of my head, but then a few days later these new developments had severe repercussions.

Jason was at the local stables riding his favorite horse, Patch. They were galloping. Jason loved to feel the wind in his face. Suddenly, another horse came galloping up behind Patch. This animal had already thrown its rider and was intent on attacking Jason. The other horse reared up, sending Jason and Patch crashing to the ground. It all happened very quickly, but Jason's instincts made him roll well clear of Patch's weight coming down, and a heavy wooden fence halted his unexpected journey. By the time other people were on the scene, Jason was standing, checking a very shaken Patch all over to make sure he was all right. The equine attacker had since charged off down the fields.

When I arrived at the yard to pick him up, I heard what had happened and swiftly went to Jason asking over and over if he was hurt. His answer stunned me. "I'm fine," he said, "but they didn't like it."

"Who?" I asked, half knowing the answer.

He smiled as he continued, "They didn't like the pain of hitting the ground like that - they don't like experiencing hurt."

Jason later explained to me that for some time he had been allowing them to share his feelings. They are somehow part of him and are able to enjoy, for example, the thrill of the gallop or a bike ride. He said that he had become accustomed to them being with him and had no objection, but on this occasion, the ride ended badly, and they didn't like feeling the pain. Apparently, the other horse had sensed the unseen riders, which is why it attacked Patch. Jason was covered in deep bruises and even had the deep imprint of a horse's hoof on his shoulder, yet he felt no pain. He would laugh at how they had absorbed it all for him.

# FIVE
# MY TURN

As Jason was becoming reconciled with his experiences, and finding strength and advice from his many conversations with Tony, we were suddenly thrown another curve. As Paul and I settled down to sleep one night, a very pale-looking Jason wandered into our room and proclaimed softly, "If you look out of that window, you will see them." Without another word, he turned and walked back out.

Paul and I were stunned by his chilling announcement, and we were immediately afraid. Neither of us wanted to be the first to look out of the window, but as I sat upright in bed my gaze wandered over to the night sky. I was so relieved that I saw nothing and told Paul, who also looked. The only thing visible in the black sky was a lone bright star, which was no more than the size of a pinhead - but then the "star" seemed to get bigger and brighter - and nearer. The very last thing that we remembered was our bedroom being flooded by a white light, and that "star," was now as big as a football and framed in the window.

When we awoke the next morning, the sun was shining, birds were singing, and the dogs were clamoring for attention. It began like any other ordinary day, so it took me a few minutes to remember the events of the previous evening. I reminded my husband about the "star," as Jason entered the room again. Looking at Paul, Jason said in a disgusted tone, "You went to sleep, but I had to go with them again." Then his tone lightened as he continued, "This time was different though. They showed me how our governments and other governments treat them. I saw people cutting into their eyes - just to see what they are made of. I saw them being kept alive in glass tanks, and bits of them being put in sealed containers. I saw soldiers shooting at them." Jason was angry at the way they were being treated and told us that he felt as if he wanted to punish those responsible. He told us that the aliens couldn't understand why they were being treated as laboratory specimens.

Then he described being taken into an enormous room where there were hundreds of other people who were all looking up at a giant screen. On it was a picture of the Earth. Paul was listening attentively, but I was experiencing a strange feeling. In my mind I could see the screen he mentioned - the hundreds of other people and Jason. Then, before he could finish, I grabbed at his arm and whispered, "It suddenly blew up didn't it? And then there was a terrible low whistling sound, a desolate sound, like a strange wind blowing. That's what happened isn't it?"

Jason nodded then smiled with relief. "I knew you were there," he said softly, "I saw you there."

For me, deep and confusing memories were stirring. I tried to convince myself that these memories were nothing more than some sort of telepathic link to my son, but I knew that I was kidding myself. When I was a child of no more than six or seven, I remembered having such a vivid dream that the memory had stayed with me into adulthood. This "dream" always had such a disturbing effect whenever I recalled it that I had stored it deep in the back of my mind, yet it would still emerge unbidden at times with crystal clear details.

When Jason left the room, Paul soon followed and although he said nothing to me, his contemptuous look was enough. Paul was trying hard to cope with all this strange stuff, and together we were trying to be strong for Jason's sake, but this latest revelation had shaken him to the core. I don't know if he thought that I was making some sort of sick joke when I spoke about the picture on the giant screen, but his look when he left said more than any words could ever say. However, I couldn't worry about that now. I needed to be alone - to think.

Images were tumbling through my mind, and I tried to make sense of them. I thought about my dad and how he had once told me that sometimes things happen to him which, though terrifying at first, had turned into something beautiful. He had said that if I should encounter such things, I must try not to be afraid. I remember asking him to explain what he meant, but he answered that he couldn't, but that I should remember his advice. I clearly remembered his words as they seemed so cryptic and confusing. I remembered too, the "dream" I had as a child, which even now, terrified me to recall it.

In the dream, I had been unable to sleep, and I asked my mother if I could sleep in her bed. My dad was working the night shift, so she sleepily agreed, but I still couldn't settle. Suddenly, I became aware that someone had entered the room and, with my heart racing, I dared to look over the top of the bed covers. There, at the foot of the bed - growing steadily taller - was a hooded figure, which I likened to that of a monk. Now standing at the height of an adult, (about 5' 8"), the "monk" seemed to glide around to the side of the bed. I felt that I wanted to scream but couldn't and was also unable to move. I remembered that I couldn't see into the hood when at that instant, long scaly fingers reached up to the hood and began to push it back to reveal large, black almond shaped eyes. That was where my memory of this "dream" always ended in the past, no matter how hard I tried to concentrate - as I always knew that there was more.

Now, more memories seemed to join this one, as if they had been there all along but just forgotten. I remembered smaller beings fussing around me and, simply by touching me, they made me float out through a closed window. My mother slept on, oblivious to all this. Even the family collie dog was snoring contentedly by the side of the bed. I even remembered the feeling of passing through the glass - it was as if my whole body was turned to a thick liquid - like treacle - and I was being squeezed through the glass as if it were a strainer - yet there was no pain, just a tickling sensation. I don't believe I had any other feelings or emotions, but it was as if time were on hold, and everything was running in slow motion. Then suddenly my body was on the other side of the glass, and I was whole again. I could feel the wind on my face, and I looked around. Realizing that I was a long way from the ground and being terrified of heights, I instinctively clutched at one of the small beings who were guiding me, but he gently pried my fingers off. More beings were still guiding me, but I couldn't recall any more than that. I could sense that there should be more - a lot more - and I could almost see it, even though it appeared very fuzzy. It's like trying to think of a word which is on the tip of your tongue, but you just can't quite recall it.

Another brief memory I always had was that of being with my father on one of our regular trips to the park. I know it was a beautiful sunny day, and I was extremely happy as I walked, holding onto his hand. We came across three normally dressed people who appeared to be waiting for us. They were all tall and fair with bright blue eyes, yet they had dark tanned skin. Even though I was only about eight, I can remember thinking that they were lucky to have been able to afford a holiday somewhere very hot. Normally it was at this point that this particularly happy memory of my childhood always finished yet now, I remembered more - much more. The "leader" of the group smiled, and Dad seemed surprised to see them there, but not shocked. Dad put his arm around my shoulder and pulled me close to him. Nothing was said, but the intensity of the situation made me giggle, for it reminded me of a cowboy film - the silent showdown before the gunfight. Nobody noticed me, and then I began to feel frightened. I looked around, and the park seemed to be getting darker very quickly. Then the sunlight had gone, and the grass had disappeared. Suddenly, I knew that we were no longer in the park, although I had no idea where we were. The three people were still standing in front of us, but now they were dressed in long white robes. They reminded me of the pictures of Jesus and his disciples that we had been given at Sunday school. Then the leader stepped forward, holding out his hand to Dad. I was extremely afraid and tried to hide behind Dad, but the man saw me and looked down at me. For some reason, I remember that I felt compelled to look into his eyes, and I couldn't turn away, no matter how hard I tried. Then, without realizing how it happened, I found that I was holding the man's hand and we were walking along together still staring into each other's eyes. I remember wondering where my dad was, and why he wasn't stopping a stranger from taking me away. The man never blinked - his gaze never faltered.

Eventually, I found myself being taken to a large room where many children were noisily playing. As the man released my hand, he broke his gaze and I could then look around. I spotted a boy about the same age as me, and I felt really happy because I knew him. He reciprocated the feeling, smiled and walked over to me. He was not a relative or a school friend, but still I was sure that I knew him well and he knew me. He took my hand. Instinctively, I knew that he was deaf. We squatted down on the floor together and began to play with some toys. This particular memory ends there.

Other personal experiences started to emerge over the forthcoming weeks. Mixed in with the many childhood memories was the reality that I would try and describe these things to my mother and, just as I had done so many times to my own child, she would comfort me and tell me they were no more than bad dreams. Perhaps for the first time in my life, I realized just what Jason had been going through - the anger and frustration he felt because his own parents wouldn't believe him. I too remembered the angst I felt when my mother wouldn't believe me yet, she was always adamant that I must not tell my dad any of this. Now all these years later, I wonder whether she didn't want me to tell my Dad because she knew about his experiences, and didn't want to face the possibility that one of her own children might now be involved in this bizarre situation.

After the revelation that I, too, was having experiences, I couldn't wait to phone Tony. My head was about to explode. Why was I remembering things? Could it be just imagination? Was I just sympathizing psychically with Jason?

Tony wasn't surprised by anything I was saying and confirmed that I wasn't imagining anything - these were my own true memories, which were now being allowed to emerge. He repeated what I already knew - that alien abduction does usually run in families. Tony believed that my own experiences were being triggered, and that the beings responsible for successfully blocking them had now decided to unleash them. He explained that a lot of abductees can have mere snatches of memories, and that some abductees never even realize that they have experiences unless something triggers them. One likely reason, he felt, was that Jason had reached a point at which he needed my full support and understanding - real empathy, not just sympathy - and I was being given back my own memories in order to help me to cope with his experiences.

It took Paul a long time to come to terms with this new event that his wife was also a victim of alien abduction. The atmosphere between us was strained for days, and he spent a lot of time on his own trying to sort out his thoughts and feelings about all of this. He knew that I wasn't making it up, even before I told him that I had spoken to Tony. Although he accepted the truth of the situation, he didn't like it one bit, and he blamed me for somehow allowing it to happen. I tried to talk to him - to confide in him as I had always done in the past, but I could feel the unease between us. Eventually though, it was the memory of an awful experience that brought us closer together than we were before.

It was such a vivid dream that I awoke sweating and crying, and it took Paul some time to calm me down enough to tell him what it was all about.

It was the dream of my miscarriage. The miscarriage which, I thought, only Paul and I had known about but then found out that Jason had told his psychiatrist all about his "baby brother."

When the dream opened, I saw "them" - the little ones - but they were in a haze. I could make out a taller one who seemed to be in charge, and although I could hear a lot of shuffling noise, the images were unclear. Gradually, tiredness overtook me, and I slept soundly.

Then, I felt something. I was now wide awake but gripped by fear. There was a blinding light in the room, which was so powerful that it was almost blinding, yet I sensed that "they" were present. I was paralyzed - unable to move - but my senses were on full alert. Then something cold touched my leg; and I felt a searing pain, first in my stomach and then in my lower back. In one awful moment I realized what was happening - I was losing my baby. The tears rolled silently down my face, and I was unable to lift a hand to wipe them away. Then the fear for the child was overtaken by a strong conviction that I was going to die. I shut my eyes as tight as I could in an effort to shut out the light. If I couldn't see the light, then perhaps I could convince myself that it was all just a terrible nightmare, and I would be able to wake myself up. Yet the pain was real and undeniable, and I could hear noises all around me.

Opening my eyes once again, the light was blocked by the shape of a head. For a moment, I couldn't make out the face as the light formed some sort of halo around the head, but as my eyes adjusted, I could see that it was a man. He had a shock of pale blonde hair and large, piercing blue eyes. His was a handsome, gentle face, and for some reason I felt instantly reassured. He smiled down at me, and then placed his hand on my forehead. Instantly, all the pain subsided - disappeared completely - and with it, all my fear. He stroked my hair and, although he didn't speak, I heard him tell me that "it's for the best." I was now overcome by such a deep feeling of peace that against my will, my eyes eventually closed, and I went back to sleep.

When I awoke from this "dream," I felt angry and cheated. As I replayed the events in my mind, I also felt degraded and dehumanized. I finally knew the truth about the miscarriage - and I cried for the loss of my child - a child that had been stolen from me.

Perhaps Tony was right. Perhaps I had been given back my memories in order to help me cope with Jason's experiences, but this particular memory changed the way I felt about "them." Up until that moment, my only concern was for my son's health and well being in coping with all of this. He never consciously asked for any of it - none of us did - yet we were having to find ways of dealing with the situation and - albeit grudgingly - accept our situation. I had never really considered whether "they" were good, bad or indifferent, but now I hated "them." They had no right - absolutely no right - to do any of the things they did to us. Over the years, my hatred for "them" over the loss of my baby grew. I would often rant to Jason that "they" don't have permission for any of this. A few years ago, I reiterated this main criticism to him, and I was totally struck by his answer: "'Course they have permission," he said in a matter-of-fact manner, "and we gave it to them." He explained that such permission would have been sought - and agreed to- on a soul level, yet the conscious mind would not be able to remember.

For me though, even if what he said was true and, on another level, I had given permission for "their" interference in my life, I still felt the intense anger for them for stealing our child. I would never have given permission for that. Never.

# Six
# Outer Interference

We were having enough problems trying to deal with all that had been forced upon us. We didn't need any more. We had always considered the farm to be our own little haven, a piece of the world where we could relax and be ourselves, shutting out the hustle and bustle of everyday life. Yet a few days after my revelations that I am indeed involved in all of the strangeness surrounding Jason, we became aware that our little piece of the world was under observation.

Paul and I were out in the fields repairing some fencing when astonishingly we both heard a phone ringing in the deep woodland close to the fence line. After a few rings, it stopped. Neither of us could believe our own ears. Why would someone be out there in the dense woodland? There were several clear vehicle tracks that wove their way through the woods, yet if someone were that close to our field, then they were obviously spying on us. Why?

At first, we discussed it and then quickly forgot about it, until a few days later when once again, we heard a telephone ringing not far from the fence in another field.

Over the coming weeks, the phone ringing - and always not far from where we were working - became a regular occurrence. We assumed that it had something to do with our experiences, and Paul joked that if someone wants to spend their time hiding among prickly bushes and dense undergrowth, then rather them than him! I did find it odd that whoever was spying on us and the farm would be so careless as to allow the phone to ring, hence alerting us to their presence, but Paul said that perhaps whoever was behind all this wanted us to know about it but in a subtle way. However, a few weeks later something more sinister happened.

We were still not allowed to live on our property and, according to the Council, we were not even allowed to work on our own property after dark! It was stressed to us that we would only be allowed to work "office hours" and were not allowed to stay or be at the farm after dark. We had a small trailer where we kept all the paperwork relevant to the farm, as well as medicines, horse blankets, and a few mugs and plates so that we could have something to eat when we were working there. Arriving early one morning, we noticed that its door was wide open, yet we are always careful to lock it. On closer inspection, we could see that the lock had been forced open, so we gingerly went inside, expecting the interior to be in the usual sort of mess that vandals are notorious for leaving. However, we were pleasantly surprised to find everything tidy inside. We inspected the cupboards, and soon realized that things had been moved around. The paperwork was all in the drawer - but it was obvious that someone had been through it, as it wasn't in the neat order I always keep it in. Then there was the smell of aftershave - and not one Paul uses. Rightly or wrongly, we associated this tidy break-in with the incidents of the telephone ringing in the woods, which still occurred from time to time.

Despite all these bizarre occurrences in our lives, we did not lose our sense of humor. I remember one afternoon when we were working at the farm. It had just begun to rain, when, from within the nearby undergrowth, we both heard a hearty sneeze. Paul stopped working, grinned over at me, then shouted back, "God bless you!" - but there was no reply from the silent, watcher in the woods.

We couldn't do anything to stop whoever was responsible for having us watched. We had no idea who was behind it, so we resolved to carry on regardless.

It was raining heavily one morning when we drove up to Hawksnest, and as we passed the wheat field beside the track, we noticed two people standing in the middle of the wheat crop. The rain was battering their brimmed hats and their long coats were being blown around by the heavy winds, but other than that, they remained motionless. Though Paul and I wondered what they were doing there, especially in such bad weather, we didn't feel inclined to go and ask. We carried on along the track and got out by the gate to the farm. The figures were still watching. Some hours later they were still there - still watching the farm. Paul became annoyed by their silent intrusion, and he walked angrily out of the gate towards them. Still, they didn't move. The rain was still bearing down, and the icy clutch of the wind was much more intense in the open. As Paul got closer making his way through the wheat, the two figures turned simultaneously and, without a word, walked slowly towards the woodland. By the time Paul had reached their previous position, they had already disappeared into the woods. He felt no inclination to go after them.

It was also around this time that we began making some grizzly discoveries in various parts of our fields. Wild animals such as rabbits, foxes and numerous birds were found dead but with one thing in common - each had a small, perfectly round hole in their heads. There was never any evidence of blood. Sometimes, it was obvious that the bodies had lain there for days, yet there were never any signs that carrion birds or foxes had tried to digest any part of them - they were always untouched. There was even one occasion when we discovered four dead mice all set out in a neat row by the gate - again with the holes to the head - but one of the mice had an eye missing and the jaw bone was neatly exposed. At that time, we had not yet heard of animal mutilations. If we had, we might have found some way of preventing what happened next.

As our fields yielded rich grass, we decided that we would invest in horses. As we couldn't be at the farm all the time, we figured that horses would be the answer, as they don't require round-the-clock attention. Paul had a favorite mare, a welsh cob by the name of Honey who was heavily in foal. A friend of ours living just a mile down the lane had a horse living in a 20-acre field by himself, so when she asked us if we could loan her one of our horses to keep hers company, we decided that Honey would benefit from a rest from the other horses. It was no problem to go and feed her, as we had to pass our friend's field on the way to the farm, so the arrangement was mutually beneficial to all.

Honey's foal was born on May 1st and, as the birth was so quick, Paul named the new colt "The Rocket." All the family was delighted with the newest addition to our equine family, and our friend invited her friends around to view The Rocket and his proud mum.

Then, some weeks after Honey gave birth, Jason woke up screaming in the middle of the night. Paul and I both flew to his bedroom and tried calming him down, but he wouldn't be placated. He kept screaming over and over again, "They didn't know she was ours! They didn't know she was ours!" Eventually Paul managed to calm him enough for him to tell us through his tears that Honey was dead, but it was a mistake, because "they" hadn't realized that she was ours, as she wasn't on the farm.

When we had finally gotten Jason back to sleep, I asked Paul what he had made of it all, but he was convinced that it was nothing more than a genuine night-mare. Besides, Paul said that he had fed Honey only hours earlier and that he would have noticed if anything was wrong. I agreed with him, and we both went back to sleep.

Early the next morning, the telephone rang. It was our friend who owned the field where Honey was living. Through her sobs, only four words were audible, "Honey's dead. Please come."

When we reached the field we were met by the piteous sight of the foal pawing at his mother's still body. He fled in fear as we approached. I was already crying, and everything seemed blurred, yet I could still see through my tears that Honey's stomach was a mess.

Though we were both devastated by what had happened, there were still things that needed to be done. Paul phoned the vet and asked for an autopsy. We had to know what had killed a perfectly healthy animal. Then there was The Rocket, who still needed to be fed.

Honey was taken away. The vet gave us a milk substitute for the foal, who had been successfully cornered in the yard, and was now screaming for his mother from an old stable building. Over the next few days, the foal accepted the formula from us - via a large lemonade bottle - but the two-hour-interval feeds were beginning to take their toll on us. We had to find him a substitute mother. We put an urgent appeal on the radio and contacted the national foal bank where a foster mum was found. A welsh cob mare in Surrey had recently given birth, but her foal was still born so, with a lot of luck, she might be persuaded to take The Rocket as her own. We drove our little lad to the address in Surrey where a vet was already waiting.

I won't go into too much detail about the macabre process of getting the mare to accept a foal, which isn't her own. Suffice it to say that for several days, The Rocket had to wear the skin of the dead foal, so that the mare would be fooled into believing that he was her own. If she had gotten a different scent from The Rocket other than that of her own offspring, she would have killed him. The ruse seemed to work, and, after a few days, the skin was removed, as the mare's milk had genuinely given The Rocket the mare's scent. He stayed with his new mum until he was ten months old, at which time we collected a somewhat bigger, yet very handsome colt.

In the meantime, the vet had performed the autopsy on Honey, yet his report was somewhat inconclusive. He suspected that she had suffered a double twisted gut, which is a very rare condition, but the only condition that he knew of which would have caused such devastation to her internal organs. Yet, in conclusion, he stated that her stomach appeared to have exploded.

Jason refused to talk about Honey or his nighttime outburst. He would only say that "they" did not know that Honey belonged to us because she wasn't on our farm.

It took us a long time to come to terms with our mare's death, and we believed that if something like this could happen once, then it could happen again. Yet how could we protect our animals? Jason tried to convince us that our horses at the farm were safe from "them" - as long as they stayed on the farm. He said that they may occasionally be taken for examination, but they would always be returned in a healthy state and none the worse for wear. To Paul and me this was still totally unacceptable, but, as ever, there wasn't anything we could do about it other than to trust that Jason was right.

Then, in November, 1997, I had a very strange "dream." I was awakened in the night by the sound of heavy machinery. For some reason, I was convinced that it was the garbage truck, and I jumped up out of bed to go downstairs and put the rubbish bags out for them. It never occurred to me that the rubbish wouldn't be collected at 2:30 in the morning! I remember going into the bathroom to empty the bin when suddenly the whole room was filled with intense light.

In the next instant, I was standing in a field at the farm and freezing in my night-dress. A second later and without any sensation of moving, I was in a clearing in the woods. There were large spotlights all around the clearing focused on some-

**Cardi with Jason at 18.**

thing in a makeshift pen in the middle. I could plainly see about a half dozen men in black/blue coveralls, and I accidently brushed against one of them. He pushed me away rudely saying to one of the others, "You wanted her here. You look after her." I walked slowly - as if in slow motion - while everyone around me seemed to carry on at normal speed. I was making my way towards a square-shaped white vehicle - like a Land Rover or Jeep - when one of the men grabbed my arm. He smiled at me as he led me towards the pen. In the pen, lying down, was our stallion, Cardi. I looked down at him and thought he was dead, yet I felt no emotion. Then, two of the men went inside the pen and knelt down, one by Cardi's head and the other with his back to me, alongside the horse's flank. I could not make out what they were doing, but within seconds, Cardi woke up and staggered to his feet. He tried to shake himself but wobbled unsteadily. I was aware that I ought to feel relief that he was alive, but again, I felt nothing. One of the other men opened the gate to the pen and Cardi, after a few moments, wandered slowly out and disappeared into the woods. Another of the men then said, "Let's wrap this up, people," gesturing with his hand in a circular movement. This was the last thing I remembered.

I awoke the next morning with no memory of any of this, and it was only when I went to empty the kitchen bin into the dustbin outside that I began to recollect the dream of hearing the garbage truck. Then, slowly, bit by bit, the rest came back to me. I then told Paul about it because my dream somehow had the flavor of reality, and I was afraid for Cardi.

We set out for the farm straight away and, as we drove up the lane near our track, we saw one of the girls from the local riding stables leading Cardi along the lane. She explained that she had taken a group out riding in the woods when they noticed that there was a riderless horse tagging along behind them. Instantly, she recognized the stallion and was on her way to Hawksnest Farm with him. She said that it had proved to be a long job, as the stallion was unusually slow and sluggish. Paul thanked her for her kindness and, taking the lead rope from her, began the short walk up to the farm. I drove on and waited for them by the gate. The other horses were all there, but they all seemed disturbed and anxious. When Paul and Cardi finally arrived, we inspected the horse closely yet there didn't appear to be any sign of injury on him. By late afternoon, Cardi was his old boisterous self again.

Was it pure coincidence that Cardi was wandering through the woods when I had my strange dream about him? He had never escaped before, nor could we find any break in the fence. If it was just coincidence, then why was an active stallion very quiet and subdued? The more I thought about it, the more I became convinced that, though, initially, this experience had the feel of a dream, it simply couldn't have been. Yet if it wasn't a dream, then there was a different, very frightening aspect to all of this - they were real people that I saw - not extraterrestrials.

The idea of the participation of humans - either helping the aliens or controlling them - was swiftly reinforced a few days after the incident with the stallion. It started with a strong sense of foreboding - so strong that I felt the urge to collect the boys from school to keep them safe. Jason, who was 13 at the time, shared my unease, yet neither of us understood why. He knew that an abduction wasn't imminent, yet something was approaching. The previous two days had been dominated by an escalation of paranormal activity - the sound of someone upstairs when we were all downstairs, light bulbs exploding, electrical equipment switching itself on and off, and the dogs being restless and growling at the slightest noise.

When Jason asked if he could sleep in our bedroom that night, I readily agreed.

It was 3:45 a.m. when I awoke, and I instinctively looked at the little camp bed and was relieved to see Jason was still sleeping soundly. Then, as I moved, I became aware of an acute pain in my lower left arm and wrist. It was so bad that I woke Paul. He switched on the light. We could both see that my fingers were swollen and would not move. The veins were standing out very prominently, and the skin was very red. An inch long scar ran across the main vein in my wrist and there was a large red lump, approximately 2" in diameter, and about 4" up from the scar. Paul slowly uncurled my fingers, as I appeared to have no feeling in them. Then, as my hand opened, we could see a patch of dried blood in my palm.

Paul's instinct was to call the doctor, but I refused. I knew that this was something way beyond practical medicine. I took a couple of painkillers, and I told Paul that I would be fine. I tried to go back to sleep, yet I was so afraid that whatever had happened to me might just happen again.

The next morning, I stayed in bed while Paul got the boys ready for school, telling them that I wasn't feeling well. Jason seemed disturbed telling his father that he had had an experience during the night, but unusually, he had no idea what had happened, except that it was different. He too, complained of a pain in his lower right arm, but all Paul could see was a reddening of the skin.

Later, still in pain, I settled with a cup of tea in the living room, and idly flicked on the television set. The first image on the screen was an advertisement for spectacles, and as I glanced at it, I went cold. A clear picture of my experience began to unfold. I remembered waking slowly and hearing noises, very loud, as if they were amplified. I then became aware that I was sitting in a chair, which was tilted backwards like a dentist's chair. At first, I believed that I had been in some sort of accident and was in a hospital because there were mixed smells in the room, much like disinfectant, antiseptic and anesthetic. Lying back, as I was, I could see that the ceilings were high, and there were fluorescent strip lights, which were not on. There were windows high up in the walls, and sunlight was streaming through them. I could feel the warmth of the sun on my face.

Suddenly, all my attention was focused on the pain in my left arm. I realized that my right arm was resting on the arm of the chair, but the left was outstretched, palm upwards, across a table which was adjacent to the reclining chair. I slowly turned my head to the left, and I could see a strap restraining my arm above the elbow. There were also five or six silver colored needles, about 4" long and spaced about 1" apart, protruding from the center of my arm above my wrist. A clear tube had been inserted into my vein, and blood was being drawn up the tube and deposited into a clear, sealed jar on the table.

My only thought then was to stop the pain, and I reached across with my right hand and began to grab the needles one by one, throwing them down to the floor. Suddenly, there was a lot of noise, like the sound of feet rushing towards me, and I knew, although I did not see "them" that "they" were there. I didn't have time to look around, as I was concentrating on getting the tube out of my arm. After a second or two, it moved, and I felt a searing pain in my wrist, which made me cry out. As the tube came free, blood spurted upwards and then I heard a voice say, "Oh no! She's awake!" There were more words that I couldn't make out, but I knew the tone was angry. Then I clearly heard someone say, "Someone's going to answer for this."

Someone wrenched the tube from my hand and then I saw a man's face. He wore a hood with a drawstring tightened around his face and a mask over his nose and mouth, but I knew beyond a doubt that he was human because he wore black, thick-rimmed glasses, normal glasses that you see every day - glasses just like those in the television advertisement.

The man began mopping up the bloody mess that I had caused. I could sense that he was angry that I had seen him, but he spoke to me with measured politeness. His voice was deep and authoritative, and he kept calling me "Honey" with a mid-Atlantic accent. I knew he was American, but I didn't concentrate on his words, as I was still struggling and crying. All of a sudden, I was aware of a feeling of intense cold deep inside my arm and I knew that something was wrong. The man started to panic, yelling at others to come quickly. After that, I remembered nothing until I awoke at home in bed at 3:45 a.m. with the pain in my arm.

I stared back at the television screen. The advertisement for glasses had long been replaced by some daytime show, and I began to cry uncontrollably. I was angry at myself for carrying on like that and I made myself calm down. Straight away, I dialed Tony Dodd's number and was so relieved to hear his down-to-earth Yorkshire voice answer. Tony listened. He probed for more details and though I remembered my experience with exceptional clarity, it was still painful to talk about it. Tony explained that my experience was similar to that of other abductees and that he was certain that there was a degree of co-operation between certain government agencies and "them." Tony didn't know if the man I had met was a servant to the ETs, their equal, or their master, but he had long known about similar medical tests carried out on human guinea pigs in some unexplained joint venture between humans and aliens.

I was profoundly shaken by this experience - partly because I had retrieved it so quickly after it happened, and partly because it confirmed to me the involvement of humans - our own people - with the aliens.

To this day, I have always been nervous of anyone wearing thick rimmed glasses.

# SEVEN
# CHANGES

Throughout Jason's story, there are numerous examples of his having scars or marks on his body that look serious yet disappear within hours. Between November, 1994, and May, 1995, when we still had no idea of what was really going on with him, Jason was rushed to the hospital several times complaining of severe stomach pains, and exhibiting strange, fresh scars on his body. Each time, we were quizzed by the staff about the marks on him, but as they all literally disappeared within hours - much to the bewilderment of the doctors - nothing positive was ever done about them. No reason for his pains was ever discovered either, and he was always released a few days later after the conclusion of their tests.

Once the situation became crystal clear to Paul and me, we accepted the sight of strange marks and scars on our son. The sight of an angry red weal - which would make most parents dash to the doctor's office - were mostly dismissed by us, as we knew that they wouldn't last long, and they would not cause Jason too much discomfort. There was one time, though, when we were concerned enough to call the doctor, as it appeared that even Jason wasn't going to recover well from this injury.

When Paul and I went to bed late one evening, we discovered that Jason was missing from his bed. Although our hearts always sank, we were used to this, and all we could do was retreat to our own bed, believing that, as before, he would be returned during the night. Besides, Jason wasn't as terrified of his experiences now as he once had been. He was listening more now and he was learning from his abductors. However, early the next morning, I was awakened by the sound of sobbing coming from Jason's room, and when I got there, Daniel was already there with his brother. Jason was lying face down on his bed weeping, "My legs! My legs hurt!" I looked down and saw that my son's legs were red and raw from the ankles to the back of his knees. They looked as though they were burned, and the burns were blistering. I called Paul to ring the doctor while I instructed Daniel to go downstairs and bring back the medicine chest. I rooted around in the chest until I found some antiseptic cream and carefully covered

51

on's legs with it. He was still sobbing.

Paul announced that the doctor would arrive as soon as he had finished his rounds, and meanwhile, we must let the air get to the wounds. With difficulty, the three of us helped Jason downstairs, where we waited for the doctor.

It was nearly four hours before he arrived and, by then, Jason's legs were almost completely healed. The doctor muttered something about wasting his time, and Paul and I felt guilty about bothering him in the first place. We realized again that whatever we were dealing with went far beyond the normal medical experience of a local doctor.

On another occasion, Jason went to his local school fete with a group of his friends. Being typical boys, they were fooling around, and Jason managed to fall down the trunk of a tree, gashing his hand open on the rough bark. His friends took him to the St. John's Ambulance first-aid post, where a concerned aide put five sterile butterfly stitches across the wound. He told Jason to tell me that he would have to be taken to the hospital if it did not start to heal properly. The aide then put a thick dressing on the wound and bound it neatly with a white bandage.

I looked at the gash the next day, and I saw that it was weeping. I changed the dressing, bound his hand again with the bandage, and resigned myself to take him to the hospital the next day. However, when Paul went to wake Jason the next morning to get ready for his hospital trip, he found the bandage and the dressing folded neatly on his bedside table. Paul called me to his room, and I assumed that Jason had removed them in the night, as perhaps they were too tight. "No. It's more than that," Paul said, as he put his hand under the duvet and withdrew Jason's hand. As he still slept, we scrutinized his hand, and there was no sign of a cut, gash or any evidence of the recent accident.

I have heard that many respectable researchers in this strange field of alien abduction feel that the scars and marks remain visible awhile in order for the abductee and others to witness them. This convinces people that they are not losing their minds, and that what happens to them during an abduction is real. I can understand why a lot of people would need such re-assurance.

Sometimes there is other evidence to prove the validity of their situation, like the time I went into Jason's room to wake him for school, and I saw that his room was swarming with thousands upon thousands of ladybird beetles. While opening the windows and shaking his duvet cover outside, I called to Paul and Daniel for help. Jason, now awake, seemed delighted by the number of tiny red-shelled beetles, which were crawling everywhere. It took all of us a good few hours before we were certain that we were free of the infestation. The only explanation put forward by Tony was that perhaps Jason had been returned from an abduction prematurely, and that he had perhaps been viewing an insect breeding program when he was unceremoniously dumped back in his bed with a whole consignment of "samples" accidentally delivered with him. I am just grateful that it was ladybugs and not any other insect.

I cannot stress too often throughout this narrative that we are in no way okay with everything that goes on with our family and the strange situation that has been forced upon us, but, gradually, over the years, we have been forced to accept - albeit grudgingly - that we have no choice other than to accept it. There is nothing we can do about it. So, if our actions or feelings seem strange or unorthodox to the reader, it is only because we have all endured years of strange experiences, and we have become rather complacent with the whole thing. We revel in the "normal" times although it is easy to fool ourselves into thinking that it's all over - finished. It's so easy to lull ourselves into a false sense of security as we have done so many times in the past. There have been months at a time when we have all been left alone to live a "normal" life yet after everything we have witnessed and learned, how do we define "normal" for us? We now spend a lot of our time looking for answers, although we shall be wary of someone who tells us that they have found all the answers. This, I would consider, would be even more of an impossibility than some of the things we have witnessed!

As I've stated before, Jason was becoming more at ease with his situation, even though, for me personally, things had changed dramatically when I realized that he was allowing "them" to share his emotions. I had visions of him "going over" to the alien's side, or of their controlling him. It is only in retrospect that I can see that this was a natural progression, and that there was still more to come.

One night, Paul woke me, and we could both hear the sound of someone talking. We couldn't make out the words, but we knew it was coming from Jason's room. We both crept along the landing, and stood framed in his doorway. Jason was sitting up in bed and speaking in a soft but strange language that neither of us had ever heard before. At first, he seemed oblivious to our presence, but then he suddenly stopped talking, looked across at me and said, rather coldly, "Oh yes. The mother." With that, he lay down and was soon fast asleep. His words chilled me. It was the emotionless way that he had referred to me. Not in a loving child/ parent relationship way. One of the dogs then pushed his way past us, went over to Jason and insisted on snuffling his face until, sleepily, Jason put his arm out and half stroked the dog telling him at the same time to go away. Satisfied now that his young master was okay, our big dog turned and left the room. We both laughed at the dog's antics before returning to our own bed, yet, through the laughter, I couldn't get my son's words out of my head, "Oh yes. The mother."

A few nights later we were witness to a similar occurrence late at night. Jason was mumbling the same language as before, and Paul, out of concern, went to approach him, asking as he did so if he was all right. Jason turned in Paul's direction, but in the same emotionless fashion answered, "Yes. We are whole." Then abruptly, he looked straight at Paul and me and said in an automaton fashion, "Understand. I am them, and they are me. The few are the many and the many are one." I wrote this down so that I would remember it word for word. Tony believes that "the many are one" refers to some sort of group consciousness.

Then a few weeks later, it was Paul's turn to be worried by his son's words. Jason had brought a note home from school telling us that he hadn't been doing his homework, and, when Paul confronted him with this, they got into an argument. I can't remember the exact words now apart from the following: Paul was shouting at Jason, telling him that he should do as he was told and not argue about it. Jason instantly went quiet before saying this: "Do you not understand? I am more a part of them than I'll ever be of you."

These words stunned Paul, and although I tried to convince him that they were just the words of an angry teenager, Paul wasn't convinced. It was he who decided to phone Tony days later when he just couldn't get those words out of his head.

Tony told Paul that he was very sorry, and that he really felt badly for him, but he had heard of it before. He said that he had heard from a friend of his in America that some children were saying a similar sort of thing to their parents and these parents also wanted answers. Tony tried to explain to my husband that these children are special in some way that we were not yet aware of, but they realized that they were indeed part of "them" - they were of extraterrestrial origins.

Reflecting for a moment on the time when Jason was born, and the fact that he was expected to be still born or, at least, born with serious problems, I now know the truth of what happened that day.

On Jason's eighteenth birthday, Paul and I were taking a well earned break from the organizing and arrangements for his forthcoming party that evening. Jason came into the kitchen and offered to make us a cup of tea. I thought then that this was suspicious - our youngest actually volunteering to be helpful! He sat down at the table with us and then quietly told us that he had something to say. He asked us to think back to that day, eighteen years ago, when he first came into the world. He then explained that the fetal monitor had not been faulty - it really did register correctly that no heartbeat was found. I looked at him in astonishment, and asked what on Earth he was talking about.

Jason continued, "We had been watching you and Dad closely. We knew that you and Grandad came from a long line of abductees and that alone suited our purpose, yet there was always something good - something special about you, Mum - and I knew that given time, you would be able to understand and carry out your role in all of this. On the day that `Jason' was supposed to be born, there would be many mothers all over the face of this planet who would feel the sorrow and the anguish of bearing a lifeless child, but such is the way of the Universe. Such action is beyond the control of all but the One. I had already chosen you to be my Earth parent. Understand here that we never interfered in any of this. It was always your destiny to bear a lifeless son, yet I had to wait until the precise moment when the life force departed from the unborn child. It was then, and only then, that I was able to 'step in' and use the vessel - the empty body. I could have chosen to go anywhere throughout the Universe, but I wanted to experience humankind first hand." He squeezed my hand as he continued, "I knew that I had chosen wisely when I picked you, Mum. I rarely get it wrong."

Paul had taken all of this in and, strangely, seemed to accept what his son had been saying. "I'm sorry," Jason said, "if I have been difficult to deal with in the past, but being human, I was subjected to the same ideals as both of you and had no idea at that time of the conscious choice I had made. So, when the abductions started to happen, I was rightly terrified of them because I had been brought up to believe that these sorts of things just don't happen. Now, when I am with "them," I totally understand why they had such a hard job in reminding my spirit - the force that is really me - just who I truly am. You see, unlike other `walk-ins,' as some of your people call us, I started at the very beginning. I had no memories of the previous inhabitant of the body. Most `walk-ins' occur when the subject has been involved in some sort of accident. You read in the papers sometimes about horrendous crashes where everyone is killed yet there may be someone who is miraculously thrown clear, or walks away from the debris totally unharmed, apart from a few bruises or scratches. There are those of us who wait until the instant that the current soul - or life force, if you prefer - leaves the body - when the person dies. Then, and only then, can one of us `walk-in' and use that body. We still retain all the memories of that person, and we try to learn from their emotions, too, but this can work for us or against us."

We were both totally intrigued by now, and Paul asked Jason to further explain what he meant by that. Jason continued, "Sometimes the memories of things that that person has done are nothing to be proud of, and we spend the rest of their time here in trying to put things right. You must have read accounts of people having a sort of crisis of faith after a near-fatal accident. They then change their life style and try to be a better person, and in this way we can make a difference. It's not the same as interference - although technically that person wasn't supposed to die at that precise moment. It would be a freak accident. I suppose there is a fine line between someone's destiny and changing what was never meant to be in the first place. `Walk-ins' don't happen just for the fun of it. There is a purpose to them, and for me it was two fold. Firstly, I wanted to experience what it was like to be human this time and secondly, as a human, I would be in a better position to help the rest of you - when the time comes."

I asked him what he was supposed to do here and how he could help - when the time comes - but he wouldn't be drawn further on this point, telling me that I don't need to know - yet. However, he stressed again that whatever he was here to do, it would not be done by force. He said that we were not given free will by accident and that whatever the future holds for all of us, it must be our decision - the population of the world - to make. He and his kind would never interfere. If there were enough of us to make the right decisions in the future for the betterment of mankind, then `they' would be there to assist us. Only time will tell."

Paul and I thanked him for his candor, yet we both felt strangely detached from our youngest son. We had put up with a lot over the years, but now to be told that although your child is your child, in another way, he isn't - and never was - is very disturbing. We watched him at his party later that evening - laughing and joking with his friends and betting with them how quickly it would take him to down his first legal pint of lager. We looked at Jason and then looked silently at each other, confirming just how "ordinary" he is at times. This was a revelation that would take a long, long time for us to finally accept.

However, that acceptance was still a long way off when Jason was still eleven and we were experiencing his strange episodes of talking in the foreign language. Then something happened that put a different spin on things.

I noticed that Jason had seemed edgy and bad-tempered all day - a sure-fire sign that the abductions had started again. He wasn't far from his twelfth birthday, and I tried to get him to talk about what he wanted as a present. Eventually I persuaded him to talk to me about other things as well, and I asked him why he was so tired lately. He snapped back at me, "I have to stay awake because I'm scared."

I asked if it was his abductions - "Was there something new happening with them?"

He shook his head, "No. It's in case it happens again. In case I see me again." Baffled, I asked for an explanation.

"It was Thursday," Jason said, "I woke up suddenly, got out of bed to come downstairs, looked back for a second and then I saw myself - still in bed, asleep. I was terrified. I tried to scream for you and Dad, then I thought I must get downstairs to you. As soon as I thought it, I was there - downstairs - but I don't know how I got there.

"You were in the living room talking to Dad about us all going on holiday, and you asked Dad if he thought it was a good idea to invite my mate, Allen, but Dad wasn't paying attention, because he was watching the television. In the end, you hit him with a rolled-up newspaper to get his attention."

As he told me this, I went cold. Paul and I had discussed the holiday, but as we weren't sure that we could afford it, we hadn't mentioned it to the boys. There was no way that Jason could have known about it. Even if he had somehow listened in on our conversation, how would he have been able to see me hit Paul playfully with the newspaper to attract his attention without his having been in the room with us?

Jason went on to say that as he "entered" the living room, the dogs started whining and growling and Chissum, the biggest and boldest of the Pyreneans, was snapping at him. Apparently, this frightened Jason, and he wished that he was back in his bedroom - and instantly he was. Again, my mind raced back to Thursday night and I remembered the dogs acting strangely and Chissum jumping and snapping at the air. We are used to the big dog snapping at flies, and we assumed that was what he was doing at first, but then he began growling and following something with his eyes and lunging at it every so often. After a few minutes, he stopped this, and, seeming to be more settled, he wagged his tail and lay down. Paul said that he must have heard a noise outside.

I was puzzled and frightened by what Jason had just told me, but I didn't let him know that. I gave him a cuddle and told him not to worry and said that I would ring Tony later that day, although I was sure that it wasn't important. I was concerned about this incident and told Paul, and it was he who rang Tony later that day. As ever, Tony was not fazed by this new development and explained to Paul that Jason had had an OBE, or out-of-body experience. This is a well documented supernatural phenomenon, which increasingly seems to overlap with abduction cases. There are known "psychic stars" who are tested in laboratories and are able to go out of their bodies more or less at will. In one case a person was able to read a series of numbers placed on top of a high cupboard without ever physically leaving the bed. Tony further explained that OBE's are common in times of crisis, and there are instances of patients being able to look down at themselves on the operating table - even being able to recall the conversation of the doctors and nurses. As many as one in six people have had an OBE, and it is quite "normal" for the experiencer to pass through walls, travel long distances, and pick up information they could not possibly have known any other way. According to the Bible, the prophet Elisha used his skills at going out of body to spy for the Israelites during their war with the Syrians. Many primitive cultures accept that the shaman or medicine man can use OBE skills to find out about certain things. It is a fact that back in the 1970s, American military authorities experimented with remote viewing, giving psychics map co-ordinates and asking them to describe the locations by using OBEs to travel to that place. During the Gulf War, when Saddam Hussein announced that the allies were spying on him by using psychic means, it was generally regarded as another ranting of a madman, but we know now that he was speaking the truth, as remote viewing was being used.

This was, however, a completely new event for Jason, but Tony was able to convince me that Jason's heightened psychic abilities made him a natural candidate for other paranormal experiences, as well as abduction. He also warned me that Jason's alien friends may have purposely given him the skill to have OBEs for their own ends. For once, Tony's words didn't bring me any comfort. My greatest fear was what would happen if he left his body but for some reason couldn't get back to it.

Within a few days of speaking to Tony, we were again awakened in the night by Jason calling for us. Paul and I got to his room, where he instructed me to get a pen and paper. "Write this down Mum," he instructed, "I don't want to forget any of this." Then he told us of a feeling of travelling and finding himself in a light environment, despite it being night time. He said he saw lots of corridors - long ones with shiny floors. There were lights set into the ceiling, and these were on. There were no windows along the corridors but lots of doors, some double. I have included a transcript of the notes I took down that morning:

"All the corridors are empty, like in a dream. But this is not a dream, I know I'm there. I turn a corner, but I don't know how, and there's a low humming sound. I remember looking at something on the wall, but I don't remember what it was. There is a very heavy dark-colored door with a soldier or guard on either side. They are wearing dark-blue or navy uniforms with a white belt. I can't see their arms. They have white socks over their boots and white curtain tassels on their shoulders - right I think. Dark berets with no badges or signs on them. One man is white, the other is black.

"I can enter the room without being seen, but I don't know how. They don't see me. This is a large room - a hall. Very high ceilings, but no windows. The floor is still shiny. There's a small switch panel by the door and a bank of television sets and buttons immediately to the left of the switches. There are two more soldiers in front of the screens, both white. There's a small staircase leading from this balcony thing to the main room.

"Now I'm in the big room, and there are two people wearing white stuff next to these tanks. There's six, maybe eight, of these tanks, and they look like dumpy milk bottles. I can't remember clearly, but there are long shelves with smaller milk bottles with large numbers underneath. Each one has a number. There are lots and lots of little red lights on the ceiling and some switch on and off as I look at them. Some of the jars have things floating in them in some sort of water or liquid."

At this point, Jason began to cry, and I told him to forget about it, but he snapped back at me that it was important, and he was determined to remember it all. He carried on:

"I know what they are. I know what they are. They're bits of them - the aliens. I'm angry, very angry, and then all the red lights start to flash on and off, and then there's a noise, like a ship's siren, and it goes on and on and it won't stop. People are rushing around and more people come in but nobody seems to know what is happening.

"The very last thing that I remember is a fantastic flash of light, then I'm in the light and I have this incredible sensation of speed, and I can't hear the siren any more. Then I woke up and yelled for you and Dad because I didn't want to forget anything."

When I look back on that night, my emotions are mixed. I was relieved that Jason seemed comfortable with his new experience, and I also understood his feelings of anger over the way his "friends" were treated by certain factions of mankind. Yet I felt overwhelmed with sadness that he should be identifying with "them" so much, and I had a deep seated fear that, one day, he might switch his allegiance completely.

Eight years on from that time, I am relieved to know that my fears where un-founded.

# EIGHT
## FAMILY EXPERIENCES

I have questions - lots of them, and I know that Jason has the answers to most of them. A short time ago I asked him why people bother trying to be more spiritual - more enlightened. Why should anyone of us try to think differently, to change the world, when the majority of the world doesn't wish to change, and the powers that be hold the upper hand anyway? What's the point?

I should point out that on this occasion I felt particularly sorry for myself as I overheard someone in the village refer to me as "that strange woman with the funny ideas."

I slumped down in the armchair in the living room - still asking my question - though not really expecting that Jason would furnish me with an answer. He had been idly watching wrestling on the television when he switched it off and leaned forward in his seat.

"Have you ever watched a flock of birds, Mum, - like seagulls on a beach or pigeons on a field?" he asked. I sat quietly and listened. "You know when they take flight because something has scared them. Have you ever noticed that they all seem to take flight at the same time? They don't wait and watch each other, then gradually follow the one that started it, do they? All the birds are individuals, yet when they burst into flight, their cohesiveness is a sight to behold. Even though they take flight at precisely the same moment, they never go off in different directions - they fly together, as a whole, in the same direction. Yet there is no leader - no one bird which organizes the others. There is no boss. This is ultimate proof of the power of collective thought - a collective consciousness. The birds are governed by a collective force - the spirit which runs through all the individuals. It needs just one bird to create the thought that there is danger close by, and that thought immediately manifests in all the birds, and they act as one. That individual bird transcends self to become one with the whole flock. So really, the bird moves within the flock, and the flock moves within the bird. This same force is possible within mankind, as just one person's idea can turn society in a different direction. So, don't sit there and complain that no one person can make a difference because you all can. It is the difference that you wish to make to society that is important. When enough of you are going in the same direction, you will be able to influence the flock - you will help to create the whole consciousness of the new collective."

His words were very profound and helped me to snap out of my depressed mood. It was wonderful being able to talk to Jason about such things, even though there were still times when he would hold conversations with other people that would go way over my head. I feel that he is now quietly confident about himself and the way he handles the things that still happen to him and around him - but it hasn't always been this way.

I wrote in my diary, several years ago, "I am beginning to feel that I cannot cope. I have to be there constantly for Jason - but who is there for me? Paul is always supportive but sometimes it's too much even for him. There are others, but they are only voices down the telephone. If there is a God - and if You are there - please do something and put a stop to all this."

I remember that we - as a family - were soon feeling alienated by our own close relatives, and again I confided in my diary. "Wally (Mum's partner) has asked me not to bring the boys to visit them in the evenings anymore. He claims that whenever we leave, we also leave something behind us in their home - strange noises, strange smells and sometimes, seeing strange things that are terrifying him. What can I do? Is it me? Am I doing this subconsciously? I would never wish to do anything to hurt any of my family, and I need them around me more than ever, otherwise I just don't know if I can cope with all this. However if I am the cause of their fear - if it is me - what can I do?"

It was suggested to us all years ago that we should tell our close family members the truth of what is really happening to our family - especially to Jason. It was felt that if our families where told, then Jason would feel more comfortable with his situation, and he would be able to talk openly about his experiences to people other than just us and the few professionals who were helping us. Paul's mother's reaction was predictable, I suppose - she didn't believe a word about "aliens" or "paranormal happenings" but, to her credit, she maintained that whatever Jason's problems, she would always be there for him, and she vowed to do whatever she could to help. Years later, this is still the case with my mother in law.

My mother though, was totally the opposite. She accepted what we were telling her - acting almost as if she were relieved that it was all out in the open. She later told us that she had suspected since Jason's fourth birthday party that he would grow up enduring the same sort of experiences that had plagued his grandad throughout his life. She told me about the nights when he, too, would be missing from their bed, yet he always refused to discuss any of this with her. I thought back to the time when he had given me the cryptic message about there being something that I would, at first, be very afraid of, but then I would come to see it as being something very beautiful - as he had done. I felt certain that this was what he mean - the alien experiences.

Poor Mum. Although she kept repeating that she knew something was going on, though she wasn't quite sure what - it was obvious that she was trying hard to deny to herself the truth of the situation. "I've seen too much," she would state to me, "There's too much going on around your family to deny the existence of `weird happenings.' She quizzed Jason about his abductors - particularly about how "they" communicate with him. She was fascinated by his answer that "they" talk to him telepathically - in his head - and she asked if he understood what they were saying - in his head. He nodded in the affirmative.

"That's all right then," she sighed. Puzzled, Jason asked her what she meant by this comment. "Well, isn't it obvious?" she laughed. "If you can understand what "they" are saying to you, then "they" must be talking to you in English. So, if they are speaking English, then they must be English aliens and that makes "them" all right with me."

Jason chuckled and kissed his grandmother gently on the cheek. "I can always rely on you, Nan, to keep me cheerful," he said.

However, it was not long before Mum witnessed more events, which, if she had any residual doubts about our situation - fully convinced her that Jason was telling the truth.

She had booked a week-long holiday for herself, her friend and her four grandchildren: Daniel, Jason, and my brother's two daughters, Sarah and Kayleigh. Mum's friend had to pull out at the last minute because of illness so I was invited to fill the breach - much to my boy's consternation. My boys knew they wouldn't be able to get away with as much with me along as they would with their beloved grandmother.

We duly arrived at the caravan park at the beginning of July. It was still quite early in the holiday season, so there were not many caravans apart from ours that were occupied. This didn't stop the kids though, and they delighted in having the swimming pool virtually to themselves.

It was Jason's thirteenth birthday that Tuesday, so, the previous night, he went to bed early in the twin room he was sharing with me. I, too, went to bed early, but it was because of a severe headache. I must have fallen asleep almost immediately, as I didn't wake up until early the next morning when sunlight drifted through a crack in the curtains. However, my headache was so bad that I could hardly see. I staggered out of bed, stopping to pick Jason's duvet off the floor and re-cover him. Then I made my way to the narrow galley kitchen to find some pain killers.

Turning on the tap for a glass of water, I was surprised to hear Mum call out nervously, "Who's there?"

"It's only me, Mum," I replied. "Sorry to wake you. I was just getting some aspirin."

The door to the room Mum was sharing with one of her granddaughters opened slowly, and Mum emerged, holding a blood-soaked tissue to her nose. Her long white nightdress had large blood stains down the front. She then peered around as if making sure I was alone before she made her way slowly across the kitchen to the table where she sat down heavily on the bench. I quickly put the kettle on before joining her, asking her all the while if she was okay and what had happened. I sat down opposite her, and she looked at me with fear in her eyes. Her nosebleed seemed to have abated by then, and she gradually coaxed herself to tell me what had happened.

She said that she had woken suddenly in the night. A hairslide she had used to clip her hair back off her face was digging in the back of her head and she assumed this was what woke her. She pulled it free and leaned over to place it on the bedside table, but as she did so, she noticed a very bright light coming from under the door. Almost at the same moment, she flopped back on the pillows, dropping the hairslide. She was totally unable to move - paralyzed completely - apart from her eyes, which remained open. "I felt so heavy," she cried, "and there was so much light, so much light. I really felt that I'd had a stroke. I tried to call out for help, but my face was paralyzed. The light was so bright, overwhelming. All I could do was lie there. Then I heard all this noise, like shuffling, coming from the living room. Then suddenly, the light was gone, as if someone had switched it off. Immediately, I was able to move, but as I did, my nose started to bleed and the blood just kept coming." There was blood not only on her nightdress but it was all over the sheets and even the carpet in the bedroom. Mum went on to say that she had stayed awake for the rest of the night - too afraid to close her eyes in case it should happen again. It was only when she heard me moving around in the kitchen with the daylight that she felt confident enough to come out.

I persuaded her to go back to bed and, as she felt safe now because it was daylight, she agreed. I immediately checked on Jason, but he was still sleeping soundly.

When the other children got up, I cajoled them all into being quiet to allow their Nan to sleep, but I was surprised when Sarah announced indignantly, "Nannie isn't the only one who needs some sleep." The ten-year old then went on to say that she had been kept awake by "all those noisy motorcycles going round and round the caravan." She said that there were hundreds of them because she could see all their lights zooming past when she looked out of the window. "I was coming in to wake you up to see them, too," she explained, "but then I think I must have fallen asleep again."

At that point, Jason wandered wearily into the room, sleepily rubbing his eyes. Daniel and the two girls joined together in a muted chorus of "Happy Birthday" while Jason went through the motion of opening his cards and presents. After the girls excitedly arranged the cards along the window ledge, I asked Daniel to take them outside. I could sense that something was disturbing Jason and, as soon as the others left, he fell into my arms sobbing bitterly, "They came on my birthday, Mum. Why? Why can't I just have my birthday? A holiday?"

As I hugged and comforted him, we were interrupted by my six-year-old niece running in and demanding we go outside to see the "big helicopter planes." Jason went to the bathroom to hide his tears, while I followed Kayleigh outside. There were eight Chinook helicopters flying extremely low over the campsite, followed closely by a small completely black helicopter. Daniel and I estimated that the machines were only about a 100 feet above the tops of the caravans and seemed to be circling the area. The display continued for quite a while, and I eventually left Daniel in charge of the girls, while I went back inside to look after Jason. He had emerged from the bathroom saying that he felt better, but his mood had changed - it was like he was somehow defiant. At that moment, Mum appeared, still looking pale but feeling much better in the daylight. She wished her grandson a happy birthday and went to hug him. To our surprise, Jason pulled away from her, squealing in pain. When we lifted his shirt, we were both shocked to see a large, angry red swelling on his side. Mum wanted to call the doctor, but, true to form, there was no sign of the swelling by the end of the day.

Another abduction had taken place - that much was obvious - but then I found that I had a new problem. Instantly, all Jason's anger was focused on me. He went out of his way to be rude, disobedient, and insolent. This was much more than the usual teenage resentment about the rules and regulations parents inflict on them. His fury was deep - and personal.

Embarrassed that Mum and the girls were witnessing Jason's vitriol, I tried to make light of it, but this technique fell flat with him. In the end, to minimize the discomfort everyone was feeling, I tried to stay out of his way. I explained to Paul what was happening, and he agreed with my actions, saying that we would deal with this when we got home.

However, the last evening when we were all having dinner in a pizza restaurant, Jason found a flimsy excuse for a row - then suddenly started screaming at me that this was all my fault - if he hadn't been born to me, then "they" wouldn't come for him. He would be normal - like all his friends. He glared at me, face flushed, with angry tears starting down his cheeks, then he turned and fled the restaurant leaving the rest of the family shell-shocked and embarrassed, as all the other diners had watched the drama unfold, and the room was now shrouded in an uncomfortable silence. Daniel was the first to get up and follow his brother, muttering to me that it would be all right. Mum, shocked and angry also went after him, announcing that however bad things got, Jason had no right to treat me like that. I felt the tears starting to flow, but the frightened looks on the faces of the girls - who had stopped eating - made me try to suppress them and what I was feeling. Deep down, I knew he was right. He had inherited from me the color of his hair, his fair complexion - and he had received a more deadly inheritance - he was an abductee. I felt wretched, guilty and helpless to do anything about it. I too, felt the resentment because the abductions were not something that I had consciously chosen. I was as much a victim as him - and there was nothing I could do about it.

We travelled home the next day - a more subdued party. I dropped Mum off at her home, and, although she insisted that she had enjoyed the holiday even after her night of terror and Jason's behavior, it was also perhaps the first time that she had fully appreciated what Paul and I have to live with on a daily basis.

Unfortunately, it is not only Mum who has been a first-hand witness to our strange situation. My younger brother, David, a University lecturer, has his own story to tell, although he still remains skeptical of the alien-involvement issue.

It began one night in August, 1997, when he and his wife, Ruth, were watching television one evening. It was quite late and both girls had been in bed for hours, so they were more than surprised when they heard heavy footsteps running down the stairs. They both assumed it was Kayleigh, who is an active little girl and sometimes has trouble settling down. David was so sure it was Kayleigh that he found himself shouting, "Kayleigh, get back to bed." The footsteps stopped. Puzzled, David got up to check and opened the door. There was no one on the stairs. He went upstairs, yet both girls were clearly sound asleep in their beds. He came back down and told Ruth. They were both startled - the noise of the footsteps had been crystal clear. Though he shrugged it off and went back to watching television, Ruth was very afraid.

During the night, David was unable to sleep and at 3:00 A.M., he went downstairs. The security light that is triggered if somebody approaches the house was on, so David opened the door to check. A large, black cat was sitting on the doorstep quietly looking up at him. David noticed that Ruth had left a full rubbish bag outside and, thinking that the bag had attracted the cat, he moved the bag back inside to prevent it from being split open by the animal. While doing this, the cat remained immobile, eyes fixed on David. When he was done, he tried to shoo the cat away, but it refused to move. With every movement David made, the cat followed him with its glare, and when David locked eyes with the cat, he found it hard to break away from its gaze. Eventually, he shut the door, left the cat outside, and he went back to bed.

Despite feeling very unsettled by the cat, David quickly went to sleep and dreamed that he was with his family and my family in a large house. Around the house was a dangerous swamp, but he wanted to explore it. In the dream, I apparently told him not to explore it but he insisted. However, when he went outside, he found that an invisible force prevented him from going any further. At this point, he woke up very distressed. Since he was fully awake now, he propped himself up with pillows, intending to read.

As he sat in bed, he saw some lights coming toward him. They seemed to be coming from a long way off, although common sense told him that the walls of his bedroom were only 10 feet away. As the lights came closer, they changed - elongating into thin, upright humanoid shapes with large heads and huge dark eyes. David then struggled to wake up from his "dream" but realized that his eyes were already open.

Soon afterwards, and without realizing it - he was asleep again. This time he dreamt that he was back in his old bedroom that he occupied at Mum's house before he got married. He walked out of the room and went downstairs, passing his parents' room and seeing a shape in the bed that he thought was Dad. Downstairs, our brother Stephen came in, and David asked him what year it was. Stephen said it was 1985, and he started to talk about a football match that was due to come on the television. David replied that Stephen was wrong and the year was 1997. Mum then laughed and stated that there must be something wrong with him to think that. Looking around the room, David recognized some old furniture that Mum had long since replaced. At that precise moment, the cat - the same one he had seen outside his door - walked in and David screamed at it to get out, yelling that he knew it was making all this happen. He tried to hit the cat, but the animal retaliated and seemed to be growing larger and changing shape. As David began to fight with the cat, he woke up suddenly in a sweat, his heart beating wildly.

This sequence of dreams and happenings disturbed David greatly. Although he instinctively rang me the next day to tell me of this experience while it was still fresh in his mind, he rejects any suggestion that any part of the experience was anything other than a dream. He knew that I would comfort and reassure him, and he desperately needed someone to talk to - to try to make sense of what had gone on. Personally, I have my own theories about all this - but I didn't share them with him. He wasn't ready yet to accept the unacceptable.

I once read that sometimes dreams can be the reality of the subconscious mind, that occasionally we can only find the courage to confront things from our conscious reality in dreams. On rare occasions, our dreams can predict the future. I have heard of people predicting earthquakes and other disasters by dreaming about them - and such predictions have come true. After my brother's revelations of his strange experiences, I, too, began having strange dreams which even now, defy explanation. For nearly two weeks, I had the same dream. Even though I would wake from this dream before it finished, I would always go back to sleep and continue the dream at the exact time I left it.

In the dream, I am always on the patio of a large house with about thirty other people. Jason is there with me, and I know that Paul and Daniel are not far away. They cannot be present, as they are not part of the chosen collective (and I have no idea where that comes from). One man is clearly the leader, although no matter how hard I try, I cannot see his face clearly. There is silence, and we are all looking toward a city in the distance when suddenly, a series of bright flashes lights up the city. There appear to be massive explosions, and the whole city is burning. I cry out in panic and despair to the leader that we should be there with our families and friends, suffering with them. He coldly replies that I must remember what I have been taught, and that I cannot be wasted.

When this dream subsided, I began having a similar dream for a number of days, and it's almost a continuation of the first dream. This time, Jason and I are in a large hall, and again I know that Paul and Daniel are close. The same people are around us, and, together with the same leader, we watch in awe as huge fires and great tidal waves happen around us, although we are all untouched by these events. Without any knowledge of being specifically told, I know that Antarctica is on fire, the ice cap is melting, and the Earth's axis has moved by 2°. Again, I cry out at the devastation but this time it is Jason who responds. Staring at the catastrophes happening around him, he coldly states, "It begins."

Five days after the dreams subsided, a strange orange light was seen above our house. It approached slowly, as a large oblong shape in the sky. Then, as it hovered over the house, it tipped to one side and fragmented into dozens of small orange lights, which formed a circle. Although I was on my own at home, I felt no fear - just curiosity. Shortly afterwards, Jason came in, and we watched them together. Daniel came home some time later, and he too, had witnessed this event with his friends. It soon became clear that this particular sighting had been witnessed by many people locally and had even made the local news. However, I believed that somehow this sighting was personal to me. I don't know why, but I believed that it had something to do with my strange dreams.

# NINE
# THE DOLPHIN STORY

Quite a few years ago, we found that we were able to finally afford the trip that we had always dreamed of taking the boys on when they were much younger - Disneyworld in Florida. Although they were no longer children, we still felt that, as we are all young at heart, Disneyworld would still be the wonderful, magical dream that it's said to be. None of us were disappointed.

We flew out from Gatwick one July morning, and it was the first time that the boys had ever flown, so that in itself was a unique experience for them. They spent the whole twelve hours on the plane delighting in the technology of having their own private video screen, and taking naps in between favorite films.

The hotel was just outside of the resort, and, to cut down on the expense, we had booked a family room, which consisted of a large room with two double beds. However, Daniel and Jason refused to sleep in the same bed, and every night we went through the ritual of dragging the mattress on the floor for one of them while the other slept on the base of the bed. Although this seemed most uncomfortable, they were both adamant that there was no way that they were ever going to share a bed - claiming that "men" don't do that.

We had a marvelous time. Even getting lost many times in the rental car was great fun, as it enabled us to explore more places.

Disneyworld itself was truly magical, although it seemed to impress Paul and me more than either of the boys. Obviously, the fast rides were more appealing to them, and they relished this, even if they occasionally felt very ill afterwards. It was all considered to be part of the thrill!

It was during the second week, however, that something changed - Jason had another abduction experience.

It was late at night, and we were all in bed. We had opened the balcony doors, as the humidity - even at night - was exceptional.

I remember Paul waking me to tell me that Jason wasn't in the room. I automatically got up and went to the bathroom, even though I expected it to be empty. Paul threw on some clothes and went down to the reception desk thinking that maybe Jason was thirsty and had gone down to the beverage machine in the lobby. He returned alone. Daniel had stirred during the commotion, but had resigned himself to sleep again after muttering that his brother would be back - as usual. I knew he was right and wished that I had his confidence, but for me it was the awful realization that it didn't matter where we were in the world - if they wanted Jason - or any of us - they could find him. Paul was half propped up on the bed, his face held in his hands. He was angry and upset. After all, we had been free of this for so long now, but, for it to come back while Jason was on holiday again - in Paul's mind, this was so unfair.

I cuddled up to Paul, and we sat in silence watching the breeze caressing the net curtains. A storm was beginning, and I don't know how long we watched the lightning weaving across the skyline before we were both asleep.

When we awoke next morning, Jason was curled up on one of the small armchairs by the balcony. Paul was first to reach him and, on waking him, started to inspect him for marks of some kind, but none could be found.

Jason was clearly upset - though more so at the intrusion into his first holiday abroad. He said that he couldn't remember much about his latest experience other than the fact that the procedure was the same as always. Daniel woke up at this point and reached for his wristwatch to check the time. He called out in alarm, asking if one of us had accidently knocked his watch off of the dresser, as the watch had stopped and the glass face was smashed. Paul went over to look at it and then checked his own wristwatch - which he was still wearing - and although the face was intact, his watch had also stopped - at precisely the same time as Daniel's - 3:11 A.M. I went to the dresser for my watch (Jason can't wear one, as it stops after a few days), and, sure enough, the hands were stuck on just past 3:10. Paul and Daniel ended up buying new watches in one of the massive markets, as no end of new batteries were able to jump start the old ones. Still, Daniel didn't mind, as he bought himself the sort of watch he had always wanted - a wind-up model with Mickey Mouse in the center using his arms to tell the time!

Although Jason was still upset over his recent experience, we decided to go to one of the theme parks, feeling sure that the thrill of the rides would cheer him up again. However, after lining up for ages for the first ride, when we all finally got seated on it, the ride refused to work. The young lad operating the ride was quickly joined by another, and when neither of them could fix it, a maintenance crew arrived, but after several minutes they were as perplexed as the youngsters. Apologies were given and that particular ride was closed down for the day with the crew muttering amongst themselves that nothing like this had ever happened before. We tried another ride and again, as soon as we got near the front of the queue, the machinery refused to work, and no logical reason for it could be found. In all, we tried four of the major rides that day and all with the same result. We decided that before anyone realized we are always at the front of the queue when this happens, we would make for the exit and try another day.

We decided to give SeaWorld a try. After all, looking at marine life couldn't cause problems, could it?

We arrived there about 11:00 A.M. and all four of us were soon filled with wonder at the enormity of the place. We were just in time to see the killer whale, Shamu, give his daily performance of specialist tricks for the delight of all the audience, and Jason really seemed to be enjoying himself. Daniel has a knack of finding the fun in everything he does anyway, so we knew he would be happy wherever he was.

After the performance was finished, we all decided that we would follow the crowds along to the dolphin enclosure. The enormous pool had hundreds of people gathered around its edge, as sometimes the dolphins would swim over to be fussed by the many hands scrambling to touch one of them. As there were so many people, we decided it would be better to go down the steps first, which would take us along a passage where you can see the animals swimming underwater. There weren't many people down there, as most of the dolphins were floating on the top of the water, enjoying their contact with the humans. While Paul and I were remarking on the vastness of the pool, Jason stepped forward and put both his hands on the glass wall, which held back the many tons of water. He closed his eyes. Paul nudged me to look over, and, as I did so, a lone dolphin was swimming toward Jason. The sheer grace and beauty of the creature was stunning, and, on reaching Jason's position, the animal began swimming to and fro past him, but never far from him. Within minutes, a few more arrived, and soon we counted more than a dozen all partaking in this strange swim past Jason.

By now, a crowd had gathered alongside us, and even though people were talking loudly about what they were seeing, Jason was unperturbed - still keeping his eyes tightly shut and his fingers evenly spaced on the glass. We left him there for a while fielding questions about what he was doing - and how was he doing it. We just smiled meekly and laughed that for some reason the dolphins must like him.

After several minutes, Jason opened his eyes, and was quite shocked to see the crowd he had gathered. He moved away from the glass, and the dolphins swam away a couple at a time. The crowd also dispersed, now that the spectacle was over. None of us said a word as we made our way to the exit, and we found ourselves once again beside the dolphin pool. The crowd around the pool had thinned out considerably, although there were still a few dozen people leaning over the water trying to attract the dolphin's attention. Most of the people had lost interest in waiting around for the animals to come back up to the surface. Daniel's attention had already been seized by the nearby penguin pool, and he made his way over there. Jason remained by the dolphins' water, and again he closed his eyes and let his hands drift into the shallow blue water. Immediately, one of the dolphins came to him and, as he caressed it, I too felt something, which could only have come from this creature. I don't know what it was that I was feeling exactly, but I felt good, calm, and relaxed - in a way, I felt a great connection not only to this beautiful animal, but to other things and to the Universe itself. I told Jason as much, and still with his eyes closed, he smiled and said that this was understandable, as the dolphins were a link between mankind and the Universe - and had a strong connection to "them" - the aliens.

Before long, more dolphins were jostling to be closest to Jason, but then, as before, a crowd began to form around us. Daniel broke Jason's concentration by yelling for him to see the penguins, as they were "doing funny stuff," so before the crowd grew too inquisitive, Paul and I made our way towards Daniel, and Jason followed a few minutes later.

We did return to the theme park a few days later - and everything worked perfectly. I can only assume from this that whatever Jason's experience had been, it had changed his energies somehow, which then affected electrical operations. This wasn't the first time - it had happened several times in the past. I remembered that back in his school days, we had received a letter from his school stating that it was against all the rules for the students to make money from their fellow students. After looking into this, we discovered that after one of his experiences, Jason seemed to get some sort of energy surge - and he was making money from his classmates by charging them ten pence a time to receive a mild electric shock from him!

All in all though, the four of us loved our holiday, and Paul and I plan to return to Florida one day soon, even though we are told by our sons - who are now both "men" - that we're too old for all that childishness!

At the time I never thought to ask Jason what went on between him and the dolphins. So it wasn't until much later when I asked if he could remember if there were any messages from the dolphins, and he said "Of course there were." I asked him to elaborate:

"I sensed the emotion of tranquility which emanates from all their kind. They also 'told' me of their sadness of being where they were, but added that if people perceived them as intelligent beings, i.e. the 'tricks' they do for the public, then perhaps that would lead to a better understanding between humans and them, and their place in the scheme of things would be better recognized in time. Perhaps the greatest `emotion' they communicated to me that day - and I was elated for days afterwards - was of 'being The One.'"

I interrupted here and asked if he meant "oneness," but he said firmly "No," and he continued: "Being the One is a step up from oneness if you like, as in that instance, I was joined with the dolphins, but through them I became part of the 'collective' (if you like) that I believe is The One. It's everything - every emotion of every being throughout your universe and beyond - but without the bad emotions. For that is truly the ultimate goal. That connection is unbelievable, and I hope every human can one day grow enough to experience The One."

# TEN
# MOVE TO LINCOLNSHIRE

We came to South Lincolnshire in early December, 1998, after finally admitting defeat and realizing that, whatever we did, we would never be allowed to legally occupy our own property at Hawksnest Farm. It was a terrible acceptance for all of us, especially Paul and me, and the days leading up to signing the sale contract caused no end of arguments and recriminations between us. Questions crept into our minds like: Were we really doing the right thing? Should we keep the place and keep applying for planning permission? Were we giving in just to go for an easier lifestyle? Why should we give up on something that we both loved so much? The sad fact is that the local council - so obviously backed by the powers that be - left us little choice. We even went to great lengths to hire a land agent, who had the reputation of winning the most hopeless of planning appeals. At our first meeting, he was totally fired up about our situation, and was absolutely convinced that he could obtain the elusive planning permissions we needed to live on the farm. The man had so many contacts, both at the council offices and in local government, and, for the right price, he would utilize these assets. For the first time in years, the land agent gave us hope, and we felt our own spirits lift as we went home after that first meeting. The agent telephoned us a few days later to say that he had set certain wheels in motion, and that we should look forward to spending Christmas in our own home on the farm. We were elated. However, our new-found optimism started to flounder when we heard nothing more from him for three weeks. We telephoned his office several times, and each time we were told that he was unavailable. Eventually, knowing that something was wrong, Paul and I drove out to his office and insisted on sitting in the reception area until he was available. Grudgingly, the agent agreed to see us, and he wasn't in the "go get 'em" mood that he was in when we had first met. He sat across his desk from us and told us, in no uncertain terms, that he shouldn't even be talking to us, as certain parties wouldn't like it. He went on to say that he was wrong, and that he could think of no way to get around the planning restrictions. He offered us our money back, and he advised us to give up - before it was too late. Paul wasn't happy with this advice - or the thinly disguised threat - and demanded to know what was going on. The agent thrust his hand forward in a "stop right there" action, but Paul was determined and threatened to sit there until he was told the truth. A few minutes elapsed in total silence before the land agent sat back in his chair and said the following - and I will never forget his words. He said, and I quote: "It is not the council who are against you, but their strings are being pulled by some very big guns, and I mean really big guns. The information I received from my informant is that you are to be stopped from occupying your property at all costs - and he did stress at all costs." The man then stood up and opened the door of his office for us saying as he did so that he didn't want anything more to do with us, and that the fee that we had paid him so far would be fully refunded.

You can't begin to know what that did to us - to me and Paul - and we wandered around for several days after that meeting as if we were in a dream state. We then realized - perhaps for the first time - that these people, whoever they are, meant business, and we had to consider the safety of our family. Paul and I discussed the possible sale of the farm over and over, just as we had done for various reasons so many times in the past, but somehow we knew that this would be the final time. Yes, we had to sell, but it broke our hearts to do so. We decided that when the farm was sold, we would move well away from it, and from Kent, so that we wouldn't be reminded of things. We felt that this was the only way that we could cope. It had to be final.

Although we sold the property six times, the sale always fell through, but there was never any reason provided as to why. We were told that the prospective purchasers simply changed their minds. At the seventh attempt, things seemed to go fairly smoothly as we understood that two sisters wanted to keep their horses there. Right before the sale was settled, the solicitor rang and told us that the name on the contract wasn't either sister's name. At this point, we told him that it didn't matter to us, we had to sell.

At the time of this writing, we understand from our friend, Sue Rutland, who still lives in the old Oast House just a mile from the farm, that the only thing that has happened there is that all the fencing and buildings have been removed, and a new perimeter fence has been erected. The only livestock there are the few geese who look after themselves.

When we first moved to Lincolnshire, I received some interesting letters from people - via my English publishers - who wrote to tell me that, because of having read about us, they were very keen to visit the farm. They went on to say that although they did not trespass onto the fields and kept strictly to the public bridle paths that surround the property, it wasn't long before they were stopped by three men who arrived in a white Landrover insisting that they leave the area immediately. One letter from a young man and his fiancee stated that while they were walking on a path in sight of the farm, they suddenly felt very ill

**Front of the House in Lincolnshire.**

and nauseous. They further stated that shortly after that, they spotted a white Landrover pushing its way through the vegetation on the same bridle path. For some reason, the couple decided to hide in the undergrowth, and watched while the Landrover stopped close to their position and two men got out of the vehicle and appeared to be searching for something. The young man stated that he and his fiancee knew that the men were looking for them, and they were very frightened. He said that they stayed hidden for a good few minutes until the men got back in the vehicle and left. Then the couple decided to get away from there as quickly as possible and took a short cut across the bottom field of the farm. He said that they were terrified of being caught but more afraid of the fact that they were both now feeling so terribly ill. His letter stated that they managed to reach their car, which had been left in the pub parking lot and, while driving home, they both felt much better and were perfectly fine by the time they got home. This couple felt so strongly about what had happened to them both that they wrote to me several times, and we eventually arranged a meeting at our house.

It was a blustery day when Mick and Fiona arrived. They were actually on their way to Norfolk for a two-week holiday and had made a slight deviation to their travel plans so that they could spend the day with me.

They had so much that they wanted to tell me. They were very obviously both experiencers and had been for most of their young lives. We discussed various incidents that had happened to them, and I tried to offer advice or explanation where I could. Although they had written to me in detail about the incident at

Hawksnest, they were keen and excited to go over the details again, when we heard a low humming sound coming from outside. The noise grew louder, and the three of us realized that it was a low-flying helicopter. We went outside to have a look, and, sure enough, there was the machine in question, hovering about fifty feet above the drive. The horses were terrified by all this commotion and were galloping up and down the paddock. While we were all watching, the helicopter whirled upwards once more, circled the back field, then returned to its previous position above the drive for a good five minutes before flying off to the East. Although there is nothing remarkable or sinister in this, as there could have been a thousand reasons why a helicopter could have been in the area, the really strange thing is that the machine was totally black - even the windows - and there were no visible markings on it.

We've since encountered these helicopters on a number of occasions, and they are always connected in one way or another to our bizarre situation here. They were even present when we visited Australia in the autumn of 2000.

However, the helicopters' appearance on this occasion seemed to have the desired effect, and my young visitors - visibly spooked by this - made their excuses and left, hoping to get to their campsite before nightfall "just in case."

# Eleven
## More Goings On...

Though we were heart-broken at finally giving up on our dreams for Hawksnest, we were excited by the prospect of a new beginning in Lincolnshire.

The house we had fallen in love with was beautiful - detached, fairly secluded, and only a few years old. Surrounded on all sides by vast fields, it stands well back from the little country lane, separated from it by a large lawn. Three enormous chestnut trees stand as sentinels in lined formation across the grass. With four big bedrooms and a study as well, the house afforded us more space than we had ever had before. There was a small paddock to the back of the property which would afford us the luxury of keeping three of the horses which we could not bear to part with - including, of course, Craven. The old rogue means the world to me, as he represents the last link I have with my father. As well as being the fulfillment of a promise to a child, this gangly-legged bay yearling was given to me by my Dad just a few weeks before he died.

There was also a large concrete barn in which Paul was determined to house his ever-growing collection of cars, which he intends to restore at some point in the future. However, this barn is still used to shelter my horses at night - much to my husband's consternation!

We moved in early December 1998, and my mother, Wally, my brother David, his wife Ruth, and their two daughters, Sarah and Kayleigh, accompanied us. The idea was to help us get settled into our new home and then spend the Christmas holidays with us. Paul was still driving the rental van to and from Borough Green to collect and deposit various items of furniture - with Daniel's and Jason's help when they could manage to tear themselves away from the final farewells to friends.

The move went well, and we all revelled in the wonderful silence for which deep countryside is famous. However, a few days later, my mother was standing at the sink in the kitchen when she suddenly screamed out in alarm. Paul and Wally rushed to the kitchen, and, when they had calmed her, she related to them that she had seen a tall white figure walk slowly past the window. At that same moment, David entered the room with Kayleigh (who was visibly shaken) and described the same entity that he and his daughter had just witnessed passing the patio doors in the living room. None of us could explain this. At first it was thought that perhaps one of the family was playing a trick on all of us, but we were all accounted for. We had no near neighbors, either. So, more for Kayleighs' sake, we all decided that it must have been the effect of car headlights somehow coming across the field and creating some sort of strange pattern on the glass windows. The children readily accepted this explanation, yet we hadn't convinced ourselves. When the girls had gone to bed, my brother made the remark that this was yet another "haunted house."

We all enjoyed Christmas and New Year's Eve, and the entity at the window was soon forgotten, but this proved to be only the beginning. On January 3rd, Paul and Daniel, who were out working late in one of the culverts we had on the property, witnessed this same entity. Paul told me later that it was about seven feet tall and that Daniel had first called his attention to it as it was standing at the end of the tunnel and appeared to be watching them. None of us had any answers, and the only thing I could do was record this incident in my diary. We said nothing to the rest of the family. However, the next evening, Ruth witnessed this thing when it again passed the kitchen window. She rushed to the living room to tell the rest of the family, when Sarah screamed and pointed to the window, where we all caught sight of it briefly as it passed. We watched in silence, all eyes fixed on the patio doors, and, sure enough, the entity again appeared to move slowly past the glass. Although we were all in a frenzy over this incident, David rose to his feet announcing that he was going to get to the bottom of this. Daniel, not wanting to be branded a coward when his uncle asked him to accompany him, grabbed his coat from the cupboard and followed David outside. The rest of us made for one of the windows to see if we could see anything, but other than the blundering shapes of David and Daniel, nothing else was visible. Having checked all possible hideouts, the intrepid investigators came back inside complaining about the bitter cold. The only odd thing they had discovered was that the horses, safely shut in the barn for the night, were very restless and milling around. Nothing more was said about this incident, and I recorded the details of it in my diary.

The holidays over, my family duly left for their homes while we all tried to settle into our new home. It was now January 9th, and, as we had so much work to do in the house, Paul and I didn't take the four dogs for their evening walk until very late. We enjoyed the country air and the fact that all of the small country lanes were deserted (they weren't used much in the daytime either!), and began talking about out future plans. Suddenly, Paul drew my attention to four very bright red lights in the night sky, which seemed to be headed towards us. They were traveling slowly, one behind the other, and, as they came overhead, we could detect a soft humming noise coming from them. The dogs had paid them no attention until they stopped overhead at which point the dogs seemed to become very anxious, and they all started whining. Paul and I stood gazing into the air, partly mesmerized by the lights and partly trying to calm four very anxious dogs, when we noticed three helicopters flying in from the east. With the strange lights still motionless, the helicopters soon caught up with them and began flying between the lights, yet the lights never once broke formation, and within minutes continued on their journey.

With the dogs now calmer, we resumed our walk while still watching the helicopters flying between the red lights, which were obviously not perturbed by this action, as they stayed in formation, even though the helicopters were repeating their maneuvers over and over again. The strange procession gradually disappeared from our view.

Jason, who was, by now, totally bored with miles and miles of countryside, had managed to get himself a part-time job helping out in a burger take-out in the village. Though he had a lift home every night, he still had to walk the length of the lane on his own with only a flashlight for guidance.

On the night of January 11th, Jason rushed through the back door at about 11:30 in quite a state, yelling to us to help him "keep them out." When Paul had finally calmed him down, Jason sat on the settee with his head in his still-shaking hands, and he `described how he had been confronted by three "ghost-like entities" on the lane just before he reached the house. We asked him to explain what he meant, and he told us that they were almost shadow-like with no substance but hazy around the edges. He went on further to say that he felt very vulnerable. After everything that Jason had been through, it seemed odd that he was so frightened of these entities. For the first time in years, he asked if he could sleep in our bedroom that night, and we agreed. The night passed without incident, but Jason was clearly worried by his encounter, so I tactfully suggested that maybe it was yet another form of ET contact, but he shook his head adamantly that they had nothing to do with ETs.

Feeling somewhat at a loss to offer any help, I then suggested that perhaps he should ask his ET friends for guidance on how to deal with this new phenomenon. He agreed. That evening, he only went to work because Paul and I agreed to meet him when he was dropped off at the end of the lane. It was no hardship on us to walk the dogs a little bit later, so we duly waited for him. Sure enough, his boss dropped him off, and, after exchanging pleasantries with the man, the three of us and the dogs walked home. However, just as we reached our driveway, the dogs started to whine then began to bark at the darkness in front of us. Then, there they were, just as Jason had described - three misty-type entities gliding towards us. Jason moved closer to us while Paul and I were frantically trying to calm the dogs who were becoming uncontrollable. Within what felt like only seconds, the entities had gone, and the dogs were quiet. Again, Jason slept in our room that night, but he had already resolved to ask "the others" for help.

The next morning we saw a very different Jason. He was bright and happy, and later told me that "they" had visited him, and it was explained to him that the entities he had encountered were, in fact, lost souls. He was told that they had been drawn to him partly because of his aura, yet mainly because he was now very psychic, which meant that he was "in tune" with spiritual vibration. I won't even pretend to fully understand any of this. Suffice it to say that Jason was told how to deal with such incidents - by "them" - and, with his new understanding, duly dealt with the matter. He won't go into any details but he must have done something right, as we have never seen these entities since.

As with most of the bizarre things that go on here, I grudgingly accepted the situation, even though I felt extreme frustration at Jason for not telling me how he dealt with this incident. Yet it posed a question in my mind: Was there a connection between the spiritual world and that of the ETs? I was determined to pin my son down on this point, and eventually, totally fed up with me carrying on to him about it, he told me that while they are separate, and not necessarily one and the same, the worlds of spirit and ETs were strongly linked. Jason tried to explain to me - in a way that I could comprehend - that, because many ETs can operate on a higher vibrational level than ours, they can more easily contact spiritual beings. He further explained that there are several dimensional levels that exist within our own time-space continuum and that human spirit can transcend each level. Our own psychic abilities can open such dimensions to us while we are still in a terrestrial state via out-of-body experiences, channeling, trances, etc. Jason believes that those of us who are able to overcome our "fears of ourselves" are able to travel astrally throughout the Universe.

Again, according to my son, he knows that there are several dimensional levels, and, depending on the way we have conducted our most recent life, when we "expire" (Jason's term) or die, our spirit aspires to the next appropriate level. Apparently, we are either sent back to try to get it right next time or we have been judged to have done enough to go on to the "next round," as it were.

# TWELVE
## GEMMA

Gemma is a wonderful young Australian girl in her early twenties - shoulder length dark brown hair, clear blue eyes and at just over five feet tall, very slightly built - almost frail and delicate looking. You wouldn't call her glamorous, but her smile is so wonderfully infectious and can light up any room. That, coupled with her lovely personality, makes her one of the most beautiful people it has ever been my privilege to meet, and I'm honored that she is also a close friend in whom I can confide. More than that, she and Jason are able to help each other through the complexities of their alien experiences as she too has been an alien abductee since early childhood.

We first met Gemma in November, 1998, when she visited England to attend her best friend's wedding. We were still living in Kent then, and, as luck would have it, her friend lived in Kent and not too far away from us. She was introduced to us via Mary Rodwell, another very good friend of the family, who is the director of an organization called Australian Close Encounter Resource Network. It was Mary who first began writing to me after reading all about us and our experiences, and we became very good friends. We have all been fortunate to travel to Perth, Western Australia, to meet all these "friends from the internet," and I will go into more detail about our visit later.

As previously stated, it was Jason who recognized Gemma first when we went to meet her at the coach station - and not from a photograph. The two of them recognized each other as if they knew that they had been together many times in the past. Gemma came to stay with us often during her six-month stay in England, and she and Jason would always act more like brother and sister than good friends. The bond between them was very strong. They would stay up until the early hours of the morning talking about the difficult times they had both endured from the strange lifestyle that had been thrust upon them.

In early March of 1999, nothing much had happened at the house for about six weeks. We even tried to convince ourselves that our situation would now be normal but, as usual, we had lulled ourselves into that false sense of security yet again.

Gemma had stayed with us for the weekend and had left early that morning. However, about ten minutes after she left, the doorbell rang. As I went into the kitchen to open the back door, the caller, impatiently started hammering urgently on the door while ringing the bell again and again. Certain that something was wrong, I hurried to open the door and there before me stood a diminutive but very plump, red-faced woman. She was shabbily dressed with black hair and very dark weather-worn skin. She didn't look at me, but rather tried to push past me into the house, saying as she did so, "Where is she? Where's Gemma?" I managed to escort her back to the vicinity of the door, and without thinking, explained that Gemma had already left. The woman seemed very disappointed, muttering that she knew she would be too late. It then dawned on me that Gemma didn't know many people in this country other than her friend and a second cousin she was staying with in Stevenage. I asked the woman how she knew Gemma, but she just smiled at me, stating that she "had been sent" to speak to her. I started to enquire who had sent her when Jason wandered wearily into the kitchen. He had been awakened by the dog barking furiously from her "safe" corner in the kitchen. There was obviously something about this person that old Millie didn't like at all, and she was letting her feelings be known.

The woman again tried to push her way past me until she stood - almost in awe - in front of Jason. He had no idea who she was, but he remembered his manners and greeted her. She didn't reply. Jason looked over to me and, grinning, shrugged his shoulders as if asking what was wrong. The woman nodded at him saying, "So, you're the other one, are you?" This time Jason and I both looked at each other blankly, not knowing what was going on. The strange visitor then turned quickly and headed toward the door grasping my arm urgently as she paused for a moment. "You do know, don't you?" she whispered. I had no idea what she was talking about and just wanted to get her out of my house, as she was making me feel very uneasy. As she stepped out onto the drive, she looked back and said, "They know about you. Be careful." I thanked her for her warning, and as I closed the door, Jason and I started laughing about her seriousness, and the fact that we had no idea what she was talking about. I did find it strange that she would know about Gemma's visit and told Jason. He seemed a little disturbed by this and went outside just a couple of minutes after the woman, yet he could see no sign of her - she wasn't walking along the narrow lane, nor was there any sign of a car up or down the long roadway.

Later that afternoon, I received a phone call from Gemma who was very frightened and upset. She told me that she had arrived at her cousin's home where she was used to being alone in the house while her cousin worked all day. However, she said that a few minutes after she had arrived, the phone rang. It was a man who asked for her by name, but he wouldn't give his. He told Gemma that he knew that she had been staying with us. He gave our names and address, and then told her that it would be in her best interest not to visit us again, nor to have anything further to do with us. He did stress that, as they knew everything, it would definitely be in her best interest to take notice of him. Gemma panicked and slammed down the phone. Moments later she remembered that dialing 1471 would reveal the last number to call. She dialed it only to be told by a recording that the caller's number was withheld.

Contrary to the threats, Gemma came back to stay with us for one last time the following weekend before having to return to Australia. We were all concerned for her safety, but she insisted that by making herself very visible to the general public wherever she went, she would be safer.

We made her last weekend with us as memorable as possible, and Paul took the weekend off from work to take us all around the local historic sights of interest. However, wherever she and Jason went together, they had a very disturbing effect on all things electrical. In a local museum, they managed to set off the alarm system as well as to disrupt the soft music coming through the speakers. When we went into a local cafe for a meal, the only vacant seats were next to the fruit machine, which when we all sat down, started playing and lighting up of its own accord. One of the staff came over eventually and unplugged it, putting an "out of order" sign on it. Even popping into the local supermarket proved troublesome. When the pair of them picked up some chewing gum and tried to pay for it at the checkout, the electrical till went haywire and had to be closed down. They tried another checkout with the same result. So, before suspicions were aroused, they put the chewing gum back and asked Paul to get it for them. Needless to say, Paul had no problem.

Gemma left for home a couple of days later. Our sadness at her going was soon replaced yet again by paranormal activity.

It was now 15th March, and Jason was awakened by a loud tapping noise on his window. I, too, heard the tapping and woke Paul to hear it. He decided against further investigation - adamant that it was the television aerial that had come loose in the high winds and was tapping against the window. At Paul's insistence, we both went back to sleep. However, the next morning Jason told me that he had switched on his lamp and saw rows of birds perched along his window ledge outside, and it was the birds who were tapping with their beaks against the glass. Jason's next recollection was of a bright light illuminating the birds, after which he found himself lying on the now-so-familiar slab in a perfectly rounded room, unable to move. He said that one of the taller beings was holding his gold signet ring and was gently banging it against an implement of some kind. Jason said that he thought the being liked the sound it made. He has no other memories of this incident.

The next day, I had just finished a phone call to Gemma, who told me that she was upset, as her "alien experiences" had begun again. Shortly after this, two British Telecom (our national telephone company) vans pulled up in the drive with two men in each van. One man got out - he was tall and very burly with short cropped hair and, interestingly, highly polished black boots on his feet. The other three men got out of the vehicles and stood huddled together. The first man approached me saying that our telephone was out of order. I told him that this was incorrect, but he insisted that there was a fault on the line that had been detected and must be repaired, as it could affect other people's telephone lines. At this point, I became very suspicious. I don't know whether it was the amount of workmen that had been sent, or this man's shiny boots that I found fascinating, but I found myself insisting that I be shown a work sheet or some sort of identification. The burly man seemed thrown by this, and he said that he would retrieve some paperwork from his van. He turned, chatted briefly to the other three, then all of them hastily got back into the vehicles and drove away. At first I was dumbfounded at what had just gone on. Then I felt frightened. After all, I was in the house on my own and we have no near neighbors. Finally, I composed myself enough to vanquish such ridiculous thoughts. I telephoned the British Telecom repair line only to be told that they had no report of any fault, and that they had certainly not sent out one telephone repair man in one van let alone two vans with four workmen! Again, the fear crept back in and I couldn't wait until Jason returned from school, and Daniel from work.

The following few weeks we seemed to go through a spate of light bulbs exploding and the stereo and television having minds of their own - switching on and off whenever they felt like it. There was the added sound of footsteps running up and down the stairs when we were all in the living room. This also began the now-familiar occurrence of what we can only describe as someone using the beds upstairs as trampolines, then hitting the floor with such force as to shake the light fittings in the rooms below. Paul was so concerned that I shouldn't be alone that he started taking more time off from work, although he still had to work sometimes as, unfortunately, bills that aren't paid do not disappear like our unwelcomed visitors do! The four cats didn't help either - the sight of them hissing and arching their backs at nothing with their fur on end is enough to worry anyone.

It was now the 20th of March and Paul was working. The two boys and I were watching television in the living room when the lighting grew dimmer then brighter. We all tried not to pay much attention to this when suddenly the faint outline of a grey being seemed to be pushing its face through the wall next to the television set. The television screen had already been disrupted and was just buzzing with no picture, but sure enough, the outline of the being's face was very prominent. The wall itself seemed to be expanding with the efforts of the intruder - much like pressing your face against clear plastic. We stared in silence, then just as instantly the image was gone - the picture returned to the television set, and the lights behaved normally. We all quizzed each other that what we had just witnessed did actually happen, and it was unanimous. Jason was the first to get up and go to the area of the wall where he pushed and moved his hand across the area several times before announcing that it was a "normal" wall. Daniel later reasoned that we had all witnessed an hallucination - it had to be. It was the only explanation he was comfortable with, so we left him this comfort.

Jason and I both woke the next morning with two deep red marks on our right wrist - and no recollection of anything else happening.

A few days later, Paul and I were out late giving the four dogs their final walk before bedding them down in their kennel for the night. We had only gone a few yards along the lane when I realized that one of our cats was following. Afraid that she might get lost, I told Paul to walk on while I picked her up to take her back home. Having safely deposited the happy wanderer in the kitchen, I hurried to meet up with Paul, who was, by this time, about five hundred yards in front of me. However, as I passed the dogs' kennel run, I spotted a tall white figure standing by the gate - the same figure who had terrified my family over the Christmas holidays. At first, I wondered if it was Daniel or Jason, but I could see them both through the living-room window. I didn't want to go back, as this figure was between me and the safety of the house, so I hurried on in an effort to catch up with Paul. The figure seemed to be keeping level with me, but about fifty feet away on the field. I could see that Paul had already turned the corner of the lane, and I realized that I was alone with this apparition. My steps were getting faster, and I could hear my own heartbeat as I was calling out for Paul. Although he didn't hear me, one of the dogs, Bronte, did and I felt such relief as I saw her come trotting round the corner. I called her again, and she came running toward me, tail wagging and happy to see me. It was a further relief when I saw Paul rounding the corner with the other three dogs - obviously going after Bronte, whom Paul thought was being disobedient and going home on her own. I quickly caught up to him, and after fussing over our canine crew, blurted out to him what I had seen even though the figure had vanished at some point after I had first seen Bronte. We walked back together with no further apparitions to bar our way.

The next evening there was a strange atmosphere inside the house, although nothing really happened. Even the animals seemed to notice it and they were clearly uncomfortable. Jason refused to sleep in his own room that night as the energy or atmosphere seemed strongest in his room, so we agreed that the camp bed should be revived for his use in our room once again. The next morning, however, Jason woke with a three-inch-long gash on his right leg. Although it appeared to be quite deep, there was only dried blood around the wound. At first I was concerned, but Jason told me that, as usual, it would disappear as the day wore on and it wasn't giving him any pain - he just wanted me to witness this and record it, which I did. He also told me that he vaguely remembered "them" collecting him the previous evening. He said that he had no memory of how he got there, but he found himself standing in the top field back at Hawksnest Farm. He remembered that he was freezing and trying to huddle into the bushes by the fence to escape the wind when he found himself confronted by lots of grasshopper-type entities. (Jason recognizes these forms now as resembling preying mantis insects, although when he was younger, he did liken their appearance to that of grasshoppers, as he was not familiar with preying mantis.) He described them as insectoid, ranging in height from eight feet to over fifteen feet. He said that the smaller ones seemed to be a dark green in color and the very small ones were grey, although he felt - and he doesn't know why - that these variations in color would turn to black as the creatures grew and matured. According to Jason, they all walked upright, and though it wasn't visibly obvious, he felt also that they were extremely intelligent.

On first seeing these creatures, Jason was terrified and started to scream. He was able to move easily and tried to run toward the gate. He said that they made no attempt to stop him, but rather told him telepathically that they would not harm him and were sorry if their appearance offended him. This seemed to calm him, and he stopped running almost immediately. He told me that he was then able to talk with them sensibly. Although he was still disconcerted by their appearance - and their huge size - he listened when they told him that they were sorry that we no longer lived on the farm, as it would have been easier to meet with them there, but also that they understood the pressure we were under to part with it. Apparently, these entities had been keeping a close eye on our situation. Jason was told that certain humans would not like it if it were known that he and these entities were meeting, but it was yet another step in the progression of things, and they considered that he was now ready to meet them. They explained to him that their race was millions of years older than any other. They were highly intelligent - so much so - that they had helped to shape the known Universe and were revered by other beings who also sought their intelligence on all matters. Jason was given a lot of information concerning possible futures for this planet - most of which he was told to keep to himself for now. He has come to know these entities as "The Guardians" and met with them many times over the following months. I am told that he has visited with them since then from time to time, and that he can meet with them whenever he feels he needs to, although for the most part, he says that he tries not to bother them. He sees them as being too important to want to deal with "trivial" matters.

At the end of March, Jason was still sleeping in our bedroom. His fear of "The Guardians" subsided but the atmosphere in his bedroom was still apparent. Even

Paul - usually oblivious to such things - could feel the change in his room. Paul said that it was like walking through some sort of veil when you opened Jason's bedroom door and entered the room. It even worried him.

Just before the month finished, Jason was again abducted. It was Paul who woke me when he couldn't find his son, but as per the usual scenario, we searched the house then resigned ourselves to the fact that he would be returned by morning.

He told us the next day that he had been taken to a dimly lit room. It was much larger than his usual accommodation but still had the metallic feel to it and was still rounded. He said that although the light source was not apparent, it was enough to cast equal light onto all the occupants of the room. Babies - I assume the age of about twelve to fifteen months old since Jason said that they could all sit upright - all looked at Jason in silence. He said that there must have been over a hundred of them, and they were all blonde with large blue eyes. I asked him if their heads were large, but he wasn't sure because being a typical teenager, my son thinks that all babies have big heads. He said that he was able to walk between them, but he said it was really eerie, as they made no effort to move other than to turn their heads to watch him. Then, toward the back of the room, he spotted someone he recognized - Nathan. My son went on to tell me that he had been with "his brother" many times over the years and I was somewhat shocked by his candor. I asked him to continue his account regarding the babies, and he told me that after greeting Nathan, he asked him what was going on. According to Nathan, these babies were special. Although they were all born to human parents, part of them was alien and, as they grew, this would become apparent to each of them. At least one of their parents would be an alien abductee - whether they realized this or not. They would feel uncomfortable in their bodies - limiting almost - and would possibly find it difficult to integrate into society as other children do. Although they would, for the most part, love their parents, they would feel a longing for their "other" family. They would become confused as they would come to know that they just don't belong here. Nathan stressed that in all other respects, they would be very normal, but they would be very intelligent. They would, in time, come to realize just who they really were and, with the help of people like Jason, would come to learn what they needed to know in order to effect their survival, which would be crucial to the continuance of all human life. They were to be the start of a new "Star Nation," and Jason was to one day be instrumental in their real education and welfare.

I have since discovered that there are many institutions in both Australia and America, and possibly many other countries around the world, who know of and are currently working with many of these children. They are known as the "Star Children" or "Indigo Children" - due to the fact that their auras are a dark shade. Dr. Richard Boylan is perhaps one of the first pioneers in this strange field and is achieving incredible results with his work with some of these children.

I totally refused to discuss anything to do with Nathan. Jason was disgusted - he couldn't understand how I could basically deny his existence, but I wanted no part of this. I couldn't make Jason understand the immense anger I felt at losing Nathan, and, although deep down I had always known of his existence, I had never really totally accepted it as truth. Coupled with my disbelief and anger was the fear I had - not of a child, but of my own inner fears of perhaps not being able to cope with life if I ever dared to admit to myself the truth of this bizarre situation. No - as usual for me I went along with "what you don't know won't hurt you. Leave it be." It was safer, more comfortable, and I wanted it kept that way. Even when Jason was telling me that Nathan watches me and loves me, I lashed out verbally, causing Jason to lash back, accusing me of being a bad mother and not deserving of his love or Nathan's. This same argument carried on for weeks, but finally I think I convinced Jason that I couldn't handle it any more, and he had to stop. He did so reluctantly, saying that when Nathan himself asked Jason to drop the subject with me, he complied as he had realized that I wasn't ready for all this. Although I thought about Nathan many, many times since, it wasn't until I visited Australia that I received the help I so desperately needed and was able to, at last to not only accept my third child, but see him.

In mid-April, Jason related a strange "dream" to me. He was lying on the familiar medical table in the rounded room, and yet this time he was able to move. On the table next to him was Gemma, and as he reached out to her, she looked over, instantly recognized him and reached toward him. However, a tall human man rushed over and prevented them from touching, muttering something about it's not allowed. He can't remember anything more of the dream, but he feels that that is all it was as he has no recollection of anything else happening. However, about an hour later, Gemma phoned and related to me exactly the same dream that Jason had, even mentioning the fact that she reached toward him, but was stopped by the man telling her that it's not allowed! How can two people have the same dream when they live so far apart from each other? I suppose it may be possible - some sort of telepathic connection - or could it be some sort of interference by a very human organization with its own agenda?

# THIRTEEN
# JASON'S ROOM

Unfortunately, my mother has witnessed many strange things surrounding our family and the weekend of May 8th, 1999, was no exception. She and her partner, Wally, arrived at the house for a few day's rest. Wally was still getting over a viral infection.

It was a wet day and Paul had gone into town for some parts for his car. Both the boys were out, and Mum, Wally, and I were sitting in the living room. Mum got up and went upstairs to use the bathroom. There was nothing unusual in that until she shouted down the stairs that the door was locked, and she could hear someone in the room.

Wally and I both ventured upstairs to find Mum still desperately trying the handle and knocking on the door asking who was there. She got no reply. There were only the three of us present in the house, and I even checked to see if Paul's car was in the drive. It wasn't. We could all now hear noises coming from the bathroom - taps being turned on and off and the sound of things being picked up and put down again. Mum was starting to worry a little, although the fact that this was going on in broad daylight wasn't quite as daunting. I tried the handle shouting, as I did for whoever was there to please go. Suddenly, I felt a strong burning sensation on my hand, and promptly let go of the handle while letting out a muffled yell. Mum immediately grabbed my hand to see what was wrong, and gasped as she saw the burn blisters, which were starting to appear. She gingerly touched the door handle with one finger, and then drew her hand back quickly, announcing that the handle was red hot.

We left Wally on guard at the top of the stairs while we went to the kitchen to see to my hand, which was throbbing terribly. Wally called down the stairs to us that we should come quickly as the door had just swung open of its own accord and, though the taps were left full on - there was no one in there.

After inspecting the bathroom and turning off the taps, the three of us returned to the living room and started trying to fathom just what had gone on when Paul arrived. He was calling to me as he entered the house and told us all, as he stood framed in the doorway, that as he pulled into the drive, he was conscious of a low humming sound that appeared to be coming from all over the property. He said that he tried to look around and found nothing except for the fact that the horses and assorted poultry were all gathered at the farthest point in the paddock, and the dogs were huddled in their kennel at the farthest end also. I related to my husband what had happened while he was out - vocally confirmed by both our guests - and showed him my burns. Paul, like the rest of us, had no explanation and though we discussed it for a while, we came no closer to solving the mystery.

Things were pretty normal for the rest of that day except for the fact that Gemma telephoned me from Australia. She wanted to make sure that we were all safe, as she knew what was going on here! She explained that she had been having some very strange, vivid dreams about our family. She said that in her dreams, there was always an intruder in our house. She stated that she could never focus on the face of the intruder in her dream but felt - on waking - that this unwelcome visitor was "not one of the good guys" to quote her exactly. She had felt so strongly about her "dreams" that she wanted to tell us about the intruder and warn us to be careful!

It was also about this time that Paul and I had joined NUFOS (Norfolk UFO Society) based some eighty miles away in Norwich - a considerable distance for us - but we both now had questions for which we needed answers.

At the first few meetings, Paul and I just sat and listened. We had all learned the hard way that you have to know whom to trust. We are now good friends with a lot of the members of this club, and each of them have their own experiences - their own truth. It wouldn't be fair to discuss any of our friends here without their permission. Suffice it to say that many times they have been able to help us sift through our confusion, and for that assistance and advice, I truly thank them all.

However, there is one person who has since become my best friend, and yet the way that we met is surely bizarre.

As I stated earlier, when people first heard about us and our bizarre situation - we had been on national television quite a lot as well as appearing in many magazines and articles in Australia - we created a lot of interest, which included my first introduction to Mary Rodwell. In one of her subsequent letters to me, she told me that a very good friend of hers, Jane, was returning to England to look after her ailing mother after the sudden death of her father.

Mary explained that Jane was one of the first people that had gone to her for counseling with regard to her alien and paranormal experiences. It wasn't clear where Jane's family home was, but Mary was sure it was somewhere in the county of Norfolk. However, Norfolk is a vast county, so I didn't have any real hopes of ever meeting up with Mary's friend.

I had never met Jane and had no idea what she looked like, but on our second visit to a NUFOS meeting, I found that I was strangely drawn to a very petite, attractive looking woman in her late forties who always sat quietly sipping a glass of white wine. After a few meetings, I finally plucked up the courage to talk to her, but when I did, the first thing I said to her was, "Is your name Jane?" She stared at me, nodded, then asked if she knew me as she felt that I was familiar to her. I explained that we had a mutual friend in Mary, and Jane was ecstatic. She told me that she had written to Mary to ask her for our address, as she felt strongly that she wanted to contact me. Jane insisted that there was definitely a connection between us, and she couldn't believe the circumstances of our first meeting. Since then we have shared information on our various experiences, and I like to think that we have been there for each other to lean on while learning to cope with other bizarre incidents, which happen to both of us.

Paul and I were both enjoying the meetings held twice a month for the UFO society, and we gradually got to know most of the regular members. We found that somehow we were all kindred spirits in a way. We weren't afraid to discuss our strange situation with these people, as most of them could genuinely relate to it. Then, after a few months, Jack, the chairman of the club at that time, asked if he could visit us, as he was intrigued by our situation. We readily agreed and he came over early one Tuesday evening in June. However, Jack said that he didn't like the feel of the house, and that it felt very threatening toward him. Paul and I wondered if this was just some sort of attention grabber so we didn't really take much notice of this statement. We showed Jack around the house, and then we showed him Jason's room. Immediately Jack started to have a bad fit of coughing, but he felt strongly that it was somehow being induced. At first we weren't sure what to make of it, but then we realized that this was genuine. He then began to have trouble breathing, and was turning quite blue in the face by the time Paul and I helped him out of Jason's room. Once we were all standing on the upstairs landing however, his coughing fit began to subside and he slowly regained his composure. He left shortly afterwards.

Though we had said nothing to our guest, Paul and I were well aware that there is indeed a strange and heavy atmosphere in Jason's room. We asked him about this, and he told us that it is "their" atmosphere, and, though he found it hard going at first, he was now very comfortable sleeping in this atmosphere. In fact, he couldn't imagine sleeping in his room without it now. To this day, wherever Jason sleeps, this strange energy/atmosphere manifests itself and becomes heavier, maybe to help facilitate his slumber. We have grown accustomed to this atmosphere, even when Jason sleeps in our room. However, car journeys are hazardous with Jason if he decides to fall asleep in the back seat, as the smaller space makes it much more difficult to breathe sometimes. After a while, Paul and I get overwhelmed with the strange heavy energies emanating in our vehicle and eventually, we have to pull the car over and get out just so that we can breathe properly. Needless to say, we have to wake Jason in order to continue on our journey. Fortunately, he very rarely travels on long journeys with us any longer!

A few days after Jack's first visit, we were contacted by a well-known spiritualist - who is also a friend of Jack's - and she told us that she was receiving messages telepathically, which were related to our son and the problem with his room. She had obtained our telephone number from Jack and was very eager and curious to visit the house - and Jason. Again, Paul and I did wonder whether what she said was true or whether she had just gleaned information from Jack and was curious to visit the house. However, we decided that we should allow her to visit just in case she did have genuine information about the problem of the atmosphere in Jason's room. So, we then made arrangements for her and Jack and a few others to visit as soon as possible. I have included the following account of events which I recorded of that visit as they happened:

JUNE 22ND, 1999

Just to recap on a few weeks ago, Jack, the chairman of the UFO Society that Paul and I attend, came to visit us at the house. I showed him around the house, but on reaching Jason's room he said that there was a very powerful and strange energy in there. He found it very hard to breathe suddenly and started to choke. I was obviously well aware of the energy change in Jason's room but had said nothing to Jack. We were also well aware of a similar atmosphere around the front of the house. Although this felt less threatening. Jack seemed to recover well when he came out of Jason's bedroom, but he left soon afterwards.

A few days later, while tidying Jason's room, I was physically "pushed out" of the door by force or forces unseen. This was totally unbelievable to me, but before I could decide whether to be afraid or intrigued, the telephone rang and it was a lady by the name of Dianne who introduced herself as a medium/spiritualist. I've since discovered that Dianne is very famous for her gifts. Dianne told me that she was experiencing problems related to our energy situation and was being "told" not to interfere. However, she felt so strongly about what was happening here that she asked to visit. She also explained that she was a good friend of Jack's. Paul and I wondered if we should allow this visit, as we really weren't sure what to make of it all, but we decided that, just on the off chance that this may all be genuine, then perhaps we should agree. So, on this day, she, Jack, Sarah (another psychic) and David, a mutual friend arrived there to take notes.

Immediately, they asked if they could visit Jason's room and Paul and I readily agreed. The other three went upstairs while I followed Dianne out into the hall. She stopped at the foot of the stairs and calmly told me that she was totally unable to move. She said that she felt perfectly fine but her feet were "stuck." She is only a small, slightly built woman, and Paul and I tried gently to move her back into the relative safety of the living room but, she was right, her feet were stuck fast to that spot. Suddenly Jack raced out of Jason's room shouting "Dianne, they're out here!"

She replied, "I know. They're coming at me." Standing next to Dianne, I was instantly aware of feeling very cold - freezing, in fact. It was like we had suddenly been hit by some sort of unseen entity. Dianne then began shaking violently and I was afraid for her safety but she said to leave her alone and she would be okay. She said that "they" were communicating with her and I, too, became aware that something had changed though I didn't know what. Then both Jack and Sarah confirmed this by saying that they could see an entity materializing just behind her. Dianne said that it was to the right of her and a little behind her, and they agreed. Then the small figure could vaguely be seen by all of us present and the large head and pitch-black eyes were unmistakable. Jack also confirmed that he had seen two of these figures materialize in the bedroom. Dianne then said that she was being told in no uncertain terms that "this is NOT a joke. It's a matter of life and death." She said this was repeated to her over and over and, though it wasn't aggressive, it was very serious.

After what seemed like an age, Dianne found that the entities had gone and she could move again. She was then "told" that she would now be allowed in Jason's room, because she understood. She duly went upstairs.

All five of us were now in the room. Paul stood framed in the doorway, as he felt for some reason that he shouldn't enter. Although Paul was brilliant throughout this whole bizarre visit, I really don't think he knew quite what to make of it. Jack sat cross legged on the floor, closed his eyes and tried to "tune in" to the energy. Dianne stood to one side and did the same. Sarah and David sat on the bed. David had his notebook ready to take down whatever was said or happened.

Dianne said that she felt that the energy was centered in the middle of the floor; Jack agreed. Dianne then said that "they" were present in order to protect Jason. She was told that Jason was important and must be protected at all costs. They explained that they were aggressive to Jack at their first meeting, because they did not understand his intentions towards Jason. The Pleiades system was mentioned, as were the words "matrix" and "mainstream." Other information was volunteered, but it was felt that this should be researched before being mentioned here. As this was going on, the room was alternately plunged into extreme heat then freezing cold. Our three guests then became aware at precisely the same moment that the energy/entities had completely gone.

Dianne had to leave shortly afterwards, but the others stayed, as they were anxious to meet Jason. Jack asked Paul if he could go with him to collect Jason from school and through the melee of students pouring out of the building, Jack was able to pinpoint Jason's exact position by tuning into his aura. Dianne had told me when she first telephoned that she could find Jason anywhere, as he had an aura or energy which was totally unlike any other persons. She said it was a cold-looking blue or indigo color, most unique.

Jack introduced himself to our son, and though Jason was polite, he was suspicious telling Paul and Jack that he sensed that something had happened and didn't know if it was good or bad.

When they arrived home, Jason was still suspicious and raced around the house. He came back and demanded to know what they had done, as "they" were no longer present in his room. It was explained to him that "they" had left of their own accord. Jason didn't believe this, so he acted slightly hostile and guarded for a time. He then went off on his own for a while, but when he came back, he was much more relaxed and friendlier and pleased to chat about his experiences. He later told Paul and me that he "had checked them out" with his alien entities and was assured that he could trust them.

Jason and Jack seemed very drawn to each other and seemed to have an insight into each other's thoughts. Jack tried sitting on the floor opposite Jason, who was also sitting on the floor, but Jason said that Jack couldn't do this, as Jack's energy was affecting him badly. They talked extensively about Jason's many and varied experiences, then Jack, out of the blue, asked Jason if he could heal a bad pain in the back of his neck, which he had suffered from for years. Jason pinpointed the exact position of the pain and began working on it. He simply closed his eyes and concentrated. Jack did the same and was amazed at the way Jason was working on his neck - without once having to get up and put his hands on it. Jack said it felt like treacle or molasses was flowing through his neck. He then became aware that it had stopped and looked at Jason who had also opened his eyes. Jason told Jack that he would be able to "finish off for himself," but Jack said he couldn't, so Jason continued until the pain was gone. He was also able to cure David's headache by similar means.

Later, Jack and Jason went for a walk and Jack later recounted to everyone that he had been given an example of Jason's power to project things. Jason had been talking earlier of a poem that he had published when he was much younger about a robin. When Jack had asked Jason to give him an example of his projection abilities, Jason asked him to think about something, anything that was mentioned in previous conversations. Jack remembered the poem about the robin.

Jason then pointed to a small bush directly left of him and asked Jack to relate what he saw. Jack was shocked to see a small robin! Robins breed this time of year and are rarely seen in England in June.

Our three visitors left late that evening, and they all said how impressed they were with Jason. Even shaking Jason's hand on the way out, they said they could feel the electricity coming from him. Things that Jason had told them should have come from someone many times his age. Jack was most impressed with Jason, saying how incredibly powerful he was - and knowledgeable. Jack had already arranged to meet with Jason again and was looking forward to it.

Later that night, Jason wandered wearily into our bedroom announcing that everything was all right because "they" had returned. Sure enough, on entering his room, I was aware that the atmosphere was indeed back.

As far as Jason was concerned, everything was now how it should be.

# FOURTEEN
# MYSTERIES

Among the assortment of post we receive regularly, I received letters from people both in the U.K. and as far afield as Australia and South Africa who begin by telling me that they are experiencers. However, in these particular letters, the writers then ask me to thank Jason for them - and thank me for allowing him to do what he does! I discovered that all of these people claim that they have always been terrified of their abductors, but the last time it happened to them was different - because Jason was there - with the aliens! Apparently, he was calm and peaceful and told these people that they wouldn't be harmed and to trust him. He then invited these people to go with him - and with "them" - and they did! These people were so grateful that, through Jason being with "them," they were no longer afraid of their experiences and were starting to learn from their abductors. Apparently, Jason is with these people in such a real sense that he holds conversations with them - as if he were discussing the weather! He talks to them about his own experiences - his own fears and eventually - his trust in "them." He tells these people about the house we live in - even giving the address. They discuss ordinary everyday subjects just like good friends.

I have kept many of these letters, and I would like to quote directly from some of them just to give you an idea of the sort of things these people were trying to tell me:

"Then suddenly, there he was - Jason was with the aliens. And I was not frightened at all, rather, I was exhilarated and filled with a special feeling of really strong sharing that is difficult to describe in words, but I got the very clear feeling of invitation from the aliens and from Jason himself."
-Gentleman in Sydney, Australia

"...something then happened which caught me completely unaware. I became aware of a very strong feeling in my mind. It was a little like someone had come into the room; not an unwelcome person at all, just someone there, but it did not alarm me, it just surprised me. I had the feeling that I was being watched but this didn't bother me either. The feeling grew to being watched - not from the outside - but from the inside. It was of another consciousness within my own mind. It was very gentle and very soothing. Pacifying would describe it well. At first I saw nothing but I sensed something. Very strongly. What I sensed was someone sending very calm, very soothing feelings. Very beautiful, peaceful feelings. Then I felt his presence very strongly. It was Jason who was contacting me. I experienced the calming, the care, and then I saw something which made me realize that this was not imagination. I saw "them" - the aliens. It was, most significantly, the first time that I have ever seen them without an initial feeling of fear. I could see "them" clearly, and I knew that it was Jason who was communicating with me; I just knew that it was. I just felt his presence, very strongly, and sending those very calming thoughts and feelings. It was very beautiful and has made a very deep impression on me."

-Lady in Pretoria

"I feel that in the area of intuition, Jason has a great deal to teach me. That he can affect my mind development and help me to understand and learn what I need."

-Gentleman in Melbourne

"I felt Jason's care, his concern, his understanding. I feel that his power is such that just his thoughts can guide me, can teach me. And I would dearly love that teaching from him if it is possible - and you are happy for him to do so."

-Gentleman in Gibraltar

Once again, I couldn't cope with this, and I didn't understand what was happening. With everything that we had been through, this I couldn't accept. How? Even the concept was unimaginable to me, and I slumped down on a chair then burst into tears clutching these letters tightly in my hand.

I couldn't sleep properly either, nor could I bring myself to question Jason about this, as I was so afraid of his answer. However, the letters kept coming and my anxiety grew, but this was all about to change just a few weeks later.

I was awakened from a restless sleep by a noise downstairs. As Paul was working away, I took it upon myself to investigate, believing that one of the cats had mistakenly been left in the living room. As I wearily entered the room and reached for the light, there, in the centre of the room was Hannah, Jason's dog who had died. I was overwhelmed with joy to see her and, rather than questioning the rationality of the situation, I rushed to her. She was very real, and I fussed over her: her beautiful white coat was silkier than I ever remembered and her eyes were just so full of life. I didn't question the reality of what was happening - I was just so ecstatic to be with her again. In her excitement, her massive tail was wagging so much that it was clearing everything from the coffee table

- including some half-filled cups! The tears were welling up inside of me, and I reached up to my face for a second to wipe the tears, and when I turned back, she was gone. I stood up and called to her, begging her not to go, not yet, and that is when I noticed a man standing in the corner. The light was dim, I couldn't see his face, but he was wearing some sort of flowing dark garment. He spoke to me in a soft, authoritative voice and instructed me to get a pen and paper and write down the following:

"ALL THINGS ARE POSSIBLE BEYOND THE LIMITS OF
YOUR EARTHBOUND CONSCIOUSNESS.

OPEN YOUR HEART AND YOUR MIND TO SEE THE
TRUTH OF WHAT I AM TELLING YOU.

IF YOU SEEK THE TRUTH, YOU MUST HAVE FAITH;
BELIEF IN THE UNIVERSE.

LEARN TO LOOK BEYOND WHAT YOUR EYES CAN SEE
AND DRAW UPON THE ANCIENT KNOWLEDGE OF YOUR
OWN INNER BEING; YOUR SOUL SELF.

FOR ONLY THEN WILL THE TRUTH EMERGE.

EMBRACE IT LOVINGLY, FOR IT IS A DESTINY
RETRIEVED FROM TIME - YOUR TIME."

When I woke in the morning, I didn't remember any of this until I went into the living room where the sight of the spilled coffee cups jogged my memory. I stood there awhile, wondering about my "weird dream," when I noticed a notebook open on the table - with my writing on it. I read the above and remembered everything - Hannah, the man, and what he told me to write down.

I have now memorized the words I was given and though I don't pretend to totally understand their true meaning, I must admit that I do find comfort in them. Whenever things seem to be getting too much for me personally, I often repeat them to myself and find that it helps. The events of that night also gave me the courage to speak to Jason about all this, and he asked to see the letters. I gave them to him and he flitted through each one stopping briefly to read paragraphs thoroughly and at times a wry smile would appear on his face. "Cool," he muttered, as he handed me the letters.

"Cool?" I replied angrily, "is that it? Cool?" He turned and looked at me, expecting more of my verbal barrage. I didn't disappoint him as I continued, "Do you know how upset I have been over all this stuff? It's one thing that these things happen to you, but this... you're actually willingly going with "them" to help to abduct other people? Are you mad?" My new-found anger was unstoppable.

"Mum," he said softly, "it's what I do. It's part of who I am and why I am here. "They" have helped me to see that. Remember how terrified I used to be whenever I was taken? Well, even though in the beginning you wouldn't believe me about what was really going on, you were always there for me, but it's not like that for everyone. Most of these experiencers who have written these letters have no one to turn to about any of this, and some of them are so terrified by what happens to them that they are close to taking their own lives. Yet I can make the difference; by seeing me and being with me these people relate to another human being, and I can convince them for the most part that they have nothing to fear. Just as it was for me, when I got over the fear and the terror, I started to listen, to learn, and, most importantly, to accept that this is my life now. It is the same for all these people. I believe that we are never given more than we can handle by "them," but this can be the truth on a sub-conscious level sometimes rather than in our own reality. So, when I was asked to assist and try and help these people understand, I readily accepted - and I will continue to help as many people as I can."

His words were powerful, and, though I felt immense pride for him, this was still tinged with a little anger. Why him? Why my son? He's still only a child himself, so why should he carry the burden of looking out for adults? These were all unanswered questions swirling through my head, yet the only question I relayed to him was "So how can you be in all these places all over the world in such a short space of time?" He smiled again before reminding me that he has the ability for. OBE's (out-of-body experiences). He explained that this is all relevant, but he goes further than simple OBE's now - he has perfected the ability to travel astrally and has mastered astral projection - with "their" help. He painstakingly explained both concepts to me, but I shan't reiterate this information, as it has been mentioned in detail already within these pages. Suffice it to say, Jason told me that to understand the concept in simple terms, perhaps I should remember the childhood stories of my belief in Father Christmas.

"You accepted without question," he began, "that Santa Clause could deliver presents to every child in the world in one night yet whenever you worked out the time schedule realizing that this feat is impossible, you were then told that Santa can make time stand still hence enabling him to make his millions of house calls. Yet, how many kids just accept that? You did. I did. This is the same sort of thing, but the ETs are not fantasy and they really do manipulate time which, as I've told you before Mum, doesn't exist. It's only that you - the human race - need it to plan your days, and it prevents various events and situations all happening at once. You limit yourselves so much and, amazingly, you do it deliberately."

I was still deep in thought when he got up and left the room saying it was "time" for his favorite TV program. I will admit to still being baffled over the concept of time not existing, but with my limited intelligence on such matters, I had no more questions for my son - for then at least.

It was now July 15th to be exact, and though I was still not comfortable with Jason's "new job" I had, like most things, grudgingly accepted it. That day he returned from school and asked me if his best friend, Alan, could stay the night. I agreed, and both boys slept on the floor in the living room - the atmosphere in Jason's room seems to "allow" no one but Jason to sleep in there. However, Jason had an experience during the night, and apparently, while he was being returned to the house by the greys, his friend Alan woke up. Jason explained that although Alan could watch everything, he was totally unable to move. The three of them - Jason between the two greys - then glided through the wall and the patio doors, and one of the entities didn't seem to notice Alan's leg stretched across his path and seemed to glide effortlessly through the bottom of it! Jason had no ill effects the next day except for a bloodied perfect half circle around his navel. This incident though, affected Alan very badly. Without a word to anyone, he was gone by first light and refused to see Jason or talk to him. Jason was really upset when I entered the living room that morning and, when I asked where his friend was, he related the night's events to me. Alan was also absent from school the following week.

When Alan did return to school, however, he made no secret about what had happened at his former best friend's house, and soon both he and others were treating Jason with the utmost contempt. Alan never let up making fun of his former best friend, and the phrases "space boy" and "weirdo" became commonplace in Jason's presence. Jason felt that he could do nothing about the experience that his friend had witnessed and tried hard to understand his anger and confusion. The only time Alan would talk about that night was in the presence of other boys, but then only to turn it against Jason and subject him to even more ridicule. The constant barraging coming from Alan and other former school mates was now really starting to get to Jason. One day he turned angrily on his classmates, telling them that if indeed they required proof of alien existence, then, if any of them were brave enough, they should accompany him on a car journey that evening. Apparently, the room became very quiet but gradually a few of the lads accepted his challenge, putting on a brave face in front of their now silent colleagues. It was eventually decided that three of the boys and an older brother - because he owned a car - and Jason, would take a short trip that same evening.

Five of them managed to squeeze into a small car and Jason instructed the driver to drive out into the countryside and then turn off onto a trackway, which went through the middle of an enormous barley field. Jason then asked the older boy to stop the car about a thousand yards into the field and to switch off the engine. They then all sat quietly waiting and watching the clear skies. When nothing happened in what seemed like an eternity, the boys began their mocking again, but Jason, who had closed his eyes the whole time, now opened them and told the boys to look to their left.

At first, they could see nothing and again the barraging began, but then one of them yelled out that there was a red light coming their way. They all piled across each other in order to see the approaching light and sure enough, there it was. Soon, the light was positioned almost above the car, at which point it began to descend, becoming bigger and brighter as it did so. This was too much for the other four occupants of the car and Jason later related to me - through his laughter - how all four doors had swung open at the same time, which resulted in each boy running for his life in a different direction only to realize that there is nowhere to run to in the middle of a barley field. Realizing this fact at almost the same moment, the boys turned and ran back to the car, piled in and screamed to the driver to "Go! Go! Go!" The light, meanwhile, was still hanging motionless in the sky though I understand that it disappeared, or could not be seen through the vast amount of dust that was being thrown up by the car in the boys' attempt to get as far away as possible.

This incident was the talk of the whole school for the next couple of weeks. Even teachers were intrigued by the tale, which seemed to have expanded a little on the truth. However, whenever Jason entered the room, he was met with silence. He felt that he had gained the respect of his classmates at last and their belief in what happens to him, but, in fact, they were also a little afraid of him. From then on until the day he left school, he never had any more problems about his alien experiences, and his classmates were respectful, but he never did gain more friends.

July 28th was a strange day - well, stranger than usual, shall I say! I was awakened early that morning by the telephone and was greeted by the voice of a Mrs. Bradshaw. She told me that she had gotten our telephone number from the telephone directory and was sorry to trouble me that early in the morning. She explained that she lived in one of the houses at the beginning of our road. She sounded extremely worried. She then went on to tell me that during the early morning hours, both she and her husband had been awakened by a noise coming from the inside of their garage. They both got up, looked out of the window, and were surprised to see that the lights in the garage were on. The husband told her to telephone the police while he made his way out to the garage armed with a bat of some kind in order to confront, he believed, teenagers. Mrs. Bradshaw continued to tell me that when her husband entered the garage, he was shocked to see an impeccably dressed man in a black suit and tie rummaging through some boxes in the corner. She told me that the man was quite tall, though not too thin, and he looked to be in his early thirties, but the remarkable thing was that he didn't even stop what he was doing when Mr. Bradshaw entered the garage. She said it was more like "an inconvenience" as far as he was concerned. Her husband demanded to know who he was and what he was doing, but the man looked up briefly, smiled, and asked politely if he could see Ann Andrews. Mr. Bradshaw told him that he didn't know anybody by that name, and the man smiled again and asked Mr. Bradshaw if he was sure. The husband affirmed this.

At this point, Mrs. Bradshaw went into the garage and told her husband that the police were on their way. The stranger had by now moved on to rummaging through another box and didn't seem perturbed by this news at all. She said that her husband started to wave his bat in the air and demanded that the man leave their things alone, but yet again, the stranger smiled at them and carried on. Mr. Bradshaw made several more demands for the man to stay where he was until the police arrived, but they were both very frightened at this point. She said that it was more to do with the strange way that the man behaved, something that they couldn't explain. However, after about ten minutes, the man stopped what he was doing, turned toward the pair, and again, smiling, informed them that it was now time for him to go. Mr. Bradshaw tried to threaten him into staying put until the imminent arrival of the police, but the stranger walked confidently up to them both, stared at one and then the other, then gently pushed past them and walked calmly out of the garage.

Mrs. Bradshaw told me that neither she nor her husband made any attempt to stop him. She said that, although he didn't threaten them or touch them, they instinctively felt that they must not anger him. This was a strange feeling, she told me, and they couldn't explain how they knew this - they just knew. The couple quickly followed him, expecting to take down the registration number of the car the man had arrived in. However, the well-dressed stranger walked off into the darkness - not toward the main road, which would have made sense, but in the other direction where there are only fields. The Bradshaws watched him disappear into the darkness and listened for the sound of a car, but they never heard one. As they walked back to their house, the police arrived. The officers duly took down the particulars of the incident, which they agreed was strange, although they said that no damage had really been done and nothing had been taken. The Bradshaws stressed to the officers that the stranger had asked to see me repeatedly, and the police assured them both that they would contact me to either warn me or to see if I knew who he was. I never heard anything from the police, which Mrs. Bradshaw couldn't understand, when she rang me later that day. Neither could I. It was easy to obtain our telephone number and address from the telephone directory - as Mrs. Bradshaw had done - but neither the stranger in the Bradshaw's garage nor the police apparently thought of that. Why?

When I heard nothing from the police all that day, I took it upon myself to phone them. I explained the circumstances and was passed to three different officers. Finally, I was told that the police didn't need to speak to me anymore, as the incident had been "sorted." I tried to ask what was going on and why my name was mentioned in the first place, but no one seemed willing or able to explain it to me. Mrs. Bradshaw told me days later that she had received the same treatment when she rang the police station, and it was confirmed that no further action was warranted.

I have kept in touch with Mrs. Bradshaw who still puzzles over that frightening incident, but fortunately, neither she nor her husband has had any recurrence of such strange incidents.

It was just a few days later and in the middle of a beautiful sunny afternoon that Paul and I returned from a short unscheduled shopping trip to find that our back door was wide open. We could hear old Millie barking, and it soon became apparent that she had been shut in the utility room. Although we were both horrified at what we might find - or not find - in the house, our first priority was to let Millie out and to check that she wasn't harmed in any way. We opened the door and though still barking furiously, she seemed so relieved to see that it was us and with her tail wagging vigorously, Paul checked her over while she nuzzled into my arm as if to say, "well, I did try and do my bit." Satisfied that our old dog was none the worse for wear, we then got on with searching the house and went from room to room, but we got an even bigger surprise than we were expecting - the house was exactly as we had left it - nothing was missing. It hadn't been ransacked either - until we went into the study. Letters from other experiencers had been selectively taken while everything else was scattered over the floor. The computer had been left switched on and again a lot of other correspondence connected with our paranormal situation had been wiped. All of the private and confidential matters I was trying to help others deal with had all been erased - and probably copied first. Fortunately, my diary is kept with me at all times, so at least I still had it, although I suspect that it may have been high on the list of things to find!

Paul phoned the police straight away, but, as it obviously wasn't a priority, they arrived several hours later. They stayed long enough to jot down a few particulars and then inspected the door where the intruder or intruders had gained entry. One of the officers then came back into the kitchen and asked us if we had a valuable collection of any kind. We didn't understand what he meant so he explained that having inspected the door, it was obvious to them that this was not the work of either youngsters or burglars. We were told that whoever broke into the house really knew what they were doing, as the door in question had a security lock and deadbolt on it and both devices had been professionally removed! Neither Paul nor I mentioned the fact that certain papers and information on my computer were missing, as we didn't want to be thought of as strange - so we kept quiet. The officer asked again what we kept in the house that was so valuable, but he eventually seemed to be content with Paul's suggestion that perhaps the intruders had made a mistake and had come to the wrong house. They left us with a crime report that we would have to send to our house insurers along with a couple of estimates for a replacement door, which we were also told to obtain as soon as possible.

Paul screwed an old bolt lock to the inside of the door so that we had some semblance of security. We also started bringing the other dogs in from the kennel at night, for as Paul said, who in their right mind would argue with a twelve-stone (150 lbs.) Pyrenean Mountain dog guarding the house! The insurance company quickly agreed on a quotation for the new door and it was duly fitted about a week later though even the fitter commented on the professional way that the door had been opened.

In light of what was "taken," I am convinced that this was not a wrong address case. I believe that this whole incident had something to do with the strange visitor in the Bradshaw's garage.

# FIFTEEN
# TRIANGLES & TELEPHONES

Since even before we moved here, we have had more than our fair share of problems with the telephone service, so we weren't really surprised to discover that our telephone was out of order yet again just a week after the "break in." I rang to report it and was told that a technician was already en route as the fault had already been reported. We later found out that my mother had called in when she couldn't get through to us. The technician duly arrived and, with the use of various gadgetry, informed us that the problem must lie underground. He further informed us that, according to their records, since we moved in, we have used up four life-time batteries - a feat, apparently, not achieved by anyone else in the country! Anyway, he continued his work but, after an hour, he walked into the kitchen and related a telephone number to me, asking if this was our number. I told him no and gave our telephone number back to him. He looked somewhat perplexed and asked if I knew the first number he mentioned. Again, I told him no and asked why. He then told me that another telephone line was spliced into our line, and he had no explanation. The technician then decided to inform his superiors, and he and I made idle chat over a cup of tea until the arrival some minutes later of the man's supervisor. They both went outside to chat, then the supervisor came back in to tell me that they were having the other number traced. Both men then left, with the promise of returning later that afternoon. They were true to their word, and both men returned within the hour and told me that they had managed to trace the other number on our line to an address nearby. However, when another of their technicians visited the given address, it was found to be an empty, dilapidated house, though the telephone equipment was all new.

They had no explanation, even though I cornered them on this point at every opportunity as they continued working to get our telephone service up and running again. All the technician would say was that it was very strange, very strange indeed, and something he had never come across before.

When the line was finally repaired, the two men left, promising us that we now had a very private line - but strange clicks and buzzes are even now still heard on our line - maybe someone is still listening!

Although our summer weather is not renowned for being predictable, I remember that it had indeed been a beautiful summer's day which had turned into a warm, star-filled evening when we decided to make a trip to Norwich to visit some good friends. We stayed rather late, not leaving their home until around 2:30 the next morning. We thought it would be a nice drive home, as apart from a few lorries, we had the roads to ourselves.

We had reached the dual carriageway when we first heard the whirring noise of a helicopter, and I craned my neck to look around the night skies for it. I finally spotted it coming in from behind us. It was flying very low and seemed to have some sort of strobe light emanating from the front of it. Paul then saw it as it made several sweeps back and forth over the car at low altitude. However, after a few minutes of this erratic behavior, it turned and flew back the way it had come. Paul made a joke that perhaps the government was keeping tabs on us again, as this wasn't long after the incident with the telephone lines. I laughed and agreed, but we soon went on to chat about other things, and the helicopter was forgotten.

About thirty minutes later, Paul heard what he described as a low humming noise. I could hear nothing, but Paul often seems to pick up low sounds, which he claims actually hurt his ears at times. I then became aware of lights flashing in my side-view mirror. I told Paul and, checking his interior mirror, he confirmed that it was a lorry some thousand yards behind us flashing his headlights at us. The lorry was persistent, so I put my head out of the window to see if I could spot anything that might be wrong, and I was amazed to see a large shape in the sky just a little behind the car and to the left. My first thought was that it was a jumbo jet crashing, as it was only about a hundred yards high, but then I realized that it was moving far too slowly for that. Excitedly, I related everything to Paul and he leaned across me slightly so that he could see what I was talking about. We also noticed that the lorry was a lot further back now and had indeed probably stopped. The "plane" was making no noise, and as I watched, it seemed to tilt slightly and was now positioned directly above our car.

As it was a full moon that night, it was easy to distinguish the object in the sky but it wasn't until it was above us that I reached the awful realization that the craft was actually triangular in shape and certainly bigger than any jumbo jet - bigger than half a dozen of them! The enormous shape seemed to blot out all the stars completely and take over the whole sky. I could see the craft clearly now and could see that it appeared to have a bright light on each angle with an enormous bluish light in the centre. This light also seemed to be emitting some sort of smoke - very similar to the effect of dry ice. Then the strangeness of the situation seemed to hit me all of a sudden, and my reaction was one of hysteria - and in an effort to "remain safe," I stupidly closed my window and sat in my seat, eyes streaming with tears - though I have no idea why - and listening to my heart beating loudly. Paul had witnessed the same thing when the craft effortlessly passed over the front of the car and his suggestion was to try and outrun it. Stupid, I know, but at the time, it seemed the right thing to do. Though our speed increased, the craft seemed to be keeping with us and continued to do so for what seemed like an age, but was really only about five minutes. It then seemed to be gathering momentum as it moved away from us and began ascending.

I don't recall what happened to the craft after that, as suddenly our car veered across the road and sped along the right hand shoulder. Paul was slumped over the wheel hardly conscious. I grabbed at the wheel trying to steer the car, while screaming at him to hit the brake. Somehow between us, we managed to slow the car until it finally came to a complete halt. Paul was barely conscious and babbling wildly, but we managed to get him into the passenger seat. My first concern was to get the car back on the correct side of the road and with that accomplished, I switched off the engine and searched for the phone to call for an ambulance.

Paul was now more awake, had stopped babbling, and was insisting that he was fine except for feeling exceptionally tired. We both sat there for a while scouring the skies for any sign of the craft before Paul announced that he couldn't keep his eyes open, and I would have to drive while he slept. I did as he asked, started the engine and pulled away slowly. There was still no other traffic on that road, and I wasn't sure whether I should head home or drive to the nearest village in case the craft returned. Then, I was aware of lights flashing in my mirror, and I felt my heart jump right up into my throat until I realized that it was lorry headlights. I further realized that it was the lorry that had been flashing us earlier, though this time he was gaining on our car rapidly. Still flashing his lights, he was now close behind us, so I pulled over for a minute. The lorry screeched to a stop beside the car, and the driver peered across and asked if we were okay. I blurted out that Paul was now out cold and hurriedly asked if he had witnessed the same events as us. He shakily confirmed this and added that he had been flashing his lights in an effort to warn us. Again, I asked him to confirm that he too had witnessed this craft, but he was already starting to pull away as he answered that he didn't know what he saw except that it terrified him. He said he was heading for the nearest garage, where he would hole up until morning and advised me to do the same thing. I decided to take his advice and started to follow behind the lorry, but he was fast pulling away from me and when he turned off the main road. I decided to continue on and drive for home.

We passed just a couple of lorries coming the other way and I made pit stops at all the service stations on our route. None of them were open, but somehow the lights seemed comforting.

Finally, we reached home, though I was very aware that the solitude of our house might prompt the reappearance of the enormous craft.

I was easily able to wake Paul when we rolled to a stop on the drive, and we both wearily made it up the stairs to bed. However, that night, I had odd dreams concerning strange entities and symbols, and these images continued throughout the next day. Paul mentioned to me that he too had strange dreams, and he described the same things as were in my dreams. He also said that these images were still plaguing him. Whenever we closed our eyes, the images would come tumbling out through our minds and we found it hard to concentrate on anything else that day. When Jason came home from work, we related the previous evening's events to him, and he grinned and said that he wasn't surprised as the electricity had been - to quote him correctly, "playing silly buggars." I asked him how we could be free of the images, and he smiled again, stating that obviously, we are being shown these images in detail so that we don't forget, and, though the purpose of the images was as yet unclear, if we transfer them to paper - in other words, draw them - the images in our heads would stop. Paul rose immediately to get paper and pencils, and he agreed that the entities and symbols I was transferring to paper were exactly the same as the images he was seeing. Yet again, Jason was right, and soon the images stopped coming to us.

**The faces Ann drew to get them out of her head.**

# Sixteen
# Fear Manifests

It was now mid-August. Mum, Wally and my brother David and his wife and family were staying with us for a few days, and my niece, Kayleigh, was frightened in the night by a "black, misty-type sort of man" standing over her while she was in bed. I managed to convince her that she must have had a bad dream, although I did record what she had told me in my diary, as I knew that she hadn't dreamt it - it happened just as she had said. Other visitors to our home had reported the same strange "dream" to me - a hazy dark shadow which resembled a person.

Later that same morning, Paul and I were sitting talking in the living room when my mother started screaming hysterically. We both rushed to the kitchen. My mother was standing in a corner, her eyes streaming, her hands held up to her wet face as she begged us to do something. Jason was lying on the floor at the other end of the kitchen and seemed to be writhing in pain. Paul and I both rushed to him and tried to pick him up, but he was adamant that he had to be left alone. He pushed us both roughly away and though it was only our intention to help him, Paul and I both instinctively backed off and left him, as he had asked us to do. I then rushed over and asked my mother what had happened, and she tried to explain as best she could that she "had witnessed the attack." I didn't understand. I took hold of her hands in an effort to calm her, and I asked her again to explain. She told me that "it was like a sweeping shadow had suddenly come over Jason and he collapsed onto the floor." By this time, Jason, obviously feeling better, was on his feet and comforting his grandmother, telling her how sorry he was that she should have witnessed that. My brother and his family returned from their walk at that moment and wanted to know what was going on. We couldn't tell them - we didn't know.

When things calmed down a little, we asked Jason what had happened, but he told us that he didn't know, other than the fact that this "entity" - for want of a better word - had attacked him several times in the recent past. He had absolutely no idea what it was nor what it wanted. He said that he had sought help from "them," but was told to look within himself as he knew the answer.

When all the family had gone home, we were still pondering this matter, as neither Jason nor I had any answers. Although he wasn't "attacked" so violently now, Jason said that the entity was still very prominent at odd times. We asked Jack to look into this matter and he even asked some members of NUFOS if anyone had any answers, but they could come up with nothing. Jason was still suffering from the attentions of whatever this was, and I could see that the pressure was getting to him. He was angry that "they" wouldn't help him in this, telling him only that he was strong enough to deal with it - and stating again that he knew exactly what was going on deep down inside himself. In passing, I mentioned all this to Jane and was more than surprised when she immediately understood exactly what was going on. She told us that the same thing had happened to her many years ago. She went into certain detail about the incident, which we hadn't mentioned, and her incidents were exactly the same! Intrigued, I asked her if she could explain it, which she did, and yet when I heard her explanation, I found it totally unbelievable.

Jane's understanding of the incidents was that this "entity" was in fact, a part of Jason. It was his own fears from long ago - many years - which were manifesting as an energy form. Jane told Jason that to combat this, he must face it, tell it he knows what it is and that he doesn't need it anymore. As I listened, it sounded like really pushing the bounds of reality to me and, with all respect to Jane, I just couldn't believe that this sort of thing happened. Obviously by now I was almost totally open to most things, but such an explanation just couldn't possibly be correct. Yet, Jason listened, quietly nodded in agreement, then put his hands to his head as if he had just realized something and mumbled, "Of course. It has to be."

As far fetched as this may sound to a lot of people - including me - Jason did confront this entity as Jane had instructed him to do, and it has never returned.

Now, I never doubt Jane, and I am sorry that I ever did. She has proved time and time again just how true a friend she is, and I'm lucky to know her.

# SEVENTEEN
# THE COTTAGE

Whether it is because the house we now live in is more remote than any of our previous homes, or whether the increase in paranormal occurrences in and around our home are greatly increased as a natural progression of things, I'm not at all certain. One thing is certain however. More and more people are becoming involved with us and our strange situation. A lot more people are usually unwilling witnesses to certain events. In one way, this is good news for us in that it is not only our word which readers can believe or not believe, but the confirmation of others, who - for the most part - have no pre-conceived ideas about the paranormal happenings here or yet, have no interest or belief in any aspect of this.

A good example would be Fay, her husband Brian, and some of their five children. Fay is actually my cousin but we have always been more like sisters. Even now, we confide in each other and are there for each other all the time. I know and love her family in the same way that she knows and loves mine, and Brian is very dear to me. We have basically grown up together, even making up foursomes to go out on a Saturday night with our respective husbands. We knew Brian years before he and Fay married and, like ours, theirs is a marriage which has stood the test of time. In that alone, Fay and I consider ourselves extremely lucky.

Anyway, it was late summer in 1999 when Fay rang and announced that she, Brian, and two of the youngest children would be undertaking their first visit to us in our new home. They were travelling from Kent, so it would take them about three hours. She said that she would ring me when they had turned off the main road in order to get further instructions on how to find the house. She did call, gave me their current location, and I explained, in great detail, the directions that would bring them to our door. However, when the time had elapsed when they should have arrived, I began to get concerned, wondering if anything had happened to them. A further two hours passed before I received a frantic phone call from Fay saying they were hopelessly lost. It transpired that although they were only minutes away from the house, Fay insisted that, though they had followed my directions to the letter, they could not find the house.

I directed them to the house from their current position but Fay was adamant that they had twice turned into our lane and proceeded to the very end of it before turning back (our lane ends in a large farm yard), and our house was not there. Again, I emphasized the directions, saying that our property could be found by going straight over the small crossroads and our house - which is a new building - would be the first one on the right-hand side after about five hundred metres. Again, my cousin insisted that this information was incorrect, stating that on both trips down this same lane, the only property they had come across at all was a small single story whitewashed cottage. She said that the cottage sat well back from the lane, thus affording it a large front garden, which was strewn with an assortment of flowering bushes interspersed with overgrown lawns. Fay told me that there were several large chestnut trees to the front and side of the cottage, and a wooden swing was hanging from the lower branches of the biggest tree in the front garden. A small girl was leaning on the rickety front gate. According to Fay, the girl was about eleven or twelve and dressed in some type of white smock linen dress. She said she had noticed her dress, as it was very unusual for our day and age. On the second trip down our lane, Fay had asked Brian to stop the car so that she could ask the child if she knew of our house, and though Brian obliged, Fay was met with absolute silence when she tried to talk to the girl.

Still believing that Fay and Brian had taken a wrong turn, I persuaded her to try once more and said that I would wait in the road for them. She grudgingly agreed. I duly waited for a few minutes and, sure enough, their car drove over the crossroads and came toward me.

After the usual greetings and hugs from the kids, Fay, Brian and myself made for the quiet of the living room while the two kids busied themselves chasing chickens and patting horses. We sat chatting over coffee and I made several jokes about their sense of direction being worse than mine but they weren't laughing. They both insisted that ours was the lane they had driven down twice before. They passed the row of houses at the beginning of the lane and came over the crossroads. However, they were both adamant that this small whitewashed cottage was the only property there and was roughly where our house now stood. They also stated that when they drove to the end of the lane, they did indeed come to a large farmyard, but it was totally empty. They remembered seeing some old horse harnesses hanging on the walls, but no one was around to ask directions from. I found this very odd, as the farm yard is always filled with tractors, trailers and combines and there are always a few people working around there. However, they were both rather perplexed by all this, and I could see that it worried them so I tactfully changed the subject.

Later that day, however, Fay told me confidentially how frightened she was by the young girl in the white smock. She said it wasn't because the girl said nothing, but more that it was how the child had looked at her - with eyes that seemed cold and empty.

I must admit that I didn't give too much thought to their account of the white-washed cottage and the child with the empty stare other than to later record it in my diary as yet another strange occurrence in the annals of the Andrews family. It wasn't until many months later that I realized that there was a connection between this strange child and the manifestation of a similar child that haunted Jason for a long time before culminating in the fire in the wheat field that will be documented further on in this work.

Fay and Brian enjoyed their visit and had intended to stay the night. The two children, Aimee and Andrew, were lying on the floor in front of the television. Neither Daniel nor Jason had returned home, as both of them were staying at friends until late that evening, so this left the five of us in the house. We were generally talking and making sleeping arrangements, as Andrew was starting to get a little tired, when Brian asked, almost tongue in cheek, if we had ever had any "problems" with this house as we had in our previous home. I knew that the "problems" he referred to were of the paranormal kind. I laughed and said no we had never had a problem - which, in hindsight, was a foolish thing to do. The word "no" had hardly left my mouth when there was an almighty crash on the floor upstairs. Our four visitors turned to me for an explanation. Thinking quickly, I blamed one of the cats for having escaped from the kitchen, gone upstairs, and knocked something over. This was believed, and they all seemed to breathe a sigh of relief when suddenly heavy footsteps were heard going up the stairs, across the hallway and into the main bedroom. This time I couldn't explain it and could see that Fay and Brian were becoming more nervous. I suggested making more coffee, and as I got up, the lights in the room dimmed and resumed their brightness a few times. I could see from their faces that they were not going to believe any excuse I had for this, so I continued into the kitchen to make the coffee.

When I returned, the room was very quiet. Then Fay said that she and Brian had realized that they couldn't stay overnight after all. They had obviously spent the time while I was in the kitchen coming up with an excuse, which they both agreed on but really I couldn't blame them.

I saw them to their car and hugged them both and, as the car pulled away, Fay was waving out of the window, promising to come back soon.

True to her word, she, Brian and all the children have been back to visit - but they never stay in the house. There is a small camping site about a mile from us and this is where, whenever they visit, they pitch their tent - even in the winter months. They visit the house - in daylight hours - after which time, I have to go and sit in their tent with them. As Fay so eloquently puts it, "We love you dearly, but nothing will make us stay in that house with you."

# EIGHTEEN
# THE WHEAT FIELD

It was the middle of September, and the evenings were starting to draw in once more. Robert, a friend of Jason's, had come round to see him that evening on his motorbike. However, barely had he gotten through the door when he started excitedly telling us all about a strange girl that he had seen just before he reached the house. He said that he thought it odd that she should be out alone, but when he looked in his bike mirror, she had gone. Robert had convinced himself that he had seen a ghost and vowed never to come to our house again in the dark.

Paul, Daniel and I made fun of him and his apparent lack of bravery, but Jason found nothing amusing and asked where Robert had first seen the girl. His friend told him that she was standing almost opposite the house, but was on the edge of the huge wheat field that covers many acres of land and is situated to the front of the house. Nothing more was said on the matter, and Robert returned home a few hours later - insisting that someone go outside with him to see him safely away.

Strangely enough, Jason has always been intensely afraid of this huge wheat field to the front of the house. Even though it was now high with the crop, he would go nowhere near it. He seemed so distressed one day when this field was mentioned that I was able finally to coax him into confiding to me what was wrong. He told me that, many years ago, a young girl had been cruelly murdered in this area where this field now existed. He further related to me that he believed that in her dying moments, she had been able to drag herself to the edge of the road where she pleaded with a passerby to help her. However, for whatever reason, the passerby ignored her pleas and went quickly on his way, thus allowing the girl's murderer to catch up with her and effectively finish her off. Jason went on to tell me that this girl was now consumed with anger and rage at the way she had been shunned and was not able to rest peacefully. Apparently, she had been able to make contact with Jason due to his psychic nature, but he said that he was afraid of her. He didn't know what she wanted or how to help her, but he was terrified of her rage. He looked at me with tear-filled eyes and asked me if I had any ideas what he should do. My heart went out to him, and I pulled him close and hugged him. For the first time in years, my "young man" cuddled up to me, desperate for comfort in the midst of his fears, and we sat in silence for what seemed an age. Later, I suggested to him that perhaps he should contact some of the psychics who had made themselves known to us over the years, or had visited the house with their array of gadgets and paraphernalia in the hope of experiencing or capturing evidence of some of the strangeness of our situation. Jason and I both spoke to several people about our problem, which according to Jason, was gathering momentum in as much as she was visible to him every time he went outside. Apparently, she was unable to enter our house, as I understand it is somehow protected. Anyway, apart from the fact that most people we spoke to wanted to come and visit us again and try to experience this phenomenon for themselves, we gave up on this idea and Jason said that he would have to find a way of handling this situation by himself.

I didn't know exactly how to help with this situation, but I decided that it may be of some use if I could find out a little more about this child. The local library seemed the answer, and one Thursday afternoon I made my way there. Being a small village, the library is the size of someone's living room, and its contents are minimal to say the least, but it does contain many old, historical volumes.

I asked the elderly librarian if there were any books or records specifically on the history of our village, and she directed me to a bookcase, which was kept locked. She found the key in her desk and opened the bookcase and directed me to dozens of volumes of immaculately kept red-leather-bound books. Each one was titled History of the Fen Villages around the Wash - the Wash is a large inlet of sea water, similar to a bay, and is only a few miles from where we live. The only thing which made each volume different from the rest was which ten-year span each one covered. They began with the 1700s, so that is where I started.

About the only interesting things that I had come across were the many reports of flooding which occurred in those times and how many cattle and sheep were lost. Relentlessly, I continued my quest until I came across an account from the 1880s that told of a prominent doctor who was returning from London by horseback. As far as I could determine, the location would have been about right to have put him in the immediate vicinity of where our house now stood when he was apparently brutally attacked by two men intent on robbery. As the account goes, this attack was either witnessed by a young serving girl on her way to or from the house where she worked, or she happened upon the fatally wounded doctor after the attack; the account wasn't clear. Nothing further was mentioned about the young girl as, in those days, the doctor - being financially affluent - would have been the center of this tragic news. After all, no one would much care about what happened to a lowly serving girl. The final thing stated in this report was that the murderers were never found, which leads me to wonder whether said murderers would have killed her to stop her identifying them. Although, how did people know that there were two perpetrators and not one? Did the doctor divulge this information to a passerby with his dying breath? Is this why she was ignored? Or did she tell someone and was later killed when one of the murderers came back to shut her up? Perhaps this wasn't the same child at all and I had gotten it completely wrong, so I continued trawling through the volumes up to 1950, but the only other account I could come up with was that of a terrible storm in 1905 that swept the county and actually picked up a small dwelling in our immediate area and carried it about five hundred metres before it came crashing down to the ground. It was totally different from the previous account except that a young girl had been trapped inside the house and was killed when the house impacted with the ground, and it was in our immediate vicinity.

It wasn't until the following day, when I was talking to Fay, that I made the connection between Jason's tormentor and the child that Fay had seen. I told her what I had found at the library and she remarked that it couldn't have been anything to do with the young girl who was killed in the storm as the cottage where she had seen the girl was of solid construction and couldn't possibly have been moved by high winds - at least not in a complete form as the report I had read suggested. Something clicked in my brain and I realized that the child that she and her family had met had to be the same girl. Although Fay's "meeting" with this girl had taken place over a month ago, Fay told me that there was something about her, and she hadn't been able to get the image of her out of her head. When I began talking about the apparition that was tormenting Jason, she assumed that it was one and the same. It was too much of a coincidence not to be the truth. This was the first time that I mentioned Fay's encounter and my findings at the library to Jason. I thought, assuming that I had indeed found details of the right incident, somehow this news and Fay's story would be of help. On the contrary - Jason thanked me for the information but it clearly had no impact and he was becoming more and more depressed, saying that the girl's dark energies were getting to him and pulling him down. He didn't know how much longer he could bear it.

A few days later, while sweeping upstairs, I suddenly felt compelled to go downstairs and get my camera. It still had a couple of snaps left on the roll and I duly retrieved it from the cupboard and brought it back upstairs. Then, for no apparent reason, I felt further compelled to take a photograph of our front garden through Jason's window. Afterwards, I returned my camera and continued with the housework, never giving this strange compulsion another thought - until the film was processed several weeks later. It took me a while to even remember taking this certain picture, and yet this didn't make me look at it properly. It wasn't until some friends were looking through the photographs that one of them brought something to my attention. Not only can images of alien faces be made out, but also an image of a small person standing in the shadows on the front lawn. Jason looked at the picture and is adamant that this indeed is his nemesis - the angry child.

However, I digress. The very next day after taking the photograph, a fire began on the far side of this enormous wheat field. It spread from a small flame until it was six feet tall and many metres wide - a wall of fire sweeping across the field toward the house.

By the time the smoke was too thick to see through, the fire brigade had arrived and began hosing and beating the flames back, but the fire was resilient and determined to sweep across the lane thus threatening our property. We had, by now, rounded up as many cats, chickens, ducks and dogs as we could find and put them all together in the kitchen to keep them safe. We had no option but to open the gate to the horse's paddock so that they could be chased out if the fire threatened, but for now they were milling around at the far end of the paddock whinnying as if asking what was going on. Through all of this panic and worry that we might lose the house if the fire did actually continue to get a hold, Jason stayed calm sitting in the living room reading a book. When asked if he would help with the animals if we had to move them, he replied that we were worrying for nothing as there was no way that the fire would be "allowed" to cross our property boundaries. He calmly reminded us that the house was protected and that we should "chill."

What happened then may be thought of as pure coincidence by anyone reading this account, but I seriously have my doubts that that is all it is.

The fire brigade had parked one of their trucks on the burntout part of the field behind the fire when suddenly, the fire appeared to burn back on itself. In other words, it was reversing and burning land which had already been ravaged - but only to the front of our house! The fire wall seemed to split and began to burn fresh vegetation on either side of the lane - except near the boundaries of our property! The fire brigade had to act quickly to get their vehicle to safety and thought it totally unbelievable that the fire could burn back over previously scorched ground.

The fight continued but was eventually won and when the last flames were extinguished, I made tea and coffee for the brave firefighters. I casually asked them about their moment of panic when they had to quickly move their fire truck or risk losing it. I asked casually if they had ever experienced this sort of thing before, and they all told me that it was the weirdest thing that they had ever witnessed. They said that there was no wind to change the course of the fire; that they had never known fire to burn across land previously burnt; and they couldn't explain why the fire had only back burned to the front of our house while it continued to burn fresh material either side of our property. They had no explanation. One of them even joked that perhaps we were charmed.

The next day, I related the events of the fire to Jane. Though she initially had no ideas on how to help, she did say to me - which I took as being rather tongue in cheek - that "divine intervention" was called for in this matter. As I was speaking to her on the telephone that day, she was very quiet for a moment, but then told me in her calm and knowledgeable voice that, though she found the events of the fire I described as unbelievable, she suggested that as the fire had acted so strangely, then perhaps this was indeed an act of God - Divine intervention. Jane explained that she felt that, as this child was so full of rage, she had been cleansed and released by the fire. Jane believed that this was the only way, and that the girl would not be seen again. As far as I am aware, this is indeed the case.

Many years later I asked Jason about this incident and why when he was so accustomed to the multidimensionality of the ETs, why were the disincarnate beings so scary?

"Well, Mum, although I had accepted the ET side of my life, at that point, I was still learning. Back then it was quite scary to suddenly encounter one of these beings because I knew that they were nothing to do with ETs, as the energies were entirely different. I did ask for help, but was told that this was something that I would and could handle on my own - I needed to come to my own understanding of this new phenomenon - and I have. Some souls are drawn to me or, more correctly, to my energy and I have had to learn how to help them to move on. It's not unlike my work when I am present at accidents or tragedies, only at those times, I do my best to help the living, too, by doing healing work until physical help arrives."

# NINETEEN
# REPTILIANS

On November, 21st, 1999, I had an experience with reptilian beings. I know that this statement alone will be extremely hard for people to take in. I know that I will appear to be pushing the bounds of all realities. I agree. I still cannot fully take in just what happened that night. It still fills me with fear, confusion and with many questions. Did it really happen, or was it just, as I first thought, some kind of awful nightmare or dream sequence which somehow, my son picked up on? If it was a dream sequence then was it perhaps induced by other entities or even human adversaries? If so, why? If it was real, what was the point of the exercise? And then my greatest fear - whatever it was, could it happen again? Then again, it had to be more than a dream because of the awful smells which lingered in the house throughout the next day. The simple answer is that I have no answer, so I shall relate the details of that awful night and I shall leave the reader to decide on the depth of this particular experience and whatever they decide, I'm sure that they will agree that this one experience - whatever it was - has to be one of the most chilling yet.

It had been a perfectly normal day. Both the boys were at work, so I was able to get on with mundane things around the house. Paul was working away down South and wouldn't be back until the weekend. The evening also passed without incident. In fact, nothing much in the way of paranormal activity had happened for weeks.

The boys had gone to bed while I stayed up for a little while watching television. After a while, idly flicking channels to confirm that there was nothing of interest to watch, I, too, went to bed.

I had just come out of the bathroom into the bedroom and put back the curtain tie, which had come undone. I opened the curtains a little wider, as the sun always came up first on this side of the house and I loved to greet the morning. I thought to myself how dark the night was and then retired to bed. I was just beginning to doze when suddenly all the downstairs lights came on. The brightness filled the back garden, and the light became apparent through my bedroom window. Jason, too, had been jolted back to reality on realizing that the lights from downstairs were filling the front gardens. He called to me, but I was already up and looking out of the window. He came into my room and said that he would go downstairs and have a look around.

As I pulled on my dressing gown, I told him categorically that he wasn't to go down there alone and that he must wait until I had awakened Daniel, so that we would all go. He murmured in agreement as I was entering Daniel's room, and, though I tried very hard, I couldn't wake him. He seemed to be in a dead sleep. I tried shaking him, gently at first, then a little more roughly, but his eyes remained closed and his body limp and a low snore was the only sign that he was alive. I left his room certain in the knowledge that whatever was going to happen would not include Daniel and that he would be safe.

Jason was just coming up the stairs, and I scolded him for not waiting for me before venturing downstairs. My scolding didn't worry him, but there were clearly more important things which did. He told me that as he went from room to room turning off the lights - even the table lamps - as soon as he left the room, they would be switched on again. He also said that Millie was sound asleep in the kitchen and couldn't be awakened. I related to him that the same could be said of Daniel. He then added that, after giving up on the lighting situation, he had gone out into the hallway to start back up the stairs and noticed that there was a lot of heat at the foot of the stairs, which he couldn't explain. In an effort to make myself feel better, I suggested that it was probably the energies of his alien visitors and that perhaps he should prepare himself for a visit. He shook his head, stating that it was a strange feeling of heat that he had never experienced before and it clearly worried him. His concern soon infected me with fear and, in desperation, I suggested that we should somehow take Daniel with us outside to the car and try and drive to civilization somewhere. Jason shook his head and reminded me that when such a phenomenon starts to happen, things such as car engines, telephones, radios, etc., proved to be totally useless, and his only suggestion was to wait it out. Naturally, I wasn't keen, but like Jason, I could see no other alternative so we both returned to our rooms whereupon I switched on all the lights, radio, and television set. Although the television was displaying white noise disruption, as was the radio, I still found the noise comforting while lying in bed jumping at every innocent noise the immersion heater made in the airing cupboard.

Inevitably, sleep overtook fear, but then my next recollection was of standing at the top of our staircase. From my position, I could see straight into my room, and it was obvious that there was someone lying in my bed. Around the bed were three figures, and, as the room was now in darkness, they were difficult to make out, but I could see that they were very tall - about seven to eight feet

- and very heavy in build. I remember squinting my eyes a little to try to distinguish things better, when I heard Jason calling to me. His voice was fearful and urgent, although it didn't seem to be coming from anywhere in particular. I looked around the hallway for Jason but could see nothing. Again, his urgent voice was calling to me, telling me that I must wake up, I must wake up. Still trying to pinpoint where his voice was coming from, I asked why, but he just continued with his command to wake up, adding that he couldn't be with me as "they" were protecting him and keeping him away. Again, I cried out to him and begged to know what was happening. One of the entities must have heard me because I noticed that one of the muscular figures was moving toward the doorway.

Then, there it was, framed in the doorway so that its awful features could be captured by the light on the hallway landing. Its appearance was so terrifying that I gasped and stepped backwards, nearly falling down the stairs. I steadied myself by grabbing the bannister rail and looked again. He looked like something straight out of a sci-fi movie. He was reptilian - greyish brown in color with a heavy physique which was very human like in shape but clearly not covered in skin, but rather scales. His toes were almost as long as his fingers, and each of them ended with long curved claws. I felt his eyes fixed on me and reluctantly met his glare. His eyes were those of a crocodile, and, like a crocodile, they didn't miss any detail at all. He didn't really seem to have a nose, as all I could see was a wide ridge or bump just beneath his eyes and the two holes, which I took to be nostrils seemed to be palpitating slowly.

Although his appearance was abhorrent to me, I felt that his eyes were more menacing. It was like he was staring at me and able to see right through me into my very soul, and yet, I found it hard to escape his glare. If it hadn't been for Jason's voice begging me once again to wake up, I don't know what would have happened. Again, I scoured the hallway landing for sight of my youngest son, but I was already willing myself to do as he asked. Now convinced that I was indeed dreaming, I remembered closing my eyes and telling myself over and over again to wake up - you must wake up.

Slowly, I seemed to be coming round and my first recollection was of lying on my bed, but feeling like I was suffocating, as there seemed to be some sort of immense weight lying on top of me. The more conscious I became, the more the suffocating feeling wore off until I was wide awake and looking anxiously around my room. I could feel my heart beating wildly, and I felt like I was aching all over. With only the dim light from the landing filtering through the doorway, I switched on my bedside lamp and discovered that all my pillows were scattered all over the floor. The duvet cover was half over me but was upside down - something which I was sure I would have noticed when getting into bed. Becoming calmer now, I got up to pick up the pillows when I noticed a strange smell, which seemed to be emanating from everywhere in my room and from the hallway near my room. It was that of mint but not the conventional minty smell. This was like the smell of a mint plant which was mixed with the smell of the soil from which it had perhaps just been plucked. This smell could be detected around the rest of the house for the whole of the next day but remained really strong in my bedroom and the hallway upstairs for a few days - so much so that Paul remarked on it when he returned that weekend.

Back in bed now, after checking on both the boys who were sound asleep, I sat up on my pillows and again listened for any noise and found my heart beat rising at every explainable sound. I could see from the window that the lights downstairs were still on, but I found this somehow comforting. At this point, I still didn't know what had gone on and found it best not to question that night's events - at least not in the dark.

After what seemed like forever, the vague light of dawn started to creep over the back fields, and I decided that it would be safe to sleep now.

I woke as a result of Jason shaking me awake and, as I rubbed my eyes, he seemed so relieved that I was okay. He then related to me all the events of that previous night saying that he saw me standing on the stairs looking into my room. He said that he felt that one of these beings came over to the doorway as he may have heard Jason calling to me. I was hearing what Jason was saying, but my mind could not take it all in. I grabbed at his arm and asked how it was possible that we could have had the same dream or nightmare - for I was trying to convince myself that that was indeed what it was. He looked at me hard for a few moments then told me categorically that it wasn't a dream, and also that I had to be honest with myself this time, as deep down inside, I knew that it had happened. I felt the fear surge upwards again and frantically asked him why - what was the purpose of this intrusion? Again, he gave me a hard look, but when he shook his head and said he didn't know, I felt that he wasn't telling me the truth, and this worried me more than anything else.

Jason tried changing the mood to a lighter one as he gave me his "order" for breakfast, and although I smiled back and answered glibly that he would be lucky and would have to settle for cereal as usual, I felt really uneasy.

Alone once again in my room, I got up and almost instantly felt a compulsion to take a bath or shower as quickly as possible, although to this day I don't know why. I remember that I entered the shower before the water had warmed to the right temperature. Although I was shivering with the cold, again I felt compelled to wash scrupulously, and I remained in the shower for almost an hour until I was satisfied that I had accomplished this.

The events of that night played over and over in my mind for days, but I still found it hard to decide just what the truth of it all was. I told Paul all about it when he came home, and he cuddled me and told me that he was home now and would protect me. All very well, I thought, but what happens when he goes back to work?

I lived in fear of this incident repeating itself for several weeks. Jason didn't seem happy to discuss it either, and this worried me more. Then, one day I got up the courage to ask him if he didn't talk about it because he didn't know what was going on.

"Course I know," he replied indignantly. "There are many species of reptilian beings. Some are indigenous to this planet and live among us while others are visitors - though they have their own agendas and should be avoided. Unfortunately, Mum, it was members of the latter who visited us that night."

I felt my heart hit my mouth, but then I swallowed hard, and, trying to make light of the situation glibly answered, "bloody typical. Just my luck." Jason wasn't smiling as he continued to talk about these beings. It wasn't often these days that he would be so forthcoming with information, so I knew that I was in for a long lecture. I ushered him into the living room with instructions to make himself comfortable, and I did the same as he began.

"You know by now that the human race was genetically engineered by an alien race, don't you? These people are even mentioned in your own Bible and are referred to as the Elohim - or, if you prefer, the Annunaki. As I understand this, they originally came from the star system that you know as Aldebaran and, not surprisingly, you have met some of them on a number of occasions. Daniel's soldier man Junus is part of the race of the Elohim, and they are all similar in appearance: tall, slim and attractive humanoids with fair hair. Anyway, when they began their experiments in genetic engineering, this planet was already inhabited by another species - apart from the animals. These beings were the real inhabitants of planet Earth and were known as Terrans. Originally evolving from a similar species to that of Iguanadon, they were already quite technologically advanced, but they were a peaceful race and didn't mind sharing the planet with the newly evolved humans. You all lived in harmony but then around 65 million years ago, the first war was fought for the rights to harvest the natural minerals of this world - namely copper. Copper was important to both the warring races - one race being humanoid and supposedly from the star system you know today as Procyon. The other race were reptilian but had no affiliation to the reptilian race already on the planet."

At this point, I interrupted Jason, asking him why these races where fighting over copper. In his usual matter-of-fact way, he replied, "According to the laws of physics, unstable materials can produce stable elements if you induce a high electromagnetic field with a high nuclear radiation field to produce an over-crossing of fluctuating fields. The fusion of copper with other elements in a magnetic/radiation field chamber can produce a force field that is very useful for various technological tasks. However, this is an extremely complex formula that your kind are not able to discover due to the restrictions of your own primitive minds. This is why you back engineer alien technology, but even then you don't fully understand the complexities of it all - which is why your machines and technology will, more often than not, crash and burn - literally. Also, you're not worthy of such information. We have tried to help you in the not-too-distant past - we gave you nuclear power with the explicit instructions to only harness eighty percent, as any more than that would be extremely dangerous to your planet. So, what do you do? Predictably, you ignore our instructions and harness one hundred per cent due to your innate greed. Chernobyl is one outcome which would have been so much more serious if it hadn't been for our assistance. However, I'm going off the subject here. So, anyway, that is why copper was so important to both sides in this war, which was fought in Earth's upper atmosphere.

"In desperation, the reptilians - who were losing the war - decided to use an experimental bomb, which detonated on Earth in one of the oceans close to North America. However, when detonated, the bomb unpredictably created fusion with hydrogen. Deadly radiation - created by an overproduction of fusion and oxygen - then produced a 200-year nuclear winter which killed the dinosaurs and most other life on this planet. Science predictably got it wrong with their asteroid theory, as it was the fallout that dropped the iridium, not asteroids, but anyway let's get back to the reptiles. A few of the Earth race survived and went underground. It is suggested that the radiation caused genetic mutations of this race which ultimately helped them to acclimatize to their new surroundings.

"The human race though, was annihilated, and it was only when the Elohim returned that they began the second creation of man. In fact, you have been "redesigned" seven times now. After each new creation, you would advance technologically and achieve wonderful things, yet each time you blew it - literally. It would always end in wars of one sort or another, and you would end up destroying not only your enemies - who were usually your own kind who had different opinions or suffered from greed - something, as I've already stated, which is common to most of your race - but they would also destroy themselves.

"You're not all unique to this planet, you know. For example, the Cherokee Nation of America believe that they walked to the surface of the world from deep underground and that before that, they had come from the Pleiades system. Think about it. Would they not have had to go underground in order to survive a nuclear war many thousands of years ago? It was you, Mum, who told me years ago that all myths and legends have a basis in truth.

"The Terrans for the most part, still live amongst you but remain underground. Humans tend to be very intolerant of any one different. Look how you ostracize mentally or physically handicapped people even in these times -that is the only reason why magazines are interested in interviewing me - because I'm different from most other people. So, there would be no way that you would "be nice" to a reptilian race found to be inhabiting your planet with you, would there?

"As you know, many species come to your planet, and for the most part, they have your interests at heart, but, unfortunately, not all of them do. Some, like certain reptilian races - who have nothing to do with the Terrans - come here with their own agenda. Remember, it was reptilians who were involved in the first war and were responsible for wiping out all life on this planet.

"The ones who were in the house back in November - and they were here - were up to no good. They knew that I had been working with "the others" and that - not to sound big-headed here - I was important to them. So important, that "they" kept me safe from the reptilians, but you weren't protected. Prior to coming into your room, they tried several times to get into my room, but they were prevented from doing so because of the atmosphere in there. Now you know why it is so important that it is always with me.

"I don't think they will come here again. After all, it was me that they wanted and when that couldn't be achieved, they went to you more out of curiosity. They appeared as in a dream state because that is the way it is most comfortable for them to get here. Some species can come from within our planet as well as from without. I suppose you would refer to it as another dimension, although technically this is the wrong word but the only one I can think of which fits at the moment. Some species have to use technology to "walk" between these levels, whilst others are advanced enough to use their minds. Thousands of years ago, the appearance of such a being would be perceived as magic, and that being would be worshipped as some sort of God and again, there were good guys and bad guys. This is why there are so many different stories throughout the legends of many countries.

"The ones that came here by the way, no longer exist. That's not to say that they were ghosts or anything like that, but basically what's happened is this species - for whatever reason - has evolved to the point of extinction, yet some of them have learned how to manipulate time so that they can travel back to any past. I think it's in an effort to try and stop their race from dying out - you know, find out what went wrong and correct it somehow. Yet this is simply not allowed and is against all laws of the Universe, but they don't care. They will do what they want and hang the consequences. They're not nice - which is probably why they no longer exist anyway - but still these few "refugees" go where they like and do what they like."

His lecture now ended, Jason sat back in his chair. I knew how hard it had been for him to explain all this to me - in layman's terms - and I thanked him for the information and told him I was grateful. Then, in my typical non-confident fashion, I asked again if he could promise me that these beings would not return. He looked at me, shaking his head and smiling, then muttered, "You're hopeless, Mother. Bloody hopeless."

# TWENTY
## SUCH IS OUR LIVES

Such is our lives - such is the strange world we live in. That's not to say that it's an on-going situation all the time - it isn't - we do get huge snatches of normality. We do go to the supermarket every week just like most people. We occasionally enjoy a quiet drink in the local pub, and we keep in touch with all the relatives. We still have the mortgage to pay, council tax, car tax, insurance, etc. In short, we're ordinary people who just have to sometimes cope with extraordinary situations.

It's not all doom and gloom though, and I apologize if I've ever given that illusion. It's like most things in life, I suppose, and once you get used to something, you can become more accepting of it - whatever it is.

I remember one experience, which though frightening at the time, does prompt a wry smile when I recall it.

It was a Friday evening late in the year, and I was alone in the house. Both the boys had gone round to friends for the evening, so I naturally left the back door unlocked for them. I recall that I went into the kitchen to make myself some tea when old Millie sat up and began growling at the back door. She was growling softly at first, but this soon became louder and more intense when the two cats who had been asleep on the chair, jumped up in alarm and, with their backs arched, started hissing vigorously also in the direction of the door. Obviously, I was becoming quite alarmed, as I knew that the animals' reactions weren't heralding the boys' return, and then suddenly, the door flew open to reveal nothing but the blackness of the night. The cats ran for cover under the table, and Millie bravely hid behind me. Tentatively, I moved towards the door, then spurted the final couple of yards in order to grab the handle and slam the door shut. I then quickly turned the key in the lock, and charged like a lunatic back along the rear passageway and into the kitchen. Everything was quiet for a few minutes before the lights in the kitchen started flicking on and off on their own. The stove top started burning hot and then, almost as if to alleviate the situation, the radio started playing very loudly of its own accord. My reaction was one of relief and almost laughter when I heard that the song playing on the radio at that moment was one of David Bowie's classics: "Starman." Even now, when I hear the lyrics "There's a starman waiting in the sky. He'd like to come and meet you, but he thinks he'll blow your mind," I always smile to myself. The message couldn't have been clearer, and I feel that at some sub-conscious level, I thanked "them" for their consideration. I know that one day soon I will consciously meet with "them" on a one-to-one basis - as my son does - but I also feel that "they" will know when the time is right and I am ready for that.

Shortly after that, I had another problem to contend with, though strangely, I wasn't frightened - which is rare for me! Anyway, Paul and I were sitting in the living room one evening watching television when I noticed a large shape walk past the patio doors. As we have Pyrenean Mountain dogs, I was worried that maybe one of them had gotten out and was going off for a walk on his own.

Just as I went to get up to put the exterior light on, the shape walked back past the patio doors and stood facing into the room. It was light grey against the blackness of the night but then I could see that it was much bigger than any Pyrenean. I called Paul's attention to it. I felt safe inside the house with Paul there, so I got up and walked towards the doors. I reached for the switch that illuminated the patio and garden and looked down. Staring back up at me was a huge wolf. Paul and I were speechless. I looked at Paul then stared back at the wolf. He was magnificent - in the light we could see his head was a pale grey color, which darkened towards his rear end. He didn't move, and his beautiful yellow eyes held my gaze for several minutes. Paul sat in a nearby chair saying nothing but trying to make sense of it all. After a while, the wolf looked around then backed away from the windows into the darkness. He was gone.

Then Paul mentioned that the wolf was much bigger than normal and, though it was the first time I had thought about it, I had to agree. As wolves go, he was huge. We decided to talk to friends about his appearance, and it was suggested that perhaps the wolf was some sort of guide or protector assuming the guise of a creature that they knew I would be more comfortable with, due to my love of animals. This made sense, and I accepted that explanation, but then several weeks later, I was walking the dogs with Paul when we noticed a huge "dog" keeping pace with us across the field. It was a full moon that night so it was easy to see relatively clearly. The wolf had returned. Paul felt a little vulnerable being out in the open with this animal, and, wanting to protect his dogs "just in case," he decided that we should return home. The dogs too had spotted the intruder and were barking and straining at their leads so much that Paul and I had quite a job persuading them to return home. The wolf also turned for home, and, as we went through the back door with the dogs, the wolf positioned himself at the front of the drive - and watched. The next morning while walking the dogs, Paul called my attention to a huge paw print in the mud by the side of the lane. Even the biggest of our Pyreneans' paws was dwarfed in comparison to this print. Obviously, whatever this wolf was - spirit, guide, protector in disguise - he was real enough to leave such prominent paw prints.

For several weeks, Paul decided that we should not take the dogs out for walks in the dark. Strangely, I had never felt threatened by the wolf's presence and instinctively knew he would never harm us, but I went along with Paul. Curiously though, some of my chickens started disappearing around this time. Of course, this could just be coincidence but then if the paw prints were real enough....

Some weeks later, Terry, a friend of Paul's, came to visit. Over coffee he related to us how he had been driving at a moderate speed along our lane looking for our house when it was just getting really dark outside. Terry then told us how he had to brake quickly when a huge German Shepherd dog charged out of the field on the right-hand side and shot straight across in front of the car before disappearing at full speed into the enormous field to the left. Terry couldn't get over the size of this "dog" he had seen and asked us if we had any idea whom he belonged to. We told him we had no idea who owned him, but that we had also seen this "dog" on a number of occasions. Terry kept talking about the size and magnificence of such a creature before going on to other more mundane subjects.

To this day, the wolf visits us occasionally - maybe two or three times in a year, and we have never gotten to the bottom of the mystery. I have noticed though that around the time of the visits, we also notice tiny red "fairy lights" - about a dozen of them - outside the windows, which can even be seen from the upstairs windows. They seem to travel together as a group, although each one acts individually. Again, they are just another of the strange anomalies which occur here and for the most part are noticed by us and others sometimes - and then dismissed. We discovered a long, long time ago that there are no answers for all the strangeness in our lives, and I am always wary of anyone who has the answer. To quote Deepak Chopra, "Walk with those seeking the truth. Run from those who claim they have found it."

As I've already stated, many friends and relatives have been witness to the strange events happening here and our good friends, Michael and Carl were no exception. We have known them both for a number of years, and, when they both decided to visit us in the summer of '99, we eagerly awaited their arrival.

They got here round about midday, and after the initial bout of hugs and coffee, we gave them the "royal tour" of the house. They were impressed and said that the house had a wonderful atmosphere.

Later that day, they decided to go exploring the neighborhood. As I had dinner to organize, I said that I would see them when they got back.

It was about seven in the evening when they returned and both of them spoke about the beautiful - though somewhat flat - part of the world in which we lived. Then Michael said something which took me completely by surprise, "You didn't tell us that you had an ancient stone circle in your back yard!" I looked at him and then Carl, who nodded in agreement.

"A what?" I replied.

"Yeah," he continued, "we were driving along the lane by the big field out the back of your place, and there they were - about fifty yards into the wheat field. Like a mini Stonehenge."

I was convinced by now that although Michael wasn't known to be a joker, this was indeed a wind up.

Then Carl picked up the story. "We pulled up next to the stones and noticed that there was like a little land bridge onto this part of the field, so we tucked the car well into the hedge, got out and walked over to the stones." Carl went on to say that the stones numbered about thirty of equal height - about eight feet tall - and that the circle they formed was about fifty feet across.

"Man" Carl smiled, "such wonderful energies coming off those things. It was amazing."

I looked at them and grinned, telling them that their wind up wouldn't work, but they didn't laugh. In fact, Michael insisted on escorting me upstairs to the guest bedroom and instructed me to look at them for myself. Realizing how serious they both were, I did look but wasn't surprised to see nothing other than the wheat field. Our friends looked, too, and went on to discuss with each other that the stone circle should be visible from this vantage point. They were so adamant that the circle was there that they made me go back there with them in the car.

We drove up and down that lane for almost an hour stopping at every land bridge onto this field but none of us saw anything even resembling a big rock. We could see for miles across the countryside, and the flatness was undisturbed. Michael and Carl were seriously confused, and, after dropping me off at home, they drove away again determined to solve their mystery. They never did.

They stayed with us for the weekend, but by the time they departed for home, they were still confused and swore that it wasn't a joke - the stone circle was real - they walked up to it - they stood in it - they touched the stones and were exhilarated by the energies of the place. Even now, when we meet up, they still talk about the mystery of "our Stonehenge" and ponder why they should have been allowed to visit it when no one else even knows of its existence.

It has been explained to me that "time slips" do occur - especially near ley lines (natural lines of energy running across the globe) - and thanks to another friend whose forte is energy dousing, we know that our house is actually built on top of one such ley line. Even so, I did find it extremely hard to accept the possibility of 'time slips or time distortions." However, something happened a few days after the Stonehenge incident which does make me wonder.

Photo by Paola Harris

**Time Distortion example, notice how the bed and wall are out of focus
yet the lamp and table are clearly in focus!**

This day was ordinary: Paul had gone back down South to work, Daniel was at work, and Jason and his friend, Robert, were by the back door fixing Jason's motorbike. After washing up, I decided to go outside and retrieve the buckets for the horse's feeds from behind the back of the barn but as I opened the door, both boys were staring at me in disbelief. I laughed and asked them what was wrong and, after what seemed an age, Robert uttered, "How did you get back inside?" I laughed again and said that I didn't know what he was talking about but Jason confirmed his friend's story, which was that I had opened the back door about fifteen minutes ago and walked round to the back of the barn. Apparently, the boys had spoken to me asking me to bring them some tool, which was in a box behind the barn, but I had totally ignored them both and just walked straight past them. Puzzled by my lack of communication, Jason followed me to the rear of the barn while Robert carried on with the repairs to the bike. However, according to my son, when he rounded the corner of the barn, I was nowhere to be seen and, after searching for a few minutes, he returned to ask Robert if he had seen me. It was at this point that I supposedly emerged for a second time through the back door on my mission to the back of the barn. Again, both boys swear that they weren't joking, and I feel that this was confirmed by their expressions.

Another strange "time slip" occurred again just a week later when my mother and Wally were staying with us for a few days only this time it was my mother who was perplexed by the events.

We were sitting in the living room when we saw, through the window that a red car had turned into the drive. Mum got up and said that she would answer the doorbell. Moments later, we saw the car drive off again as Mum came back into the room announcing that the driver was lost and had wanted directions. She had been able to direct him back along the lane to the address he was seeking.

About twenty minutes later, we all witnessed this same car again turning into the drive. This time, thinking that Mum had perhaps given the driver the wrong details, I accompanied her outside when the doorbell was rung again by the driver. He was very polite and asked for an address not far away from us. Mum interrupted this poor man and informed him that he had previously asked for this address and she had directed him. The driver, a well dressed man in his late forties, looked puzzled and insisted that he had never been to our house before and had, in fact, only just turned down our lane a few minutes ago. Mum was adamant that the man had been here already, so before she called him a liar, I shuffled her back inside and told the man where to find the address he was looking for. He thanked me and strode back to his car, but I sensed that he was still very puzzled by my mother's outburst.

Back inside, Mum was confirming that Wally had seen the car and heard the doorbell the first time. When I entered the room, she looked at me in dismay and said, "Ann, I'm not going mad. Wally heard the doorbell and saw the car pull in, so why was that bloke lying?" I sat her down and tried to explain one possibility, that of the "time slip" and though at first she found it incredulous to say the least, she did later admit that judging by the man's reaction, it was a possibility.

Mum reasoned that the man had no reason to lie or to deliberately fool her so, yes, this was a possibility even though it was way out there.

Something similar happened the next morning when Mum maintains that Wally entered the kitchen, said nothing when she spoke to him, and went out again, only for him to walk back a few minutes later and do exactly the same things as she had witnessed him doing previously. The only difference was that this time he answered when she spoke to him.

I am no expert on any of these paranormal happenings and can only report them to the reader as they happened. However, I do have a theory of my own.

I believe that the visitors have certain powers, which at present, are far beyond our comprehension, although Jason assures me that this will not always be so. It is a well-known fact that we only use less than thirty percent of our brains capacity, whereas the visitors seem to use one hundred per cent of theirs. According to the eminent Dr. Richard Boylan, more than 350,000 years ago, the primitive ape life on this earth were the subject of an experiment - and we are the result! It is around this point in time that the first human emerged, scientifically known as Cro-Magnon man, yet his direct predecessor is a Neanderthal - little more than an upright ape. For centuries, science has been searching for the "missing link" - the bridge between these two species, and yet no such link has ever been found. With today's technology, it would seem plausible that if such a link existed, then some proof of it would have been found by now.

It is my belief - as well as that of many - that indeed we have been - in a sense - created by another life form. Even the Bible bears witness to this and the book of Genesis, Chapter One, Verse 26 states, "And God said, Let us make man in our image, after our likeness." There are further examples to be gleaned from the book of Genesis: Chapter Three, Verse 22 states, "And the Lord God said, Behold, the man is become as one of us, to know good and evil." This verse is spoken just after Adam and Eve commit "original sin" (sexual relations), and after they have "eaten" of the tree of knowledge (the power of reproduction). Eminent scholars have suggested that the serpent in the Garden of Eden is actually the symbol for human DNA - in other words, the double helix strands of life itself. This is further backed up by our present day symbol of medicine, the Greek caduceus is seen as two snakes entwined with a flying disc at the top. Snakes are also a powerful symbol of the Goddess. The Sumerian Goddess Tiamat is represented by two entwined snakes. The Sumerian equivalent of our own Bible actually relates the story of creation - much in the same way as Genesis - but they talk of a race known as the EL-Ohim (which means "combined Gods and Goddesses." In translation to English - for the Holy Bible - scholars have substituted the word EL-Ohim with the word God, which means the singular of EL-Ohim. The name Adam is Hebrew and means "man of earth." If further proof of genetic manipulation were needed, again this can be found and confirmed in Genesis, Chapter Six, Verses 2 and 4. "That the Sons of God saw the daughters of men that they were fair; and they took them wives of all which they chose." "There were giants in the earth in those days, (referred to throughout the Old Testament as `the Nephilim'); and also after that, when the Sons of God came in unto the daughters of men, and they bare children to them, the same became mighty men which were of old, men of renown." It seems clear to me that the translators slipped up quite a few times. Rather than re-enforcing the views of the church - that there is but one God - they have left plenty of room for doubt.

It would seem logical to assume then that if we are a hybrid of the visitor's creation, then one day we would learn how to use all of our brain capacity as they do. For instance, their ships are "powered" by thought and the old saying that "faith can move mountains" springs to mind. I believe that faith - the collective thoughts of many - is capable of such a feat.

There are many theories around regarding the propulsion system employed by the ETs - most theories from very eminent scientists, nuclear physicists, rocket scientists and university professors - and I have great respect for their knowledge, but as my recent path has been learning more of both the alien and spiritual worlds, then to me, the power of thought can be an incredibly versatile tool. As Jason stated in his interview "you really don't know how powerful you all are without all this rubbish (technology), do you?"

I have never - as far as I'm aware - been as "up close and personal" with one of their craft as my son has. He tells me that to touch any part of the outer hull is like gently pressing your hand on a sheet of satin, which has been spread out over still water. No matter how hard or gently you distort the material, as soon as you remove your hand, the material will spring straight back into its shape. It is like the ships themselves are living matter. Could this be why so many people have seen so many different shapes and substances: disc shaped, cigar shaped, small discs which seemingly fly towards each other and then seem to "join" together as a whole.

Even my friends, Sue and Billy Rutland, described their sighting in 1997 as "moving like a shoal of fish." Perhaps buttons and levers are not often seen by abductees on ships because the inhabitants have little need of them. Jason also tells me that the openings for the craft can appear wherever the aliens wish them to appear. I once asked Jason how it is that occasionally their ships do come down (for instance, Roswell), and he replied that they are not invulnerable, and can be brought down by military force if they're hit in the right place and they crash - as at Roswell - because they are not used to our severe weather conditions such as lightning strikes. Yet, he stresses, for the most part they are protected well against our "defences" unless a ship coming down is supposed to happen. He further explained that with their brain capacity, the visitors are able to manipulate time as we understand it, because for them, time does not exist. Due to such manipulation, their ships are visible sometimes, and on occasion, only to certain people. Huge ships could be sitting above residential areas at any time, but having engineered time distortions, we would never be able to see them. Some people are able to see them, but these people are already one step ahead of most as they are embarking on a more spiritual path. The experiencers, abductees, clairvoyants, mediums, psychics, spiritualists, healers are all embarking on their own journeys of truth - truth of the Universe and not the man-made truth of society.

So, how would all of this affect the possibility that "timeslips" might really have happened at our little house in South Lincolnshire? Simply this; could some of the energy of the thought collective have dropped off onto us when a ship was hidden overhead - a veritable sprinkling of fairy dust in a way? This would seem to me to be a big possibility, but then that would mean that the reader would first of all have to believe that aliens and UFOs are real. If Father Corraddo Balducci - advisor to the Pope as well as chief exorcist to the Vatican - believes in their existence, then, it seems that perhaps belief in such things is well on the increase and skeptics may soon be in a minority. You decide.

It was decided that we should hold a meditation evening here back in August 2000. The word was put out among the Norfolk UFO Club, and the idea was well received. So, that Saturday, I prepared a buffet, along with wine and soft drinks, and waited patiently for my guests to turn up. In all, eleven people arrived and the afternoon was taken up with a friendly social time with every one eating, drinking, laughing and chatting. The early evening saw us all getting ready for some meditation work and whatever came from that.

Greg was one of my guests that weekend. He is a really sweet person in his late thirties who used to be in the Army. He was seated on a dining room chair in front of the fireplace in the living room. Everyone had come out of meditation and was discussing their "experiences" - except for Greg who was definitely in a deep sleep, with his head slumped forward onto his chest. At first, we all ignored him expecting him to come round with all the noise and chatter going on, but then we started to become a little alarmed when he didn't. Someone was saying that we shouldn't wake him from such a deep sleep as it might be dangerous, and someone else was saying that we must try and wake him, when all of a sudden, Valerie, who was sitting in the armchair beside the patio doors, cried out in alarm that there was someone standing on the patio facing the side of the house. We all got up and went over to the doors to see for ourselves. Sure enough, there was a man standing there. His features couldn't be made out at first as it was starting to get quite dark outside, but then as the man turned slightly towards us all, we could see that it looked like Greg! How was this possible? Greg was still slumped over in his chair by the fireplace! A few minutes went by while we were all confirming that there could be no mistake - this was definitely Greg - when the man on the patio seemed to walk forward and then straight into the side of the house. Our attention then quickly focused to the "Greg in the chair" - and we were stunned into silence as "the other Greg" appeared briefly behind him, leant forward, and moved into the body on the chair. Almost instantly, Greg sat upright, yawned and then announced to us all that he "had been on one hell of a journey." He claimed that while he was trying to meditate, a small grey being had approached him and asked if he would go with him. He answered yes. The being then helped Greg to step away from his physical body and escorted him outside. The being pointed skywards and Greg saw a display of lights at first but then, realizing that he was already ascending with the being, the lights betrayed a large disc-shaped object hovering above the house. Somehow, he found himself on board and went on to tell everyone how he had been shown around the ship. He described what the Earth looked like when viewed from thousands of miles up. He explained that when it was time for him to return, the beings had put him down in the field next to the house. However, Greg became disorientated and wasn't sure where the house was as it was obscured by thick trees on that side. He said that he wandered around for a few moments while he got his bearings and ended up on the outside patio. That was the point when everyone else in the room had seen him outside, and we all knew how this story ended!

This out-of-body experience was witnessed by eleven people - including myself - in the room so unless we're all hallucinating, then it's obvious to me that something strange went on. If further proof is needed, then I'll mention the pen that I found on the floor after everyone had left. It was an expensive pen, so I put it on the window ledge intending to return it when I found out who the owner was. The next day, Greg rang and asked if I had found this pen, as he had lost it. I confirmed that I had picked it up, and would return it to him personally the following Monday when attending a club meeting, and he said that would be fine. However, a couple of days later, the pen was gone. Neither I, nor the boys, had touched it, although they had both seen it there and asked me who it belonged to. That evening, Greg rang me again and explained that at around four that morning, his doorbell rang several times denoting some sort of urgency, which naturally caused him to don his dressing gown and answer the door. It was still dark outside, but there was nobody there. He thought he heard a cat meow by his feet and when he looked down, there, on the step, was his pen - the same pen he had dropped while at our house.

There have been several instances of objects being lost or misplaced and then turning up again, but we also had a few instances of items being lost - and then returned to their owners unexpectedly.

When my Mum visited us for a few days one summer, she wore a beautiful diamond studded brooch in the shape of a guitar on her jacket. Returning from a short shopping trip one afternoon, she was horrified to learn that the brooch was no longer on her jacket. We had all seen it when we left to go out as Daniel commented to her that the safety device on the pin was undone. Mum secured the pin properly thanking Daniel for noticing that. We all assumed then that perhaps the safety device on the pin had been faulty and the pin had become unfastened and dropped out of her jacket.

Mum was devastated at the loss of such a valuable brooch, but more than that, it meant more to her for sentimental reasons. She was still upset when Paul took her home. However, the next day she phoned me - very excited - and explained that the doorbell had rung late that night and when she went to answer the door, she glanced down at the floor and there on the mat was her lost brooch!

I also had a valuable brooch returned to me. This is a tiny diamond studded brooch in the shape of a bee, and I consider it to be a sort of lucky charm. As it is quite small, I find it easy to wear with most things as I did when I went to a party at my cousin Fay's house. The brooch is unusual and many people commented on it, so I am certain that I wore it that day. However, as the evening wore on, someone asked me where my brooch was, and sure enough, it was no longer on my collar. A lot of the guests joined in the search for my brooch, but it was never found. However, a few days later, I received a phone call from some good friends of ours, Jane and John who both live in Norwich, asking me if I owned a small brooch in the shape of a bee. Jane remembered me wearing it on one occasion and commented on how pretty it was. Obviously, I said that I did have such a brooch but had lost it at a party. John then said that they had found it when sweeping their living room - sitting in a prominent position on the carpet when they moved the coffee table. They both said it would have been impossible to miss.

I know that I was wearing the brooch to my cousins as many other guests witnessed it on me - and I hadn't been to see Jane and John's house for quite a few weeks, so what is the explanation?

Greg's pen, Mum's brooch, and my brooch. These are just a few examples. How can things like this happen? It defies all logic, but it does happen. Is it some sort of game "they're" playing?

Personally, I'm just relieved to have my lucky charm back - however I got it!

# TWENTY ONE
# FARM REVISITED

People always ask for evidence - even when any unusual events are witnessed by several people - and not necessarily people we know. Sometimes, though, certain witnesses to such events are reluctant to let anyone know that they were even present. I refer, of course, to whatever organization it is that is ordered to watch us, to see what we do, who our friends are, and to see if we're a threat to the security of our nation!

These covert actions - several instances of which have already been implied throughout these pages - only serve to strengthen our beliefs that certain government bodies know a lot more about the subject of aliens and UFOs than they want the general public to know about. Of course, most people have heard about Area 51 in New Mexico, and even mention of the Roswell crash will ring a bell with most people today, but it isn't only America that has its share of the X-Files type secrecy. Great Britain does, too.

Although most of the abduction experiences and much of this story revolves around Jason, sometimes - very occasionally - other members of this family have strange experiences and encounters that defy logical explanation.

Daniel likes to sleep in his room with the curtains open at night, as he likes to see the sky. This isn't a problem for there is nothing but fields to the back of the house (all around it for that matter). However, on more than one occasion, he has noticed a very bright "star" that seems to grow larger as he looks at it. The "star" seems to Daniel to be travelling toward him, growing bigger and brighter as it does so. He tells me that his last memory is of this "star" - now the size of a football - actually coming through the window into his bedroom and hitting him with such a force that he loses consciousness and remembers nothing more until he wakes up in the morning.

There was one incident, however, which frightens him even now. It was late afternoon and he had returned home from work early, and he was casually lazing on his bed, flicking through some magazines. He told me that as he looked up, he wasn't in his room any longer. He jumped up quickly and looked hurriedly around him. He found himself in some sort of doctor's waiting room or hospital reception. Unable to move or cry out, he stood helplessly and was totally bewildered. Then he noticed a young girl walking into the area with a woman whom he presumed to be her mother. They obviously spotted him, but their reaction was one of horror as he heard them both scream. Within seconds, he was back in his room, but he was standing nervously behind the door, his heart pumping loudly, and his body shaking. He had no explanation for what had just happened to him, but he has absolutely no doubt that this experience was real. Daniel is very level-headed, and it takes a lot to faze him, but this incident did, which is why I'm convinced that he is telling the truth. He has only mentioned this event a few times in my presence, but that was mainly to tell me that he lives in fear of something like this happening again. He says it is more the fear of being powerless to act. He wonders who the girl and the woman were and - more to the point - what if he were to meet them again?

I have spoken to Jason about this incident, and he tells me that it is nothing to worry about. He explained that Daniel simply projected himself somewhere, but is afraid because he doesn't know how he did this. It's like when you hear about ordinary people who travel out-of-body when they are sleeping, but have no recollection of being able to do this when they are awake. Daniel, however, managed this feat somehow while relaxing - and it has terrified him.

Several months ago, I too had a related experience. Paul was home that evening, and we had gone to bed early, as we had an early appointment the next morning. In that comfortable state between dropping off to sleep but still slightly awake, I thought I heard hushed voices. They obviously didn't worry me too much because soon I was fast asleep and dreaming.

At first my dreams were mixed up - undecipherable as they sometimes are. Then, without warning, I was awake - wide awake - but not at home. I was standing on wet grass. I was in my nightclothes, and it was freezing with the wind whistling around me. Through the dim light offered by the moon, I could see the outline of trees about thirty yards in front of me, and I became more aware of my surroundings. I noticed the tree line extended all around this place, though the field I was standing in was vast. Then it dawned on me - I knew this place. I was back at the farm in Kent.

As I stood, confused and shivering, a man approached. For some strange reason, I didn't feel afraid, but I turned to gaze at him as he came closer to me. He looked very much like Junus, the "soldier man" but he was different. His hair was longer and fair, but his facial features were different. He was still a very handsome being, even though it was obvious that he wasn't human. He was over six feet tall, and his large eyes - like Junus - were the most beautiful blue.

He reached for my hand, and I instinctively reached up toward him. When he held my hand, however, I became aware that the wind had died down, even though the trees were still being blown about. Just by holding this stranger's hand, I couldn't feel the cold or the wind. I was neither warm nor cold - just okay. It was at this point that he seemed to look behind us along the bridle path towards the gate, and soon, I, too was focused there, as I could hear what sounded like vehicles. Lights were wavering around the gate, and it soon became apparent that they were from approaching vehicles. The man looked at me, and immediately I felt, too, that whoever was approaching wasn't good. Without question, I started to move across the field with him, but then realized that we were heading for the fence. I remember thinking that if he thought I was climbing over or through that fence, he had another think coming! However, without hesitation, we seemed to glide through the fence as if it weren't there. I found this totally unbelievable, really this whole scenario was just that - unbelievable. I remember that I turned to look back at the fence, and saw that there were now two white Landrover-type vehicles coming across the field. The stranger and I seemed to be gliding effortlessly through the assorted bracken, and even large trees didn't seem to present a problem as, we moved through them as if they weren't there. Eager to see where the vehicles were now, I turned around, but I accidently let go of the man's hand. I turned back again only to walk straight into a low branch - and felt the pain tremendously! I could also feel the wind and the coldness of my feet, which were caked in mud. The man turned and again reached for my hand, as before, I couldn't feel the cold or the wind, and we glided through the undergrowth.

Soon we came to a clearing, and if memory serves me correctly, we were quite close to the Mereworth base. We were standing still now when he told me telepathically that there was something important that I had to remember. He repeated a phrase to me over and over again until he was certain that I could pronounce it. Though I have no idea of the correct spelling, but the phrase he told me was "Maahthataoe Nouss Tsnumamoe."

I awoke in my bed with this phrase banging through my mind so clearly that I immediately got the pad from my bedside table and wrote it down. With the light now on, I noticed the filthy state of my feet, and I woke Paul to confirm this before going to the bathroom to wash them. I came back into the bedroom and told my sleepy husband to get up for a few minutes so I could change the muddy sheets. He grudgingly obliged and, while doing so, he noticed a mark on my face. Paul switched on the main light and told me to look in the mirror. I had some deep scratches around my left eye, which also was beginning to bruise up. I hastily explained to him about my "dream exploit" as he snuggled back into the bed complaining that the new sheets were cold. I could tell he wasn't really taking any of this in. The next morning, he asked me how I had bruised my face, and I had to go through it all again.

That day, I got straight onto the computer, asking for help in deciphering this strange phrase. I didn't get answers straight away as no one seemed to have any ideas but, eventually several weeks later, I received an e-mail from a linguistics expert at the University of London who told me that it is similar to an ancient Mayan language, and though the words were a little ambiguous, the general meaning was "come to know who you are." I may be way off here with my spelling, but his interpretation felt right somehow. Now whether that's because I wanted it to, I just don't know. I've never forgotten that phrase even though I didn't fully understand what it meant.

# TWENTY TWO
# AUSTRALIA

Early in October, 2000, the family was fortunate enough to set off on an eight-week holiday to Perth, Western Australia. We were invited to this part of the country because most of the good friends we had made due to our story being published in Australia lived in and around this beautiful city.

We had a marvelous time sight-seeing, visiting friends, attending the famous "Aussie Barbecues," whale watching - which was a truly breathtaking experience - and even camel riding! Interspersed within our stay were the almost ever present occurrences of paranormal happenings.

Two weeks before we were due to leave for Australia, our accommodations fell through. Our dear friend, Mary Rodwell - director of ACERN (Australian Close Encounter Resource Net work) and renowned author - worked really hard until she found us another place to stay. She somehow persuaded a friend of hers to let us stay in her home high up in the hills country. We had never met this lady before nor spoken to her, so we extend much credit to her for allowing complete strangers to invade her home for two months. Since everything was arranged for us through Mary, I was quite surprised to receive an e-mail from our hostess, a lovely French woman by the name of Isabelle, just a week before we were due to leave England. Even more surprising was the content!

Isabelle stated that Jason had been to visit her! She had never read anything about us or our situation. She didn't know what Jason looked like either, but she explained that he introduced himself! She stated that he had appeared in her living room late one evening. Being psychic herself, Isabelle wasn't afraid and spoke to Jason for quite a while. He told her that he couldn't wait for the holiday, and he wanted to find out where we would be staying, and what Isabelle was like. She disclosed more information to me - which only Jason could have known - and went on to tell me that it was perfectly okay and that she didn't mind his visit at all.

As usual for me, I had a hard time taking this sort of thing in, so I showed Jason the e-mail and asked what was going on? He grinned at me and then told me that he had wanted to "check her out" - and the house - as he really needed to know whether or not she would be able to cope with any strange events that would inevitably follow him to Australia. His verdict? Isabelle was "a really cool lady" and more than capable of understanding and accepting whatever other dimensions or alien beings threw at her. Even on the plane to Australia, he had drawn a plan of the house marking off all the rooms. His plan proved to be very accurate, as we discovered when we arrived at the house. I realized then that we were supposed to visit Perth - not just for a long holiday and to visit friends, but because we were supposed to. By the end of our time there, I was proved right.

We were met at the airport by Mary and Gemma. It was quite emotional meeting them again after such a long time, but good friends are just that - good friends. We enjoyed each other's company immensely throughout our stay. Jason and Gemma spent most of their days together, and it was wonderful for Jason to have someone to confide in and talk with about absolutely anything - knowing that she would understand and empathize.

Through their time together in Australia, they explored much more of their alien heritage. This time meant so much to both of them but more so I think to Jason.

Meanwhile, back at the ranch, as the saying goes, we were having our share of things weird and wonderful. Just a few days after settling in, I was told by Isabelle that she was detecting an energy or atmosphere that she found quite threatening. Instantly, I knew that this was the same energy force, which is often present in Jason's room back in England. I tried to explain to Isabelle what the energy force was, and that it was hostile toward her just as it had been to visitors to our house in England, that it was there to protect Jason, and it didn't know her or her intentions towards him. To tell the truth, I felt bad that this lovely lady who had opened up her home to us should have to put up with the aggressive behavior of this energy/entity. However, Isabelle said she completely understood. She planned on retiring early that evening in order to meditate in an effort to communicate with this force and make clear her intentions.

The next morning, Isabelle was up early as usual, but was full of life and genuinely happy. She told Paul and me that her efforts had been successful, and that Jason's "protectors" completely understood her intentions and accepted her immediately as not being a threat to him of any kind. She said that afterwards - perhaps as an apology for causing her to live with this awful threatening feeling- she had been filled with a wonderful feeling of warmth and love. She said that she had felt their love for him, and that it was truly wonderful. Isabelle was very happy with this new energy pervading her home, however, whenever visitors came to see her, many of them would not stay long, as they too picked up on the energy which most of them found threatening. One of Isabelle's good friends said that she found this energy so threatening that she refused to enter the house and they would sit and talk on the patio. Again, I felt terribly guilty about all this, but Isabelle was adamant that she loved the energy around her and really didn't mind what her friends thought. Besides, when we left, she knew it would go with us, so it was only a temporary problem.

Sometime later, I asked Jason why the energy was still threatening in Isabelle's house after he took the trouble to visit and "check her out?" I wondered why "they" wouldn't be happy with his findings? He gave me an interesting response.

"First of all, I should tell you that the energy or atmosphere that is generated around me does actually come from me. For a long time, I believed that the ETs placed this energy around me as protection. This was the case in the beginning, until I learned how to generate this protection for myself. It manifests in me. This is another reason why it begins to get heavy when I fall asleep in the car. It's almost automatic for me now to do this as I know that I can be vulnerable to others when I am in a sleep state. However, back then, it would have been mostly the ETs who generated this energy around me - albeit through me.

"Even though I liked Isabelle a lot, I didn't say that I totally trusted her. In fact, I never totally trust anyone and never have."

I interrupted at this point and exclaimed, "What? What about us? Your family?"

"As a family, we have a special bond and I know that we always will. There are some things which we all take on trust but no one can ever trust another with absolutely everything. There is no such thing as complete or "blind" trust. Besides, I wouldn't have been around for as long as I have if I didn't exist by this rule, would I? So, I liked Isabelle a lot, but I would never let my guard down completely.

"The ETs assist in my life, but it is me who runs my life. However, they would have left the heavy energy in place - as would I. When Isabelle meditated and connected with "them," in effect, the energy or atmosphere was still in place for my protection but it had been changed in order for Isabelle to enjoy it. That is why whenever her friends came to the house to see her, they couldn't stay in her home for long because they still perceived the energy as threatening. It was merely an illusion if you like but done out of kindness to help a nice lady."

I found this good advice for all of us in realizing a little protection is around our energy field is a wise thing.

Before we left for Australia, my good friend Jane told me where to find a little crystal/spiritual shop. She told me the name of the place and exactly where to find it, and I promised her that I would try to visit it. Jane lived in Perth for many years, but returned to England three years ago to look after her ailing mother after her father passed away. During those three years, she had not returned to Australia.

When we had some spare time, Paul and I finally managed to track down the little shop with the help of Jane's directions, and we went in to have a look around. The owner of the shop, a bright lively lady in her late forties, came over and started talking to us. She told me that she was being told by her guides that I am a powerful healer, and if I let go of my fears, I can do a lot of good for people. I thanked her for her candor, but I didn't really pay too much attention to her words. We continued chatting and went on to other things. She then told me that she had only opened the shop in July - that same year. Remembering what Jane had said about this shop, I asked the lady if she had bought it as a going concern, but she replied that it had been a green grocer's shop for many years, and that the owners had closed it down when they retired. I couldn't believe what I was hearing. How could Jane have known about this place and its difficult location when she hadn't been back to Australia for three years - yet she even described what it looked like outside and inside? I have spoken to Jane about this since we returned, but she was as shocked as we were, as she was certain that she had been in this shop many times.

I was asked to give several talks while in Perth, which I nervously consented to do. The biggest of these was held at the University auditorium where the promised thirty or so interested people turned rapidly into over two hundred! I remember feeling quite relaxed when I saw people arriving and picking their seats from a wide selection, but then when more people arrived and the seat selection became very limited, I started to panic. A lovely gentleman by the name of Professor Eustace introduced me, and I made it to the rostrum amid loud clapping. When I first spoke, even I could hear the nervousness in my voice, and I found myself clearing my throat every few seconds. I then stopped for a moment, took stock of myself and began again with the words, "I'm either going to do this or I'm not. I'll give it my best shot - so here goes." After a shaky start, my voice got stronger and once I was relating our story from the book, my nerves calmed. Even through the questions at the end, I was able to answer with knowledge and confidence. I was greeted at the end of the talk with a standing ovation (which does wonders for anyone's confidence), and other talking engagements from then on were easier and a pleasure.

There was one thing though which intrigued me, and that was that at the end of the lecture at the university, a young couple approached me and asked if we could have a quick chat. I readily agreed, and we found a quiet corner and sat down together. Brian - in his late twenties I believe - began telling me that he knew the M.O.D. base near our farm extremely well. He told me about its layout and pinpointed places of interest in the surrounding area. I asked him if he had lived in this area, as his accent was very English, and he explained that his father had been the commanding officer at the base when he was a boy. He further explained that it was never made clear to him just what the base was used for, as he was forbidden access to much of it. He said that when he had first read about us, he couldn't believe that this was the same base, and he excitedly spoke to his father - now retired - about this. Yet, he was surprised when his father, still living in England, refused to discuss his time spent at the Mereworth Base. Brian said that he could totally relate to everything that I had been talking about - particularly with regard to this base. He then seemed to look quite saddened, and when I asked him what was wrong, he said that during the five years he had spent at Mereworth with his father, he could not remember his childhood at all. He had no recollection of friends or even hobbies he might have involved himself with. He maintains that all of that is a complete blank in his memory - and something else which his father refuses to discuss with him.

Apart from all the usual strange things that happen around Jason, I did have some experiences which were uniquely mine. To start with, Mary told me that she felt strongly that she had some work to do with me to help me resolve certain issues that had been eating away at me under the surface for years. Again, my fears of the unknown welled up within me, but none the less, I, too, for some strange reason, felt that we did have work to do and agreed.

Mary is a trained counselor and midwife, with many diplomas in regression therapy, so I felt safe with her. In our first session, she helped me to become more accepting of the strange world that I and my son inhabit. She made me more aware and more "open" to my psychic side, and I will always be grateful to her for that.

The next thing we dealt with was the big one - for me anyway. In this book, there are some paragraphs regarding the baby that I lost many years ago, which I had always known deep down was very much alive somewhere with "them." In fact, while watching a baby being born on television a couple of years ago, Jason calmly asked me what I would have called our baby. I went cold and quickly answered "Nathan" then I made it clear that this was the end of that particular discussion.

He looked thoughtful for a moment then answered, "No, that doesn't sound anything like what he is called now." My only reply was to give him a withering look of confirmation that this was the end of that particular conversation, and he shrugged okay but a few minutes later asked me directly if I wanted to see him.

Again, the anger and fear surged in me and I sharply answered, "No" and that was the end of the discussion.

However, several months before going to Australia, Jason again started talking about Nathan, telling me how good he looked, and the fact that they had been good friends practically since he was born. Again, I made it clear that the subject was not to be discussed. This time Jason reacted with anger, and told me that my stupid fear and anger was stopping Nathan from coming to visit me. We had quite a furious row, and I then glibly remarked that if "they" wanted me to see my son then all "they" had to do was arrange for another abduction and take me to him.

Jason glared at me in silence for a moment then replied with sadness, "But this has to happen through love. It cannot be forced. You will only meet with him when your fear and stupid anger have gone." I stayed silent, eyes filling with tears, then he said, "You know Mum, he really loves you. Please don't deny him your love." With that, he got up and left the room.

That night I cried myself to sleep, upset that I just could not get past the anger I felt - anger at Nathan having been taken from me in the first place. What right did these beings have to do whatever they wanted to without permission? How dare they? I was still sobbing late into the night when I felt the atmosphere change in my room. Needless to say, Paul was working away that night. The room became very warm and almost became calming. I stopped sobbing and started to look around the room through the dim light - and for the first time I wasn't afraid. Then I felt as if someone gently kissed me on the cheek, and instantly I knew it was Nathan. I called out to him several times, but nothing further happened, and I must have slowly drifted off to sleep.

It is important to mention here that in October, 1999, I took a course in Reiki healing. For the uninitiated, Reiki is a very ancient form of spiritual healing which has its origins in Japan. Jane had encouraged me to do this, as she felt that Reiki would give me a better understanding of our strange situation. Jane is also a Reiki master and in October, 2001, I extended my own teaching, and I myself attained the position of Reiki master.

After qualifying in parts one and two of the Reiki course in 1999, I was eager to practice my heightened abilities and my family became willing guinea pigs. My brother David was still extremely skeptical about healing, but when he was complaining bitterly about his severe headaches again - all stress related, according to his doctor - I finally persuaded him to let me have a go. Reluctantly, he sat in a chair, and I began my work. To my surprise, he said that he could feel the energy coursing through him - praise indeed from someone like him! Then he became more intense, and announced that "someone" was in the room. Thinking that David was winding me up, I took no notice at first, but my brother persisted in this and then told me that this "person" was seeking permission to enter him. Still believing this to be a wind up, I glibly suggested that David should grant this request. He grunted in agreement. However, I felt his shoulders tighten and he said that his fingers and toes were tingling, and he didn't like this situation. Now, half believing him, I told him to "ask" his visitor to leave. After a few moments he confirmed that he had done this, and it had worked. He then told me that he was instructed to go for a walk alone, and, even though it was pouring down rain, he was adamant that he had to go. The rest of the family was worried by his behavior, and started to question my use of Reiki healing - did I really know what I was doing? I did have my own doubts - not so much about my use of Reiki, but I still wasn't sure that my brother wasn't making a fool of me. However, when he returned soaking wet from his walk, I had absolutely no reservations about his seriousness. He claimed that he had walked over to the adjacent parkland, and had gone through the woods. It was already dark outside, yet he said that he clearly saw a man standing in front of him as he rounded a bend in the track. As David got closer, he said that the man moved to cross in front of him, and he could see that he had a small child with him. My brother continued and told us all that, though neither the man nor the boy spoke, he was "told" that he was related to this boy, and that the boy is known by us as Nathan. He was further "told" that, as he was now becoming more accepting of his "gifts" and his true nature, he would come to know Nathan better and eventually work with him for the benefit of others.

I couldn't - or maybe wouldn't - understand what he was saying. I had told no one - not even my mother - about Nathan. All my family ever knew was that years ago I had had a miscarriage. Yet here was my brother talking to me about - and describing - this beautiful child - my Nathan. I felt devastated. My niece told me that I looked as if I had seen a ghost, I was so pale. My family then started fussing around me asking what was wrong, yet I couldn't bring myself to tell anyone. The devastation I felt quickly turned to anger. Why should he be introduced to my child? I was furious. Even I didn't know him - and then it dawned on me - I hadn't wanted to know him.

# TWENTY THREE
# NATHAN

It became clear to me that while I was in Australia I would deal with my "Nathan issue." Mary had been "told" by her guides that she was to help me work through this important issue in my life, and she suggested meeting when we could have the day to ourselves, without interruption. I was terrified at the thought of what I might be getting into, but again I found myself agreeing with Mary, and we arranged to meet one Monday morning at Isabelle's house. Isabelle was away for the day and, unusually, Jason wasn't with Gemma that day, so he and Paul arranged to go on a shopping trip for new jeans for both of them. Daniel had already found himself a girlfriend for the duration, so he spent much of his time with her, and we knew he wouldn't be back anytime soon.

Mary and I began by facing one another in the bedroom. I told her that I was frightened, but just as Tony Dodd had helped us all in the past with his calming voice, Mary did the same. She told me that I was perfectly safe, that she wouldn't let anything happen to me, and to close my eyes and listen to her voice. I did. Somehow, by following her instructions, I felt as if I were descending a large ornate staircase and, as I went further down, the staircase became darker until I was left standing alone in the pitch black. I make the techniques Mary used sound simple, but this is only my understanding of what happened. I don't feel that it is ethical to discuss the techniques in too much detail. Suffice it to say that, for me, they worked! Being under hypnosis is being in a state of complete aware of your physical presence, but at the same time, the place you go to is very, very real. I was always aware of Mary's voice telling me that whatever transpires, I would be safe, and I believed her.

By following her instructions, I instantly found myself back in my bed the night the miscarriage happened so long ago, yet it was like it was yesterday - the scene was so cleat I was conscious of Paul being there beside me - even hearing him snore - but then a horrible realization grasped me at my every fibre as I suddenly saw one of the small grey entities, which are now so familiar to our family. I began to cry as more entities appeared, and I knew that whatever happened, I could not move - even when I was conscious of floating above the bed, then the caravan where we were living at that time.

I described things as I journeyed on, but the tears kept coming as I knew instinctively what was about to happen. Again, Mary's voice was calming, but authoritative, as she made me move forward a little and asked me to describe what was happening. Apparently, I became very emotional while I described this scene - I could see a large flat surface - much like an operating theatre in a hospital - and I could see certain instrument-like things connected to the table. There was no instrument tray as such visible, but I could see that one of the taller greys was holding some sort of long spatula-like instrument, which glowed luminous green at one end. Again, the fear surged inside me as two smaller greys seemed to move me effortlessly onto the flat surface. I watched the procedure - I saw the tiny, tiny life and the receptacle it was placed in - but this was all too much to bear, even from the perspective of just a witness.

Mary decided that I couldn't take any more of these scenes, these memories. She again calmed me down and kept repeating that I was only observing - I wasn't going through it all again, I was only watching, but she wasn't convincing me. It is hard to put into words just how you feel in situations like this. I know a lot of skeptics will say that it is imagination, but it isn't. There is no way that anyone could ever imagine such a debilitating scene or imagine the amount of pain and anguish that you so vividly remember that you suffered. No way.

I was becoming quite anxious now but started to feel calmer when Mary instructed me to go back a few days before this happened and to try and remember other encounters. At first, there was nothing but then I realized that I was again standing in a similar sort of room as the "operating room," but I was alone, dressed only in my nightgown. I felt that it was chilly and said so, which was when I realized that a figure was approaching. At first, I was afraid again, but Mary reminded me that I was observing and would not be hurt. However, that fear dissipated completely when the figure came into view, and I realized that it was Junus, Daniel's "soldier man." Mary said that at that point I seemed to completely relax and began to relay to her my conversation with him.

She later told me that I was visibly shocked by what he was telling me - the baby I was carrying would not survive as he would be too weak, and if I went ahead with the birth, there was a good chance I would die also. His suggestion stunned me - let them take the child and raise it with them. I told him that this was not an option, and that he had no right even suggesting this. This was my and Paul's child and our decision. We would decide what was right, not him, not "them." He pleaded with me to consider this, and I believe that his concern for me was genuine. Again, and again, I heard myself refusing, but through my tears, I was already starting to consider his pleas. He touched my face very gently, and I stared into his eyes, focusing as best I could through the tears. He begged me to remember my other two boys, and how they needed a mother and that I would be selfish to leave them alone at this stage in their young lives. Somewhere along the line, I knew what he was saying was true. Paul and I had been considering abortion, but the soldier man smiled and told me that I had too gentle of a soul to go through with such a drastic thing. He promised that my unborn son (somehow I knew it was a boy), would never be kept from me. Through more tears, I heard myself agreeing with his plea to take the child, and then I remember that I kept on repeating, "Please promise me that you will love him and don't ever, ever let him think that we didn't want him." Again, I heard myself pleading with him to explain to him so that he will understand one day. Again I made him promise that "they" would love him unconditionally.

I was very conscious of my face becoming very wet with tears and again, as the emotions were mounting, Mary gently but firmly talked me out of this event until I was fully awake, safe and sitting with her in the bedroom. She offered me a tissue to wipe my face, but the tears were still trickling as I kept saying, more to myself than to Mary, "But I did give permission, didn't I? They didn't just do what they wanted, I actually gave them my permission."

This new revelation kept sinking in, and Mary found the whole thing very emotional. We sat quietly together for a long time just wiping tears from our faces. Then, when I felt a little better, Mary suggested some other techniques to help me to relax, and then she asked quietly if I wanted to see my third child. I nodded yes. We both felt the atmosphere in the room change. It was the same as it had been several months earlier in my bedroom at home when I had argued with Jason about Nathan. Then, suddenly, there he was - Nathan. He was standing in the room smiling at me. He was there with Junus, the "soldier man" and he was holding a long-stem red rose in his hand. As he spoke softly I noticed the gap in the front of his mouth where a tooth was missing and realized just how human he was. He was dressed much like, Junus with some sort of tight-fitting white coverall hidden by a type of long smock. His hair was fair, and I could see both Daniel and Jason in him. I told him how handsome he was. His eyes sparkled with life as he called me "Mum," and he told me that he had always loved me. He said that he knew that I loved red roses, as he had often witnessed Paul buying them for me. He also said that he was so glad that I had received the help I needed in order to finally accept him. I remember smiling and telling him that he needed a haircut because I didn't want other children to call him a girl. He laughed. I don't remember how long this meeting lasted, but when he and the "soldier man" left, I felt as if a great weight had been lifted off my shoulders. I have never felt as good as I did at that moment. Mary returned from the kitchen with a glass of water for me and told me to stay where I was until I felt ready to face the world again. She said that the boys had just returned from their shopping trip and were getting into a game of backgammon. Neither Mary nor I had mentioned any of the events of that day, so you can imagine my disbelief when I walked out to the living room and Jason, without even looking up from his game, asked, "So why do you think Nathan needs a haircut then, Mum? I think it suits him."

Explaining that day's events to Paul however, proved to be a lot more difficult. Although he tried hard to understand, and said that he did, I felt - and still feel - that this is still one issue that he will never come to terms with, so I have never pushed too hard in this respect. Even for me, writing about those events is terribly hard, for this is a very personal issue for me and always will be.

I have seen Nathan again since that time, and I only wish that I had sought to resolve all the issues I had with my hatred and anger years ago. I am certain that, for me, this is the main reason why I had to visit Australia.

When we returned home, I wrote the following to Mary:

"I have seen Nathan a few times since that day at Isabelle's. Strangely, I feel him more at first, and then I can see him in my mind's eye, very clearly. Usually when I am writing and getting stuck with words to express myself, he comes to me. The whole room changes, the atmosphere becomes warm and though it is hard to put into words, love and immense feelings of peace abound. It is a truly wonderful experience every time.

"I used to ask if it was Nathan and I would always get the impression of him and the answer, "Yes, Mum." Now I don't ask anymore, as I know his energy, and always there is the same love and inner peace. I know this will sound incredible, Mary, but I feel he helps me with my writing. I always get over my word block, then thoughts and details enter my head and I can't get them down fast enough. I rush through the particular piece of writing and then, exhausted, sit in silence, just enjoying what we have together.

"He always says goodbye, but I don't feel sad, as I know he will always return - and it's the greatest feeling in the whole world."

As Mary says, "That day we discovered a part of the amazing enigma of our intimate relationship with our extraterrestrial visitors, and we are still only scratching the surface of what our galactic neighbors are here to show us."

# TWENTY FOUR
# AUSTRALIAN INCIDENTS

Towards the end of our stay, something happened though its full implications still elude me.

Feeling unusually tired, I had gone to bed early but I noticed through the bedroom window that there was a bright, red light shining through the trees outside. As we were high up in the hills country, there were a few other properties scattered around the woods, but we had been there long enough to know where they were, so I knew that the light wasn't emanating from any of them - it was well into the bush. As I approached the window, the light seemed to blink out and, as tiredness overtook curiosity, I curled up in bed and was quickly asleep.

My next recollection was of waking up because something heavy was sitting on my feet. I moved my feet quickly, half believing that I was at home, and that one of the cats had sneaked upstairs and was lying on the bed. However, when the weight lifted, I became fully aware of where I was, and I sat up. Now wide awake, I rubbed my eyes and, in the dim light, I could make out the shape of a person. My first thought was that it was Paul, until I faced the terrible realization that he was asleep beside me. Before panic fully set in, the figure stepped forward and I could see that it was Junus, the "soldier man." I have learned that I have little to fear from this being, so my panic quickly subsided. He beckoned me to go with him, and without question, I found myself following him, but whether this was in a reality state or out-of-body I don't know. However, my next recollection was of being inside some sort of large vehicle, travelling slowly across a desert terrain. I remember that it was very dark both inside and outside of the vehicle, but also that it was raining heavily - not normal rain, but a black rain, which left a murky grey residue as it ran down the windows of the vehicle. As I watched the water, two small oriental-looking children approached me and, rather pitifully, asked me if I could make the black rain stop. I looked down at their tear-stained faces and, feeling totally helpless, answered, "No." Saying nothing, they turned and walked away.

I turned to look back at the rain, but then felt as if I had been gathered up almost by some sort of energy, which seemed to whirl me around until I was almost dizzy. When I regained my composure and could focus properly, I saw that I was standing on warm sand with the sun beating down. Beside me was a very tall stone block roughly ten feet or so tall. It reminded me of the massive stone monoliths at Stonehenge, and, as I walked around it, I noticed that it appeared to have a large curve cut out of it on its right-hand side. Just a few yards behind this stone, which was various shades of yellow, I could see another one. This stone wasn't quite so tall but had just as much girth as the first, although it seemed to go up into a point. Then I noticed that beyond these stones were thousands more - as far as the eye could see. I don't remember how long I stood there, but I believe that the sun was starting to go down, and, as I shielded my eyes from the sun, I found that I was now back in the familiar surroundings of the bedroom in Isabelle's house.

I was able to sleep easily, and I didn't get up until almost midday. Strangely though, Isabelle, who is always up at the crack of dawn, didn't get up until very late either and was quite upset by a dream she had had. Before she could continue, Paul surprised us both by relating that when he had gone to bed the previous evening, he had seen a large red light shining through the trees, and, when he looked closer, it appeared to change to two smaller blue lights.

Then Isabelle related her strange and vivid dream in which she was viewing a rocky desert-like place from above it. As she went on to describe what she was seeing, I joined in telling her that the landscape she was seeing was a reddish orange in color - as was the skyline. She seemed excited by my interruption, and asked what else I had seen in my vivid dream. I began to describe the scenes I had witnessed, interspersed by outbursts from Isabelle of, "Oh, my God! I saw that, too." She would then take over the conversation again describing something else we had both seen, until it became obvious that we had both been present at the same scene. The only difference between our accounts seemed to be that I was there at this place - wherever it was - and viewing events from the ground, while she was somehow viewing the same scene from above the ground.

Isabelle and I started making quick sketches of the place we had been to, and they were remarkably alike. She told Paul and me to wait while she went into her study, and she emerged with a map of the local area saying that she had an idea where this weird-looking desert may be. I was surprised to think that it may be in Australia itself, but then again, the country is so diverse in its geography that in hindsight, it made sense. Isabelle brought our attention to a place known as the Pinnacles Desert, and, although she had never been there, she had seen pictures of the place and felt strongly that this is the right place. For some reason, I too, felt that we were on the right track and Paul - totally intrigued by now - offered to drive us. We both eagerly accepted and set off an hour later.

Although it was a lot farther away than we thought, we finally arrived about an hour before sunset. I understand that the Aborigines would never go to this place, for as they believed the spirits to be evil here, and I could totally understand why - I have never seen such an eerie and desolate place. It is a flat, sandy desert filled as far as the eye can see with strange upright megalithic stones which have been standing in their places for hundreds and thousands of years - if not millions. No one seems to know just how they were formed, but here they stand like thousands of soldiers ready to move out as soon as the order is given.

I didn't like the feel of this place at all. Isabelle was indifferent, just enjoying taking pictures with her new camera. Paul preferred to wait in the car as the flies were really starting to bother him. I walked between the great stones, some as tall as fifteen feet and probably the same in girth. Though I walked aimlessly at first, I began to feel a strange guidance towards a small group of these stones, and I recognized them as the ones from my dream. I was certain of this. I felt that I had to stand beside the tall one with the curve in its side, and the stone felt hot to the touch. The sun was just beginning to descend now and was bathing the sandy landscape in the most beautiful reds and oranges imaginable. I concentrated again on the stone, and, with my hands placed on either side of it, I closed my eyes. Then I could see "them" - all of "them" - all of the entities that we had all encountered throughout our lives. The images were tumbling through my mind so fast it was hard to keep track of them, but then I knew why this place was so important. It was some sort of portal - an entry point. There are certain places throughout the World where energies facilitate easier access to our planet - much like ley lines do but here the energy was just so immense.

My concentration was broken by a large group of Japanese tourists who had descended on my little group of stones and were snapping everything in sight with their cameras - even me!

I made my way back to the car where Paul and Isabelle were waiting, and we made our way home. In Australia, the roads are long and lonely and extremely dark, but the sight of millions of stars that night were just amazing to see.

A few days later, Paul and I managed to get a little time to ourselves for a whole day. Although we loved being with the family and our many friends in Perth, we relished the idea of taking a little time for us just to wind down.

We set off in the car, ending up at a little seaside resort named Rockingham, a lovely place whose main street was dominated by a huge Union Jack denoting the little English sweet shop. We wandered around for a while and then, as the sun began to set, turning the day into a beautiful evening, we sat on a bench beside the golden beach, watching the waves lap the shore. Paul spotted a little "fish and chip" shop and suggested that we eat here on the bench, as it was so nice. I agreed, and he went off to join the queue for the fish supper.

I sat alone with my thoughts, enjoying the wonderful view and listening to the tide lapping the sand. Suddenly, I felt that my thoughts had been invaded by something outside of my awareness. Fear rose up, but I quickly realized that I was in a very public place and Paul wasn't far away, so I found it easy to relax and listen. After a few seconds, I felt compelled to get up and make my way toward an old disused walkway, which stretched out into the ocean for about five hundred yards. Without even thinking about it, I found myself walking along the planks, carefully avoiding the many holes that revealed the water beneath. This was a strange feeling - it was as if I had the will to change my mind at any time, yet for some reason I completely trusted the voice in my head, which urged me onwards to the end of the walkway. This was very notable for me, for I am very much afraid of the ocean, yet here I was making my way along a dangerous walkway that would soon stop abruptly. It did.

I stood alone on the end of this pier wondering what to expect. Then, in the dwindling light, I saw a shape coming towards me through the water. At first I only saw the adult dolphin, but I soon realized that the shape following her was her baby. I couldn't believe it. I lay down on the planks so I could reach down into the water - knowing that she had been sent to me. She swam past a couple of times then surfaced directly beneath my hand so that I connected with her head as she emerged from the water. I will never forget that feeling as long as I live. My mind raced back to the intense feeling I had had when I was close to the dolphins in SeaWorld, yet this feeling was so much more. The intensity made me cry yet through the tears the blurred shape of her head and my hand caressing it gave me such a wondrous feeling of joy that I began to laugh to myself, mumbling to her that she was beautiful - a miracle worker. I looked into her dark eyes, and for an instant I believed that I belonged with her - that I was part of her in some way. I would have gone with her had she asked. This was all in a moment. The youngster, half the size of its mother, had been keeping its distance, but now it came in beside her and allowed me to touch it, even staying still for a few seconds. For me it was as if I were in some sort of heaven, and just the touch of the dolphins seemed to be inducing in me so many emotions. I felt sadness - why, I'll never know - but then I felt immense happiness and, I wanted to drown myself in that feeling.

Paul had been watching all of this from his elevated position near the beach, and there were already several people making their way along the walkway to see my dolphins. Unexpectedly, I had become aware of the real world around me just at the moment that she and her young one decided that it was time to go home. Perhaps she would have stayed with me longer had not other people seen us. I don't know, but as I watched them both swimming away from me, I thanked them - and whoever had guided us toward each other - for my gift. If only our world could stay with the feeling I had with the dolphins, but that's not to be.

I made my way back along the rickety walkway, looking down every time anyone passed me so as to hide my tear-stained face. Paul was waiting for me on the beach. He said, "I didn't think anything would ever get you to go out there like that across the water." I nodded in agreement, and, wiping the final evidence of tears away, I looked at him and smiled. "I can see from your eyes that you have been to a wonderful place," he continued, "obviously, it was worth the risk on those old planks."

Then, just as in the movies, we put our arms around each other, walked over to our bench where dinner was waiting, and we watched the sun finally disappear beneath the calm sea as we ate.

We believe that we were all followed on a number of occasions during our stay in Perth. Jason and Gemma also told us how many times they had been out together when a small black helicopter would appear very low to the ground either in front of or behind them and would proceed to dog their movements.

When Paul, Daniel and I went to a good friend's barbecue, (the friend is also an experiencer), we were inside the house chatting to him about our mutual experiences when one of his young nephews came running into the room demanding that he go outside immediately. His young voice was so urgent that we all hurried outside, and there was a small black helicopter hovering about a hundred feet above his garden. The machine had a powerful searchlight beneath it which seemed to be snaking its way through the mystified guests. Then, when the three of us and our host appeared, the light seemed to focus on the four of us for several minutes before it seemed satisfied and then, switching off the light, whirled upwards and shot away.

Our host, Elliott, wasn't too surprised - he said that he was getting used to it as, like Gemma, he was often dogged by these mysterious helicopters.

We arrived back in England during a heavy rainstorm, and, as the light was already fading by three in the afternoon, we found our spirits also fading. We all wanted to be back in the warm sunshine of Perth among our many friends. Jason was already missing Gemma, but it was clear from his whole demeanor just how much they had learned from each other. He was different somehow, and so was she. They both believed that they were meant to eventually find each other here on Earth, and, this accomplished, they were not going to allow that bond to be broken. Nor have they. Even across that many miles, they know each other's thoughts, they travel astrally with each other on many occasions, and they talk - on the terrestrial telephone - about their exploits together. May they continue to have this wonderful relationship.

167

# TWENTY FIVE
# THE LION MAN

During the first few years of learning to cope with our strange situation, the journey we were all on was very much a personal and perhaps very lonely one. At that time, we were looking for an explanation for what was happening to us as a family. We believe that we found a satisfactory explanation, although as we have maintained all along, we are always open to any other explanation of our bizarre situation.

I still keep searching, not for an explanation, but for answers to all the different and varied pieces of the puzzle I am striving to put together.

The biggest question that people ask me is "How has all this affected your life?" and some are shocked when I say that my life has now completely changed and taken a new direction. We are all still together as a family, and both our sons still live at home with us - probably because it's cheaper than striking out on their own! But, nevertheless, we are all still together. However, my view of this world we live in has altered dramatically. Years ago, I was more than content to just enjoy my life by being a good wife and mother. I looked forward, like many people do, to an annual holiday - somewhere Paul and I could just relax for a couple of weeks before returning to our normal, little domestic lives. Whatever the governments of the world wanted to do was fine with me, after all, they only have our best interests at heart - don't they?

For me personally, I have learned not to take anything for granted. Perhaps I'm stating the obvious here when I say that the state of our world is now so fragile that it could disappear at any time. However, I am now so much more conscious about the environment, although I've always had a great love of nature and animals, I feel that I actually appreciate it even more now and want to do my part in helping to protect it.

Yet overshadowing all of this is my awareness of the vast Universe that we and so many other beings inhabit. I totally accept the concept of there being other dimensions, as it makes so much sense to me. If I hadn't been thrust unwillingly into this situation in the first place, I would never have sought to become a Reiki master. I probably never would have heard of it. I would have continued to live blissfully ignorant within my own little lifestyle, doing all the things that most "ordinary" people do.

I have found a great inner peace, which I believe comes partly from my healing work, and, in some strange way that is hard to explain. I feel that over these past few years, I am now able to get in touch with another part of myself - a deeply hidden part, which Mary Rodwell always refers to as "the part of you which knows." I do find answers there, and I am more able to go with my intuition - my gut reactions. Surprisingly, Paul is accepting this situation better, too, and relies on his own "gut feelings" a lot more now than he did years ago. I once remarked about his turnaround in the way he now views things in his life, and his reply to me was - in his usual light-hearted tone - that I've worn him down!

It's taken me years to come to terms with most everything that has happened, but I still accept help from many people to get me over my personal stumbling blocks.

I remember in particular that about a year ago Paul and I went along to a lecture being given by a very well-known clairvoyant who also claimed to be able to "channel" information from other worlds or dimensions. For me, as always, I was fascinated and wanted to know more. Paul, as usual, came along mainly to keep me company, but also because he thought it might be interesting.

We sat quietly at the back of the room as this very petite woman began. She was going to various people in the audience giving information, and, for the most part, receiving their confirmation that what she was telling them was true. Though it was quite fascinating to watch her work, when we left at the end of the evening, Paul and I were still debating whether or not it was all genuine. We don't just accept everything strange at face value. Although our minds are much more open now to such bizarre things going on in the world, it doesn't mean that we are in awe of everything all the time and accept everything at face value. Far from it. We discussed the fact that as she kept coming up with "someone here whose name begins with G. George? Graham? Gary? "etc.," and at some point someone would always jump in and shout back "Yes. It's Gary." Whereupon she would then zoom in on them and relate certain details that the person's dead relative was passing on to them. Paul said that a lot of the things she said were very general and could have referred to anyone, but even he conceded that there were some very personal details, that she imparted to people which would have been impossible to know beforehand.

Anyway, we had a nice evening and after thanking our friend John, the organizer, we made our way home.

The next day however, John rang us to say that the clairvoyant, Eleanor, had asked him who the lady sitting at the back was. Me! He said that he knew me, and asked her why she asked. She told him that towards the end of the evening, she had received certain messages that were for me, but she hadn't singled me out as these messages were from "outside the earth" - an extraterrestrial source.

When John said that Eleanor had asked him to set up a meeting between us, I was eager to accept the invitation. I anxiously awaited our appointment the following Friday.

On Friday I drove the eighty or so miles to Norwich and arrived early at John's home. It was quite late in the year so by 5:00 PM it was already very dark.

I sat in the living room: Eleanor was late. I wondered if she was still coming, and then I wondered that, if she did, would it all be worth me driving all that way to see her anyway? She arrived. John had already set up his round dining table with a cloth and had a single candle burning. After exchanging the usual pleasantries with Eleanor, I then entered the room with her, and we sat opposite each other across the table. John closed the door on his way out and the only light we had was that from the brightly burning candle.

Eleanor began. She asked to hold my wedding ring. I gave it to her, whereupon she closed her eyes, and we sat in silence for what seemed an age. She then started to moan, very quietly, and though this didn't frighten me at all, my fear soon crept in when the one single candle flame began to expand greatly in length for just a few seconds before reverting to its normal flame. This happened four times - the last time being interrupted by Eleanor seemingly passing out - her head hitting the table as she slumped in her chair. Before I could show any concern, she seemed to regain her composure almost instantly, opened her eyes and said to me "He's here."

As I was already frightened by the antics of the candle, I will accept that when I started to see a mist accumulating just behind her right shoulder, it might possibly have been my imagination. I remember reading somewhere that the adrenaline rush from being scared can sometimes cause our brainwaves to act erratically and pass false messages. However, there is no mistaking what I saw next. It was a being, well over six feet tall, dressed in loose-fitting clothing. I had time to notice a large gold-colored buckle within the clothing before I knocked my chair over in my panic to reach the door. This was enough. Fear got the better of me, and I ran.

Upon reaching the door, I was trying to turn the handle, but my hands were shaking too much. I could hear my own heart beating extremely loudly when over the sound of that, I heard a very soft, docile voice calling my name, and asking me to please return. It had the desired effect, because I looked around slowly and saw this being properly. I returned to the table, stood the chair up again, and sat down, staring at this entity. His face was so beautiful I shall never forget it, and I felt compelled to draw it later that evening. He was a very strong, powerful being, and his face was lionesque in its features. It was pale gold in color with a wide but flat nose and prominent nostrils. His mouth was small but otherwise ordinary, and he had a great shock of bright golden hair - a lion's mane falling in an unruly mess over his massive shoulders. His eyes couldn't be seen - he kept them focused towards the floor the whole time.

Eleanor had now closed her eyes again, and I then realized that the words were being spoken by him, but they were coming from her mouth. He had a wonderful way of speaking, very deep, but soft and calming, and I wanted to hear what he had to say. He began by explaining to me that he is indeed a warrior - immensely powerful and always successful in his many battles. He said that all his race were galactic warriors and that they were dispersed throughout the Universe to act as Peacekeepers and Guardians wherever they were sent. He likened his role to our own United Nations Peacekeeping Corps stressing that they preferred peaceful solutions, but were more than able to step in and defend themselves and their charges at any time if they had to. He informed me that they had been around a while - even assisting with the building of great monuments on our planet in our dim and distant past. I asked him where he was from, and he asked me why it was important for me to know that. I answered that I was curious, but he told me that his "place of origin" was far beyond my primitive comprehension. I remember that I felt rather stupid when he told me that I should be more interested in why he had come, rather than where he was from.

He talked at length about his "mission" here on this planet and that he had, in fact, been sent to look out for, and protect my son, Jason. I stupidly asked why he had chosen to come and speak to me, and not Jason, but he politely answered that he is well known to Jason. He seemed to answer with a laugh in his voice, and I saw Eleanor's mouth curl up into a smile as his voice came from within her. He continued that I was the one he had decided to talk to because I was, as usual, having a lot of trouble accepting what was going on around me. He reminded me of the words that had been told to me the night that I saw my long-dead dog Hannah, that all things were possible beyond the limits of my Earthbound consciousness and that I must learn to look beyond what my eyes can see.

My mind raced to that night, and I asked him if he was the figure in the shadows whose face I could not see. He answered that he wasn't, but did confirm that he and others were all working toward one goal - to protect my son so that he could

**Lion Man drawing by Ann.**

concentrate on what he had to do for the future, and to help those of us who arc like-minded, to protect our own planet - our Earth. They were here among us to help us save our home. I listened intrigued by everything he was saying, but when a lull occurred in our seemingly one-way conversation, I seized the opportunity and told him that I like to look into people's eyes, as I can usually see the truth of what I am being told in them. I asked if he would look at me. Without moving his head at all, he answered that he was sorry, but he could not. I asked why, and again, eyes still fixed to the floor at his feet, he told me that his home is a very hot planet, which revolves around three suns. He continued that his race had adapted their eyesight to cope with the heat from the suns and

173

their intense light. He likened his planet's surface to that of the texture of our own quartz crystal but with multi-colors. He compared his eyes to that of crystal, and he explained that to look upon his face fully would be dangerous for my own eyesight. He said that the brightness from them may cause blindness to other races, and this was why he would always keep to the shadows. He said that even Jason could only see him in shadow.

I asked him why this was, if my son was supposed to be "part of them." He confirmed that indeed this was correct, Jason is "part of them," but Jason was inhabiting a human body and was growing up experiencing human emotions. He told me that this was what "the child" had asked for - to experience being human, as he thought it might help him to understand us more, and he would be in a better position to help us when the time came. I asked him about this also - what was it that Jason was supposed to do here? Again, the smile came from Eleanor's mouth as I was told to wait and see. He said that he knew that I wasn't a very patient person, but I wasn't the only one. There were other "Indigos" here, thousands of them, all like my son, who know that they are here for a purpose and are growing up as human beings, yet they will never divulge what their purpose is in the future, only that it is to benefit the planet.

His image was beginning to fade, and I called to him to stay. He said that he would see me again and that, as we had now been introduced, he would come to me through my subconscious. He added that Jason had indeed chosen wisely when he "chose" me as his mother, and that even though I was still concerned and confused about so many things, I must try to be more confident in myself and not so afraid of what goes on around me.

As he had all but faded by now, Eleanor's lips whispered that great love for me comes from the Universe. Again, her head slumped to the table and again, almost instantly, she regained her composure, sat upright in her chair and smiled across at me. I said nothing. She then leaned across the table, took my hand and squeezed it, saying that she knew I was a very special person. She then thanked me for allowing her to be a part of a very wonderful moment. I asked her what effect all this had had on her, if any, and her eyes lit up as she said that "they" always leave her feeling fantastic for days. I then asked if she had heard any of our conversation, and she answered some, but that it was mainly for me to hear and that she was pleased that she had helped to facilitate this. She then rose from the table, found the light switch and returned to blow out the candle. Then, in her usual flamboyant way, she fiddled in her handbag for her car keys, bid me good night and poured like a whirlwind out through John's front door.

Things continued to happen here, small things for the most part, but still enough to get my attention.

There was the time, last March, when I took the two dogs for a walk down our lane. It was almost pitch black at about 8:00 P.M. We hadn't even gone past the boundary of the house, when Chissum, the big dog, started growling at something in the dark on the lane. I swung the torch up to meet nothing, and I was still peering through the darkness when Chissum decided that he had had enough of this thing, whatever it was. He pulled the lead from my hand and sprang upwards, obviously intending to connect with whatever was threatening him. However, what the big dog connected with was some sort of invisible wall. I heard the dull thud as the crumpled dog slid to the ground. Bronte, his daughter, who had been watching and barking furiously, had now replaced the barking with a whimpering noise, while she slowly backed away, not wanting to be any part of this strange situation. Chissum regained his composure and shook himself. He half-wagged his tail as he thrust a wet nose into my hand, as if assuring me that everything would be okay and he would protect me. Again he turned to face his invisible adversary and again, growling, launched himself at the darkness. For the second time, he slid to the ground.

By now, I had gathered myself enough to grab for the big dog's collar, and, while still keeping a tight hold on Bronte's lead, I was able to walk them both away from the lane and into the relative safety of the kitchen.

Both dogs seemed relaxed now, and then slumped down into their favorite sleeping positions on the tiled kitchen floor. Several times, however, Chissum adjusted his position until he was facing the back door. He continued resting while opening one eye now and again - just to check on things.

I have no explanation for what had happened, but I recorded it in my diary along with other bizarre entries, which have no explanation.

As can probably be deduced from these pages, animals mean the world to me, and, though I love my family dearly, I could never be without animals. You can imagine my anguish then when one of our older cats, Tigre, hadn't been seen for a few days. We do live in the country where there are many wonderful distractions for cats. But when the days became a week and Tigre was still missing, I became really worried and began looking for her. After searching for hours and finding no sign of her, I grudgingly gave up. Both the boys could see how upset I was, and they offered to look for her the following day. Neither of them could find any trace of her either. Eventually we had to face the possibility that she had been caught by a fox, or had been run over. We had to get used to the idea that we would never see her again.

About four weeks later, I was just returning from a long walk with the dogs, and as I approached the back door with them, Tigre came sauntering through it! She was purring loudly, and arched her back in contentment as she fussed around the dogs legs. They took no notice other than to sniff at her. Our dogs and cats all get on so well together that in the winter, the cats will often be found asleep while curled up between the great paws of either Chissum or Bronte. She came to me for her usual fuss, after which she headed off towards the stables. I went inside the house with the dogs and found both the boys sitting at the table. Daniel asked me if I had seen the cat and when I answered yes, the three of us got into a conversation about where she had been all this time. Jason told me that she had just wandered through the back door as if nothing had happened, then jumped onto his lap first for fussing, then onto Daniel's. While I relayed to the boys that the dogs and I had been fussing her outside, we could hear her calling. Jason and I went outside. Tigre was standing beside the stable block still calling. She was obviously unhappy about something. We walked over to her, at which point she turned and ran behind the building. We followed. Lying underneath some discarded pieces of timber was the distorted body of a cat. It had lain there for several weeks because when Jason got a stick to move it, thousands of maggots emerged from the carcass. Though it was badly decomposed, we could see that the back was broken, because the back legs were twisted in a grotesque way. She had been hit by some sort of vehicle, and had probably crawled to this final resting place. The mouth was wide open. This cat was Tigre. There was no mistake. Jason and I picked up what was left of the body and duly buried it.

Had the three of us imagined that the cat was there? Could it have been a different cat? To both of these questions I answer a resounding, no. It is my belief - and that of the boys - that Tigre knew I was worried and upset in not knowing what had happened to her, and this was her way of not only showing us what had happened to her but also, more importantly, of letting us know that she was okay.

# TWENTY SIX
# HOUSE GUESTS & HEALINGS

As mentioned earlier, we have met a lot of people on our journey, some good, some bad.

We have been fooled or taken in occasionally and once Jason had the misfortune of going out with a young girl, who, it turned out, wanted nothing more than to try and cash in on his "fame" by reporting to the newspapers that she had been chosen to bear his alien children! Jason got out of that relationship very quickly!

On the whole though, most people whom we've met have been great and have become good friends to us all. We have also learned a lot from each other and in some circumstances, they have inadvertently supplied me with yet another piece of my personal puzzle concerning the "alien agenda."

One such lovely lady and good friend goes is Marie Therese, who moves all over the world, yet has her roots in her native Paris. Whenever she is in London for business, she always sets aside a few days so she can come up to see us all. She is a well-known UFO researcher and writer in her native France, and we came to know her as the best friend of Isabelle with whom we stayed in Perth. The first time Marie Therese came up to see us, we were all a little nervous, for we had never met her and didn't know what to expect. As Paul and I had a prior engagement, it was left to Daniel to meet her at the train station, and they got on like a house on fire from the very beginning. Even now, Daniel takes a devilish delight in mildly winding her up by calling her Marie Celeste, to which she calmly replies in her immaculate French accent, "Daniel, I am not a ship."

Though very petite, her aristocratic breeding shines through, and on her staple diet of cigarettes and strong black coffee, we chat with her into the night.

Just before retiring to bed on her first visit, Marie Therese informed us that she would not get very much sleep. She explained that since she was a small child she had developed this problem of only needing an hour or two of sleep. Her parents had taken her to various specialists and clinics around the world, but to no avail - her sleep problem could not be cured. She apologized in advance in case her moving about in the night awoke any of us. She retired to bed at about 10:00, armed with dozens of books and various papers to keep her busy when her short sleep had been fulfilled. The next morning, however, there was no sign of her. Paul and I started to worry when it got to be 11:30 and there was still no sign of her. I remember that I had started up the stairs to see if she was all right when her door opened and a very tired-looking Marie Therese bid me good morning as she made her way along the hall to the bathroom. I returned downstairs and boiled the kettle for her coffee. She entered the kitchen looking much brighter now and sat down for her coffee. It was at that moment that she glanced at the clock and cried out in alarm - wanting confirmation with us that this was indeed the correct time. She couldn't believe it. She told us that for the first time in her life, she had slept for hours. She had switched on her light in her room when she went to bed the previous evening and had settled down to some work when she says she became extremely tired. She vaguely remembered someone calling her name, but then remembered nothing more until she awoke the following morning - at 11:30! Marie Therese was ecstatic; she claimed that she had experienced the most wonderful and sleep-filled night! She talked on and on about how good it had made her feel. To all of us, it was unbelievable.

Towards the end of her visit, she asked if she could take some photographs. We agreed. Her camera, like the lady herself, was very elite and expensive. She fiddled with zoom lenses and apertures until she was satisfied that it was set up just right. She then turned her focus to Jason, who had been sitting at the table chatting with her. He put up his hand and said that he didn't want it, but Marie Therese is a very persistent lady - very used to getting what she wants. She told him in no uncertain yet jovial terms that she was going to photograph him anyway - hand in the way or not! He looked at her, and with a wry smile told her that he would temporarily "stop" the camera from working. Laughing at his ludicrous threat, she put the camera to her eye and snapped. The flash didn't go off, and the button on the camera wouldn't depress. Puzzled, she tried again with the same result. Jason, for his part, sat smiling at her, making no attempt to shield his face from the imminent snap of the camera. Marie Therese checked her equipment and loaded another set of flash bulbs then, checking that the button depressed properly, tried again to take his picture. The result was the same. Still in utter disbelief, she took a picture of Paul who was standing by the door. The camera worked perfectly. She put down her camera and sat in silence looking at Jason for what seemed an age. Then she told him that he had made his point, but if she begged him, could she please have one photograph of him please? Smiling, he relented and said that she would be allowed to take only one picture, so she had better get it right. He stressed to her again - only one. She set up her camera and half believing that the camera wouldn't work, she snapped the button down. The flash behaved normally and the camera clicked down. Hurriedly, she mumbled to Jason that she would take another of him in case that one didn't come out, but this time the camera refused to work again. She put down the equipment, and sat back down with a wry smile on her face mumbling that she didn't believe it. Jason sat still, looking very smug with himself, and told her that she was only allowed one picture - no more. They then both laughed out loud, and she conceded that she had tried to be sneaky, but he was too good for her. She apologized for trying to fool him. They both laughed again and continued chatting until it was time to take her back to the station to catch her train to London.

She has been to visit and stay with us a few times since then, and the house always seems to have the same effect on her sleep patterns, for which she is very grateful. She claims that the house helps to recharge her batteries, for she feels wonderful after staying here.

She is a lady in the autumn of her life, yet never has she let that stop her. As I write this chapter about our dear Marie Therese, I understand that she is now spending a few months living and working in a bio-dome in Arizona! Prior to that, she spent several weeks sailing while working on a tall ship in the Pacific! As you might gather from these words, Marie Therese is a lovely person, a wonderful friend and I greatly admire for her determination and courage. Long may she reign!

As with Marie Therese, the house does seem to have an effect on certain people and word does seem to get around. We receive many requests from both here and abroad from people who ask if they may experience the house and its amazing properties. When it's convenient, we don't mind, and some people tell us that they have experienced the feeling of a presence during the night, while still others have actually seen shapes manifest. Some people tell us that they experience healings during the dark hours, while others go home disappointed in that they have experienced nothing at all. Like Marie Therese, some people have told me that they have heard their name being called, which I do believe, as I don't tell anyone what to expect, and these people have no knowledge of each other. As for anything going on here - yes, I believe certain things do happen, although I have no explanation to give to certain people when they are disappointed when they experience nothing. Why this should happen to some and not to others I don't know. Even my own mother has slept here on several occasions and tells us of being aware of "someone" holding her right foot - my mother broke her right foot many years ago, and as it was a multiple break, she has several steel pins holding it together and it does give her a lot of pain now and again. After her experience, she delights in the fact that she cannot feel any pain at all in that foot and once demonstrated that fact by holding onto our fridge door and continually bouncing up and down on said foot. Paul entered the kitchen at this point and quickly went out again, saying that he had witnessed a lot of strange things in this house, but the sight of my mother bouncing on one foot was one of the strangest! True to their mother-in-law/son-in-law relationship, Mum later chastised Paul for his comments and then thrust her foot in front of his face to prove to him that it felt wonderful! I dare not publish my husband's comments!

Another frequent and very welcome visitor to our home is our dear friend, Pat. She won't mind my saying that she is in her sixties, but still very attractive. Her silver hair is always pulled back behind her head, and her make-up and her dress are always immaculate. When we first met this lovely lady, we were all impressed by her jovial manner and her smile, which radiates warmth and kindness. Her eyes, though failing now, still glisten with the same joy her smile portrays. We met through our UFO research group where Pat is a long-standing member. She originally joined because of her own sightings of strange craft and has been interested in the subject ever since. In getting to know her, we have discovered that she has - with her husband who has now passed away - lived in most parts of the world. I feel that she and her husband were very close - soul mates perhaps - and she is still very close to her children, even though they are now grown and have moved away to live their own lives. She is a very spiritual lady and has a wealth of knowledge on all so called "new age" subjects such as paganism and Wicca and will always find time to offer advice to anyone who asks. Yet her life isn't so rosy. Apart from losing her husband and life partner, she has also lost a son to cancer, and she is constantly battling the disease herself. She tells me that ten years ago, she was told by doctors that she only had a few months to live and should get her affairs in order. She said "we'll see about that" and stands before all of us now as living proof that conventional medicine doesn't have all the answers. She has her ups and downs, good days and bad days, but generally she can hold her own. This, in my mind, makes her even more of a wonderful person, with all her problems and her losses, you would think that she would have the right to be miserable - to blame the world - yet she clearly loves life and everything and everyone in it.

Whenever she comes to our home, we ply her with her usual favorite tipple of red wine as we talk. She always says that she's only allowed one glass but never refuses another - and another. Jason always tries to make a point of being home whenever "Nannie Pat" visits, and even Daniel comments that the house feels brighter when she is around.

Jason would never allow anyone to stay overnight in his bedroom, but had no hesitation in agreeing when Pat asked if she could sleep in his room overnight one Saturday. She couldn't wait to get to bed that night. Jason took up temporary residence in the spare room, but stressed to her that he would be on hand if she needed him. None of us knew what would happen especially as the energies in his room usually react only to him. However, we needn't have worried. Pat came down the next morning looking her immaculate self, and proclaiming that she had gone to bed as a sixty something year old and had gotten up feeling like a sixteen year-old again. She said she felt wonderful. Although she felt a little nervous about staying in his room, she told us that she felt that the energies were welcoming and though she had decided to read for a while before sleeping, she heard a deep voice call out her name. She said that she could remember nothing more until she awoke in the morning.

Pat's "healing" lasted for over a month, and now, just like Marie Therese, she likes to return now and again for "her top up!"

Usually it is left to the house - or rather the strange energies contained within it - to cope with clearing people and - in many circumstances - healing them. Yet, there was one particular occasion when I was privileged to see my son work first hand.

Jason is not known for his patience in all things paranormal and cannot understand why other people cannot easily do what he does. I can only think that because all of this - astral travel, projections, healing abilities, reading people's thoughts, etc. - comes easily and naturally to him, he cannot understand why it doesn't work the same way for everyone. He is extremely knowledgeable on many subjects, particularly spiritualism, but, because he has been taught all this by "them" since early childhood, it comes easily to him. He is always telling me that my "social upbringing" and instilled fears will prevent me from reaching my true potential, and I know he is right. So many times I have found that I can go only so far, and then my fears will get the better of me.

We were asked, through a friend of a friend, if a man named Phillip could come to our house and meet with Jason with about a medical problem.

At first, Jason refused to meet with him, stating that we all have it within us to heal ourselves, but this man persisted. He told us that his problem was that he had a trapped nerve in the side of his neck, which was so painful that he was no longer able to go to work. Although he was on pain killers from the doctor, they were having little effect. He had been to many physio-therapists and sports injury specialists, but he appeared to have wasted his time and money, as his situation hadn't changed. We hadn't spoken about this person for quite a while when Jason wandered into the kitchen one day and just said, "By the way, tell your friend that I will see Phillip. Saturday would be a good day."

Our friend passed on the message, and the offer of help was gratefully received. The following Saturday saw Phillip's arrival with his partner, Karen.

Phillip seemed a little edgy - as if he didn't know what to expect. While Karen looked around the house admiring pictures and ornaments, Phillip sat quietly in the living room.

Jason came downstairs and introduced himself. He sat opposite Phillip and began talking to him about everyday things. Both supported the same football club, and they were soon rabbiting away about strikers, transfers, goals, relegation to the next division and everything else to do with their team. Karen and I held our own conversation at the other end of the room, stopping every now and again when the boys included us in their talk. It was during a lull in all conversations that Phillip said to Jason, "You do know why I'm here, don't you?" Jason smiled and nodded his head. Phillip continued, "Can you help me?"

Jason took another few gulps from his milk shake, then smiled at the man and said, "Done."

Phillip sat back in his chair looking quite stunned. He put his hand to his neck, massaging the painful area, then he gasped that Jason was right - his neck felt fine. He said that it was the first time in many months that he had felt such great relief. He thanked Jason profusely, then asked how he had done this - he never even touched him. Jason took on his boyish grin and spoke, "I don't have to touch; I went into your head to see your thoughts and feel your pain. I worked out where the blockage was occurring and fixed it." Phillip was listening intently as Jason continued, "It won't last though; it'll get blocked again. See, it's like there's this energy running through our bodies and sometimes things block its path. It can be illness or a physical injury and when that happens, all this energy crowds up against it, causing pain. So, to get the energies flowing again, you have to learn how to unblock the disturbance. If I teach you this, you will have to do this daily until the pain - even a twinge - stops returning. Now, clear your mind and accept the things I'm about to tell you without rationalizing them."

The three of us now sat silently waiting for this wise teenager to continue. "You have to go deep into your own mind - your own consciousness," he began, "and you have to clear your head of all other thoughts. Sit comfortably in a room where you know you won't be disturbed by anyone or anything. There must be no distractions. Now, see yourself in a blackened room where there is no light anywhere and then visualize your pain as being inside of a bucket or something like it. However, this particular bucket has a hole in the bottom of it which allows your energies to flow through. Your job is to make sure that your energies keep flowing so you will need to stay focused for a while. The blackness all around you will gradually grow lighter the longer you visualize the free-flowing energies running through the hole in the bucket. Inside the bucket, you must concentrate on dispelling the blockage, and in your mind you have to believe that the size of it is getting smaller and smaller each time you start the healing process. Over time, you will succeed and find that your aura is intact once more. I can see auras and blockages appear as bruises or discoloration. So, although I have sorted your trapped nerve for now, you are responsible for ultimately getting rid of it completely. Do it as I've explained, and you'll be fine."

When our guests left later that evening, Phillip still seemed a little overwhelmed by his visit here - and his conversations with Jason. Although he had believed that Jason would be the one to help him, I felt that he was still a little puzzled and confused as to how a teenager - albeit, a special teenager - could heal his long suffering without any contact, when professionals who had studied their chosen careers for many years, couldn't.

We kept in touch with Phillip and Karen, and it became clear that his meeting with Jason had stirred something inside of him, and they both began learning more about spirituality, which could make their lives richer. The last we heard from them was that they had sold their house and were touring England and Europe in a luxury camper van, meeting up with other like-minded individuals - and having the time of their lives. It's great to think that maybe that one visit and conversation with Jason had helped to change someone's life - for the better.

I remember another occasion when my son agreed - albeit reluctantly - to help a young woman who was experiencing problems connected to alien visitation. The woman, Eva, and her partner, Terry, had turned up at one of our UFO meetings one week along with Richard, a medium who had been trying to help Eva for many months. As Eva seemed quite distraught and obviously uncomfortable just being there, it was Richard who took it upon himself to explain the situation to a fascinated membership that night. Eva was being "possessed" by some sort of alien entity that was destroying her life and her sanity. Richard said that he had done everything he could think of to help Eva - even arranging an exorcism - but nothing seemed to work. He had suggested coming to our meeting to ask Paul and me for assistance in asking Jason for help. We both immediately replied that we would do what we could, and resolved to speak with Jason the next day.

Jason came wandering downstairs the next morning, and, in his usual automaton fashion, he reached for his favorite cereal, milk and a spoon. Having made his breakfast, he began eating it as he wandered slowly into the dining room. I followed him, believing this to be the best opportunity to speak to him about Eva.

He mumbled at me through a mouthful of cereal, "Well, who is it this time?" The fact that he was usually one step ahead of me was infuriating at times!

I told him about the events of the previous evening and described the state of this poor girl, but when I mentioned the supposed possession part, Jason burst out laughing, scattering corn flakes all over the table. "We don't do possessions, Mum," he smiled, "We don't need to. There are enough people out there who want to work with us voluntarily.

"Sometimes, certain alien races will channel information through humans, but you have to watch out that the channeling is authentic - if you know what I mean." He continued eating his breakfast. Then after a few minutes, he mumbled through a mouthful of cereal that he would try to help Eva, and he asked me to arrange a meeting for the following week. The meeting was duly arranged.

Paul and I accompanied Jason to a quiet pub on the outskirts of Norwich. It was easy for everyone to get to, and Monday nights were always very quiet there so we knew we wouldn't be disturbed. Eva was still upset, but she graciously thanked Jason for meeting with her. We left the three of them - Jason, Eva and Terry, her partner, to talk while we got ourselves drinks and sat in another bar.

A couple of hours drifted past before the three of them appeared, and Jason stated that it was time to go home. Eva had obviously been crying, but she looked so relaxed that you could see for the first time just how pretty she really was. Terry had grasped Jason's hand again and was thanking him profusely for what he had done and promised to stay in touch. "I'll see you out there," Jason called, as the couple left, and Eva anxiously answered that he surely will.

The journey home was relaxed and quiet until I could bear it no longer. I asked Jason what had gone on. "I don't need precise details," I told him, "but I am aching to know what happened." Paul just shook his head, and muttered that he had wondered how long it would take me before I asked.

"It's sorted," Jason began, "It was as I thought. Eva is an abductee and has been all her life. She has very strong psychic links - you know, spiritual stuff - so she sees and hears things which most "normal" people don't. She's a bit like you, Mum - if something doesn't fit in with your social upbringing, then you deny it. Then, if it persists, you start to question your own sanity and then you become afraid - because you're not "fitting in" with the dictates of society and other people will find you "weird." Can't have that. Eva was like that. She's never had anyone to confide in or back her up. Remember what it was like for me in the beginning when I was telling you things, and neither you nor anyone else would believe me? Well, it was worse for her because she doesn't have the sort of parents who would even listen, so she has had to bottle all this stuff up without ever really understanding any of it. She's had out-of-body experiences many times, but she thought she was going mad. I've convinced her that she isn't alone - nor going insane - and that she must learn to embrace her gifts. I've said that I will help her any way I can - on this plane and others. She'll be fine given time."

He has kept in touch with Eva and Terry and the three of them are good friends. In fact, the last time I saw the couple, they were planning to visiting the Scottish Highlands for a while to enjoy its absolute peace and tranquility. Eva looked really happy and relaxed - and totally at ease with her strange life. Her acceptance was total - and she was now fine with that.

Jason is a very private person. He shies away from publicity, even though he has been offered money from various television networks in an effort to get an exclusive interview with him. Only on very few occasions has he ever agreed to talk to the media - once, at the start of this work, and then to two national newspapers some years ago. The first newspaper reporter was brilliant - he was a youngish man and made a point of treating Jason like a young person, not an idiot. He discussed everything that 13-year-olds are into - football, pop music, and, rather sheepishly, girls. He was very professional and managed to broach the alien subject as if it were a casual part of their conversation. Jason responded well to this sort of treatment, and, feeling at ease with the reporter, he talked openly and honestly about his experiences.

He was happy, therefore, to talk to other reporters, and, when another major newspaper sought an interview, he expected to be treated the same way. However, he was disappointed. The reporter this paper sent obviously didn't have children, for he had no idea how to treat them. He sat Jason down in front of him, and went at him like the Spanish Inquisition. Jason didn't respond well to all the bullying, and the fact that the person sent to interview him had a very broad Scottish accent didn't help matters. Jason, for the most part, couldn't even understand what the journalist was saying to him and kept asking him to repeat the questions. Somewhat frustrated by "this young child," the reporter was not very kind in his written opinion of Jason. To make matters worse, the paper printed a picture of an "alien" which was taken from a Steven Spielberg movie with the caption reading, "and this is the alien which this boy claims to see."

On reading such rubbish the next morning, our thirteen-year-old boy could not understand just how and why some reporters were extremely nice and kind to him - and, more importantly, wrote down the truth of what he had told them - and how others, like the latter reporter, could print unkind words about him - even worse - could lie. He asked me to explain it to him, but neither Paul nor I could. We later discovered that there is such a thing as "newspaper politics," and, because other national papers had treated him well, this particular paper, possibly upset at not being given serial rights to his story, decided to make Jason and his story look ridiculous so as to make the other newspapers look ridiculous. We were given an apology by this newspaper - and compensation - but as far as our son was concerned, the damage had been done. He said that he wanted no part of any newspapers, television, magazines, etc., ever again. He said they could play their stupid games without him.

At the age of nineteen, he agreed to be interviewed by a television network but only, as he put it, because he had something to say. Even so, Jason was pretty angry at the way that the interviewer decided to end the interview, and this served to re-confirm his decision never to become involved with the media again. [See "Jason's Interview" on page 237.] He prefers to be left alone to live a relatively normal life while still continuing with his healing work, which takes place on a different level. I, on the other hand, believe that it is part of my journey to help to educate people in this subject. Jason is fine with that, telling me that I speak for him also.

People who come to our home for cleansing or healings are mostly satisfied with their experiences - they never seem to question the validity of the situation. They have learned to trust the Universe and are generally at peace with themselves. For me, I have questions all the time. I want to know if it is because our house is supposedly built on ley lines, or do extraterrestrial forces operate from here? Or is it all something to do with the gift that Jason seems to have? Or, could it be that the faith of certain people is so strong as to will these things to happen? There is an old saying that states that faith can move mountains, so maybe it can. Could it be that some of us get carried away a little with our story as a background and their own beliefs and trust are the real healers? I really have no definite answers, just theories, but I carry on witnessing such strange phenomena taking place on a fairly regular basis, and I just accept that whatever the reason, the results far outweigh the question.

# TWENTY SEVEN
# FRIENDS &
# STRANGE PHENOMENA

Chris is another good friend whom we have met through our mutual interests in alien phenomena. He lives in East London, and is quite happy to recount to like minded listeners his experiences and those of his ex-partner. Chris is not an abductee, as far as I am aware, but his paranormal experiences around this subject are becoming more frequent as time goes by. He is an ardent sky watcher, and is fortunate enough to own a state-of-the-art video camera, which is of tremendous help to him in catching moving craft on film. A lot of his sightings are made in the daylight hours - and usually when they are not expected, which is why he now keeps his camera with him at all times. Chris is also the author of an excellent book titled Intruders in the Night which focuses on his ex-partner's experiences, which sparked his almost inexhaustible enthusiasm for finding out more on this subject.

He has been to the house on several occasions, and it was during one of his skywatch sessions here that Jason asked him a question. "Instead of photographing things in the sky," he asked, "how would you like to meet them for real?" The three of us had been standing out by the back paddock looking out to the wide-open skies above the fields. It was late in the year, and it was pitch black everywhere.

Chris seemed a little taken aback for a moment then answered shakily, "Yeah - okay then."

Jason began to climb over the back fence separating our property from the farmer's vast fields. "Come on then," he called, "They're here now. Out here. Follow me."

I looked at Chris and asked gingerly if he knew what he had let himself in for. He smiled nervously back and answered that he wasn't sure, but he was already climbing over the fence to catch up to Jason.

They were gone for what seemed like an age, and, though I tried, I could see absolutely nothing through the darkness. Nor could I hear them. They returned some time later, after I had given up waiting and had gone back into the house. Jason was full of himself as usual, but Chris was quiet and subdued. I asked Chris what had happened. "I have never felt anything quite like that in my life," he began, "I just felt so overwhelmed. I could feel them around me and for the first time since I was twelve years old, I felt overcome with such emotion." Chris was genuine in what he was relating, of that I have no doubt. Jason later took him outside again, this time to the fields to the front of our house. They both walked into the fields and Chris later recounted to me the strangeness of the field - he said that he could feel a dark presence, and it scared him. Jason knew the dark energy was there, but he also knew that "they" would protect him from it. He figured that with this protection, he would also be able to keep Chris safe. Though he was right, Chris declined to go farther into the field - and I don't blame him. He had experienced enough for one night.

Chris returned to our home several weeks later hoping to see something in the clear night skies over Lincolnshire. The flatness of the land here gives incredibly vast amounts of sky - ideal for sky watching. I had also invited a few friends from the Norfolk UFO Society, John and his partner Jane, a dear friend Maddie, and, of course, our lovely "Nannie Pat." Jane is now learning a lot about all things spiritual, but at that time she had a very restricted knowledge. Yet it was she who noticed the change in the atmosphere as soon as John's car - in which they had all travelled - turned down our lane. She commented to Pat that she had felt a definite shift in the atmosphere to a warm, loving feeling which, she felt, emanated from our property. Pat's response was that she too had noticed it immediately, but had said nothing, hoping that another of their party would confirm this.

I greeted my guests and introduced them to Chris. We had a small buffet and some drinks, and soon everyone was chatting like old friends. Maddie was the only one who had not been to our home before, so I showed her around the house.

As the evening arrived, Pat, Maddie and John stepped outside the front door to smoke. I decided to leave Chris and Jane talking while I went into the kitchen to make fresh coffee for everyone.

Waiting for the kettle to boil, I suddenly became aware that someone was in the room with me. I knew it was none of our guests, as I had heard no one open the door. I turned quickly, just in time to see a pale, misty, human-sized figure, pass through the wall by the window, then pass through the wall in the corner of the room. We had all seen this entity before, and though it didn't worry me, I was concerned that some of my guests may have noticed something, and I was a little afraid of what their reaction might be. I decided not to mention the incident and to see if anyone else said anything.

I went outside to announce that coffee was ready, and the invitation was readily taken up in view of the chilly night. As the three of them walked in, Maddie paused for a moment and asked me if I had seen anything in the kitchen, explaining that that is where it went! I asked her what she meant. She told me that while standing outside on the front lawn smoking, she noticed a figure glide around the front of the trees to her left. It then travelled in a diagonal line towards the front of the house and straight towards her. She then asked me if there had ever been a path or track way, which would have been diagonal to the house but before the house was built. I said that I didn't know, and asked why? She further explained that the entity had stopped right in front of her for a moment, and told her to "move out of the way as you are obstructing my path." She immediately moved to the right and the entity continued along its chosen path-passing through the house beside the kitchen window. That was when I confirmed to her that I had seen this same entity pass through the kitchen and out again through the corner of the wall. I could see that there was no need to worry, Maddie seemed to take it all in stride, but she wouldn't be a member of a UFO Society if she weren't open-minded. Therefore, she wasn't unduly worried or frightened about seeing this figure. However, later that evening that would change, Maddie would be afraid and there was nothing I could do about it.

Pat was telling Maddie about the strange atmosphere in Jason's room and was effusing about the energies, which she found absolutely wonderful. Pat asked if they could take a look in Jason's room, for Maddie was, by now, intrigued by Pat's account and wanted to experience some of this for herself. I replied that I didn't mind, but I would ask Jason's permission, as it is his room. I called Jason - who was outside with Jacqui - and he came into the living room. Pat asked him personally and he answered that he didn't mind at all, but warned everyone that the energies would most likely not be the same to everyone, and that they should take care. I don't think anyone took his warning seriously - I know I didn't, and we all started up the stairs.

Pat was the first to enter his room, and, closing her eyes, she seemed to drink in the energy, which was very obviously there. Pat was holding on to the bottom of the bedstead, and urged Maddie to join her and drink in the wonderful energy. Maddie walked towards Pat and took hold of the metal bedstead as well, but rather than enjoying the energies, Maddie started to feel really ill and then had extreme trouble breathing. She said later that it felt as if her chest were collapsing. She released her hold of the bedstead, and, with her head down, she slowly made her, way out of the room. Realizing what was going on, I quickly went to help her and we stood on the landing. She grabbed a hold of the balustrade and although her breathing was still very labored, said that now that she was out of the room, she was beginning to feel a little better. We never make a point of telling anyone who is visiting the house about any adverse re-actions that other people experience. What poor Maddie was feeling was totally genuine. The color had drained from her face, and she was at a loss to explain why she had felt so ill. I stood with my friend for several minutes until she felt strong enough to go down the stairs. She sat down while I went to get her a glass of water. As the minutes wore on, she was feeling better until she felt perfectly fine again. Personally, I couldn't apologize enough for what had happened. Jason was sorry, too, but reiterated the fact that he had given everyone a warning. Pat had been accepted by "them" a long time ago - Maddie was someone "they" didn't know.

Maddie rang me a few days later to thank me for an enjoyable day. I apologized again for the incident in Jason's room and she admitted that she still felt a "little wobbly," but she assured me that she was now back to her old self.

Jason's friend Craig also encountered terror at our place one Sunday evening in February, 2003. He had called to pick up Jason, and the two of them had set off to get some much-needed parts for a car they were repairing. Yet scarcely had they left, when Craig came tearing through the back door with such force that the door slammed back against the wall with a resounding thud. He was shaking as he went to the window and pulled back the curtain. I began to laugh, asking him what he was playing at, but he didn't answer - instead he was scouring the skies. Realizing the situation was serious, I asked where Jason was, yet he still kept his eyes focused on the sky and said nothing. As I went to go outside to find him, Jason walked through the back door. I asked Jason what was going on. "Don't worry about it, Mum. He's frightened himself more than anything." I still wanted to know what was going on, and Jason began to recount the story.

"We had just turned out of our lane when Craig spotted three orange lights in his mirror. He called my attention to them, and immediately I thought 'Oh no, here we go,' but I told him to ignore them. However, our speed started to increase because Craig was trying to outrun these things - and the lights were by now, right up close to the back of the car - like they were chasing us."

At this point, Craig interrupted shouting, "There they are, Jase! They're back!" Jason and I moved over to the window where Craig pointed out the lights. Sure enough, three bright orange balls of light seemed to be hanging motionless in the sky above the field to the front of the house. Jason suggested that we should all go outside to get a better look, and, as Paul had now come into the kitchen to see what all the fuss was about, Craig felt safer with all of us and he agreed.

The four of us stood outside. The orange lights were still sitting above the field, but then we noticed what seemed to be search lights emanating from the middle of the field and going upwards into the night sky. Soon afterwards, a round, brightly lit patch where the lights were began to spread outwards - almost like a rippling effect similar to water - until it was about three hundred feet in diameter. It then stopped, seemed to pulsate for about ten minutes, and switched off, as if someone had suddenly thrown an off switch. Craig stayed at the house until he was convinced that all the weirdness had gone. Even then, Jason had to drive his car behind him until he reached the relative comfort of the street lights on the main road.

This exact same incident also happened just three days later. This time it was witnessed by Paul, myself and another friend.

As far as I am aware, more incidents have not happened since, although there have been quite a few times when the front of our property was lit up like the proverbial Christmas tree. When we venture outside to investigate, the lights are instantly "switched off," and the reason for them is never found. Now when this happens, we don't even bother going outside to investigate, as we know that the lights will disappear within minutes, and it will all be back to normal. We have, so far, been right.

# Twenty Eight
# Mereworth Mysteries

I have already mentioned some of the strange instances that we experienced while living near the military base of Mereworth - the base next to our farm in Kent. Unfortunately our move did not completely shield us from running into strangeness once in a while.

As you know, although we love living in Lincolnshire, Paul has to go back to Kent every few days in order to work. He has tried making a living there, but as the chief occupation locally is agriculture, it does not generate enough money to cover all the bills.

While driving his taxi in Kent one day in August of 2001, his passenger needed to go to a place that was very near to where we used to live. Paul decided to take a short cut to the address and turned down Seven Mile Lane, which coincidentally, runs alongside the base at Mereworth. However, Paul found that this lane had been blocked off, and the road block was staffed by military personnel.

Paul didn't give it much thought at that time, reversed back, and took the longer route. However, later that day, Paul mentioned it in passing to one of the other drivers. The driver told Paul that he had been asked to pick up two council surveyors early that morning, and to take them to Seven Mile Lane. On arrival at the beginning of the lane, the driver said that a rough police barricade was already in place manned by the local police, but since his two passengers were expected, the barricade was removed so that the car could drive on. Halfway down the lane, the car was flagged down by the Fire Brigade. The driver stopped and let his passengers out, at which point he was stunned to see that a massive hole had opened right across the road. He said that it was about thirty to forty feet in diameter and seemed to be very deep.

The driver stayed around while the surveyors were lowered gently into the hole in order to ascertain the structural damage to the road. After several minutes, they came back up and were both talking excitedly about the fact that they had both seen tunnels - man-made tunnels - going in all directions down there. They had noticed lights in the ceilings and switches on the walls. Other people then went down into the hole to see for themselves, and they subsequently came back up and confirmed that this was correct -there were many tunnels, all lit and very obviously man-made.

The driver told Paul that at this point, some military vehicles turned up with men dressed in dark blue/black uniforms. They pulled aside everyone who had seen what was at the bottom of the hole. After several minutes, the two surveyors returned to the car, somewhat ashen faced, and asked to be driven back. The driver had, by now, been infected with some of the excitement of the situation with the strange hole, and he asked the unusually quiet passengers what they had made of the tunnels. He asked a second time before one of his passengers sheepishly replied that they were told they were not allowed to talk about the tunnels - to anyone. The driver said that both men looked "very scared and were visibly shaken" - he assumed - not by the hole or the tunnels, but by their impromptu meeting with members of the military, because their mood changed dramatically after that encounter.

Just three days later, the military barricades were gone and the lane was open again. There was no sign that a hole had ever existed.

This base had always been strange when we lived on our neighboring farm. We were used to seeing helicopters hovering over dense woodland then seemingly coming down into trees, yet nothing was ever visible from the roadside. The barracks - which are visible from the road - are always empty, yet Paul and other drivers have witnessed great convoys of lorries entering in the early hours of the morning and disappearing into the woodland. I clearly remember one occasion when my brother, David, took my old horse, Craven, out for a ride in the woods. David is not known for his good sense of direction and inadvertently wandered onto M.O.D. property. Rounding a bend in the track, Craven was startled when a heavily, armed soldier sprang out of the undergrowth and made a grab for his bridle. David then found that he had military weapon of some kind thrust in his face as he was told in no uncertain terms that he was on M.O.D. land and the consequences would be considerable if he did not leave the area immediately. His easy-going, relaxed ride through the woods quickly turned into a desperate race for home. Having been pointed in the right direction, David swiftly urged Craven on at a fast canter in order to get away from this man as quickly as pos-sible.

In October of 2004, Jason and Jacqui had gone down south to pick up a car for Paul. The address they had to go to was just a few miles from Hawksnest Farm, and Jason was keen to take Jacqui to see it. They drove to the bottom of the track and he was surprised to see that permanent barricades had been erected across the access to stop vehicles and horses from using the track. He found this strange as, when we owned the farm, it was clearly stated in our title deed that the vehicular track leading to the farm must be open to any vehicles with business there, and for all persons who wanted to ride their horses along the track leading past the farm to the woods. This by-law had been in force for many, many years and, as far as we knew, was impossible to change.

However, Jason was not going to be put off by these barricades, so he parked the car on the road and he and Jacqui proceeded to walk along the track. Within minutes, a white Landrover arrived with two men inside. The vehicle stopped beside them, and, while one man was busily talking on a radio, the other got out and asked them what they were doing there. Jason explained that his parents used to own the land at the top of the track and that he was taking his wife up there to see it.

The man replied straight away, "So, you're Jason then?" Jason confirmed this and asked the man how he knew. The man said, "Oh we've heard all about you."

Jason asked him to elaborate, but he just smiled at him and didn't answer. The man then told them that as it was him (Jason), he would get in touch with his superiors and see if he could get "permission" for Jason to show Jacqui the farm. He spoke with the other occupant of the Landrover and got on his radio. A few minutes later, the man got out of the vehicle and told Jason and Jacqui that they could go ahead, but he would have to accompany them.

On reaching the gate, Jason wasn't surprised to find the fields empty, as he had been taken there a few times by the ETs since we moved. However, he was surprised to see a small brick building to one side. He asked their "guide" what it was for, and the man replied that it was a stable. Jason's response was that he wasn't stupid as it was nowhere near big enough for a stable, and for what? There were no animals anywhere to be seen! He then noticed that at the far end, there were a number of Army vehicles - lorries, jeeps, etc., which were all covered with camouflage netting. He asked the man what that was all about, but the guy replied that he was asking too many questions and would now have to leave.

The two of them were escorted to the end of the track, and the two men watched as they drove away in the car.

# TWENTY NINE
# THE BLACK ARTS

Someone once asked me - more as a joke - which alien race I was most afraid of. Yet the smile soon disappeared from the inquirer's face when I answered that the alien race I was most afraid of is the human race. The enquirer, a middle-aged well-dressed gentleman, seemed quite put out by this remark and asked why I would be afraid of my fellow human beings as we "are all part of the great family of humans." I briefly replied that it is human beings who work for the various agencies who keep an eye on us. It was human beings who were present at an abduction of mine. It was human beings who worked for the various agencies who made us leave our beloved Hawksnest Farm, and human beings were responsible for the death of our cattle. At that time, these were the only "crimes" I could name which had been perpetrated by my fellow human beings, but something began to happen in June, 2003, which could be added to this infamous list.

It began on the night before the summer solstice. Jason, Jacqui and their friends, Mark and Lisa, had all been out for the evening and had arrived back at Jason's mobile home at around midnight. It was decided that their friends would stay over for the night, as they were all planning to go out somewhere the following day. Jason unlocked the door and the four of them went inside. Jacqui was putting the kettle on for tea when Mark said that he could smell a fire burning. At first, none of the others could smell anything, then gradually, the smell became obvious to all four of them. They all went outside. The smell of the fire was very strong - and so too was the sound of crackling wood on the fire - so it had to be extremely close. There was no glow from a fire anywhere to be seen. Mark went back inside the caravan and emerged with two flashlights and handed one to Jason. They all then ventured out into the horse's paddock but could still see no sign of even a single flame. Lisa was becoming quite upset by all this, yet Mark found it quite fascinating. Neither of them had any connection to or any interest in the paranormal, so they all soon returned to the caravan to decide on which film they should watch on the video recorder. However, although the smell of the fire was still great, another smell attacked their senses - that of burning incense, and it was all over the caravan, present in every room.

The following morning they all rose early and made their way outside to the pad-dock to greet the beautiful sunshine we experienced for a short while. It seemed that they all spotted something at the same time - and were equally shocked by their discovery. There, in the middle of the paddock, were the glowing embers of a large fire. It had to be the fire they had all smelt the night before, yet none of them could see it then. They went over to get a closer look, and around the outside of the fire were carefully placed rusty nails. They varied in size, but it looked as if each one had been deliberately placed in certain positions and some even created certain symbols, which had no meaning to any of them. Also, they found several discarded used incense sticks. Jacqui got a pen and paper and quickly jotted down some of the symbols before the boys removed all the nails, then dispersed what was left of the fire so the horses wouldn't injure themselves. The six-foot fencing at the rear of the paddock had been cut to allow access to whomever was responsible for the fire, and, on closer examination, they could all see that the tall barley in the adjoining field had been well trampled so there had been obviously more than one perpetrator. However, the horse's safety was first and foremost in their minds, and only later did they all comment on the strange-ness of it all.

The four of them went out for the day, and it was decided that Mark and Lisa would spend the night at the caravan again. It was around 2:00 AM when they were all awakened by the sound of many voices and tapping and banging against the outside of the caravan. Though Mark and Lisa were rightly terrified, Jason and Jacqui were equally confident that whatever was happening outside, the protection from "them" was inside the caravan and would allow no harm to come to any of them. Jason told me that it sounded like some sort of repetitive chant-ing in what he thought was Latin, yet the most repeated word was "esperatto" (which we later found out through our research means "to appear" or "appear now"). The following morning, they discovered that foul smelling oil of some kind had been daubed over the walls of the caravan to create symbols similar to the ones made with the rusty nails.

That seemed to be it for a while, and the four of them dismissed the strange in-cidents as the work of cranks - or someone out to try and scare them. However, the following Sunday Paul discovered the next mind-numbing event.

He went to the paddock to put the horses away for the night. Jason, Jacqui and their friends had been out all day. Paul called to the horses, yet strangely, they wouldn't come to him. He walked over to them and discovered to his horror that our little mare, Goldie, had blood running all down her face. At first, Paul was afraid that it was her left eye, but on wiping away some of the blood, he noticed that there were three deep straight gouges to the side and beneath her eye. He called me out to tend to her. The cuts were too straight and the same distance from each other for it to have been any sort of accident. We were both sick with age that anyone could do such a thing to an innocent animal. Paul said that if he ever found out which sick moron was behind this, he would happily leave them in a pool of their own blood. All the horses were extremely spooked and upset when we put them in the barn for the night but, over time, Goldie healed and all the horses were soon back to normal.

Odd things continued to go on here, and soon it was obvious that the wonderful atmosphere we all enjoyed at the house was changing for the worse. Really dark energies seemed to linger everywhere outside, and it got to the point where even the animals didn't want to be there. The dogs even refused to go for walks.

Mark tore down the lane late one evening shouting for us all to come and look at the darkly robed "people" standing facing the house. As the moon was full, they could be clearly seen. Jason got to the door just as I did, and the monk-like characters - about thirty or so in total - soon began dispersing across the fields. We watched as they walked steadily and with purpose. Mark suggested that we should "go get the bastards," but his enthusiasm soon wore off when Jason pointed out that we were heavily outnumbered and that it was probably done to scare us. Anyway, Jason had a better idea.

That same evening, Mark and Lisa were again visiting Jason and Jacqui, but more so because Mark had felt strangely compelled to do so. Jason later told me that Mark began acting very strangely, marching up and down the caravan and wringing his hands. When asked to sit down, he kept repeating that he was bored - which wasn't like Mark at all. Then, suddenly, Mark began swaying to and fro, and, closing his eyes, he calmly announced that he wasn't Mark any longer. The other three sat back, and Lisa chastised Mark for frightening her when Jason interrupted her and calmly asked Mark who he was. Mark grinned and said that he really didn't want to be here, but he had no choice; he had been forced to "appear" and talk to them all. Half believing that maybe Mark was playing a joke on them, Jason asked his friend to prove his claim by counting backwards from ten. As Mark is dyslexic and cannot do this, the three of them were convinced when this request was easily carried out. As the girls were stunned into silence, Jason asked what this being wanted and was told, in no uncertain terms, that they must not interfere in the things that were going on recently. He was further told that their work would be finished shortly, but also that they would not tolerate any interference. Jason's reply was bold - this was his home and he would do everything in his power to stop these people in their tracks. He added that he had an idea what they were up to and would not allow it to progress any further. The being inside Mark again warned him not to interfere, and the discussion became heated. It was then that Mark tried to lunge at Jason, and the three of them then had a hard time subduing their friend. It was at this point that Mark fell into a deep sleep, and they made sure that he was comfortable on the sofa. The two girls were still very frightened but didn't want to leave the caravan, as it was extremely dark outside. They all had no choice but to sit and wait to see what happened.

After about an hour, Mark roused himself from his sleep and asked why everyone was staring at him. He found this quite amusing and asked if he snored that loudly! He was obviously feeling himself again and had no recollection of his previous activities!

It may be worth noting here that the people from the next property down the lane came and saw me the following morning and asked if we had noticed any disturbance during the night. I didn't mention any of the night's events and asked our neighbor why she had asked such a question. She said that her two dogs had awakened the whole household in the early hours by barking and growling furiously and lunging at the upstairs windows. Her husband got up and switched on the lights, and all the family strained their eyes to look out onto their paddock, yet nothing was stirring - all was quiet. My neighbor told me that she decided not to let the dogs out of the house - even though they were scratching at the back door and barking - as she feared for their safety. Apparently, after about an hour of not being able to pacify the dogs, they suddenly went quiet of their own accord and then resumed their normal sleeping positions. The rest of the family, grateful for the silence, did the same.

I asked Jason what his thoughts were on all of this, and he told me that he felt that certain cults knew of the three ley lines that run through our property and of the immense energy generated here. He said that certain people have the ability to home in on such things. He was equally certain that whoever was responsible was trying to open up a portal of some kind in order to invite or invoke some type of being or energy to enter our dimension. However, I found it quite frightening when Jason added that such a portal was already partly opened. I asked him what we could do about this situation - which was becoming more absurd by the minute - and he assured me that he was strong enough to handle the problem. I asked what he intended to do and said that I didn't want him in any danger. He laughed, gave me his sideways glance and just said softly, "Don't worry, Mum. I know what I'm doing. I'll sort it."

As usual, I didn't get any further details from Jason, but after a few days, even I noticed that the lovely atmosphere we were used to was returning to our property.

As far as I'm aware, we have had no repercussions from this human-initiated situation. I did ask Jason about it one day, but he just said glibly that it just goes to prove that he is stronger than most mortals - even those using certain powers or energies for their own causes.

A few weeks later this question of whether we fear humans or aliens more once again became apparent in a conversation I had with Jason.

While watching a program on television about alien encounters, the question of body implants was raised. The program then took a scientific turn and document- ed some of the eminent researchers who are currently taking a serious interest in removing such implants from people's bodies.

A lot has been written about such tiny instruments which have mysteriously found their way into certain abductees, and, as a matter of curiosity, I asked Ja- son if he had ever considered having his implants removed. His answer surprised me, as it was completely unexpected. "No way," he said. "That would be stupid."

I asked him why, and he further explained, "Everybody believes that these things are there to track people. It's a popular theory now that "they" find you - wher- ever you are - by tracing the implant. Haven't you ever wondered why they are never in the same place in everyone? It's because tracking is only a side line - they have a much more important function. Their correct name is bio-readers." I had by now switched the sound down on the television and was listening intently as he continued.

"They are multi-functional, but their main function is to monitor the person's body. It gives a reading of the heart rate, blood pressure, lungs and kidneys and other vital organs to make sure they are all working well, and it reads the chang- es when we are stressed or going through some very emotional stuff. This is all done for `their' research into our feelings and emotions. However, if we have any medical problems, these tiny instruments have the know-how to make our bodies stronger. They can't necessarily heal a medical condition, but they can hold it back and stop it from progressing or getting worse. People have them removed because they think that the aliens can find them by tuning in to the frequency of these things, and while this is true, the implants are not strictly necessary, be- cause `they' can find people again whenever they want anyway. See, when you are abducted, certain information is recorded about you, and one of these things is that your brainwave patterns are monitored and samples of them are stored for future reference. Everyone's brain wave pattern is different - like fingerprints - and all `they' have to do is trace the pattern of the person they are looking for. So, even when you are sleeping, your brain is still active, therefore you can be found wherever you are and, let's face it, no one can stop their thoughts can they? Simple and effective. This is why not every abductee will have an implant, because not every one is issued a bio-reader."

He ended his lecture with the words, "No way does someone get mine."

# THIRTY
# JACQUI

At twenty years of age, Jason was married to Jacqui, who is four years his junior. She knows that she is a Star Child, or Indigo. She has that certain look about her which denotes her genealogy. She is small in stature, blonde haired and fair, but her eyes give the game away: She is like Jason in where she is from. She has told me many times about seeing strange lights and craft in the sky when she was a child. She remembers encounters which, when mentioned to her parents, were quickly dismissed as dreams or wild imaginings. Like Jason, she has learned the hard way that you keep this sort of thing to yourself - unless you are sure of the people you are talking to.

They met when she was only twelve, but they remained only passing acquaintances. She always liked it when he was around, but the feeling wasn't reciprocated. It wasn't until a few years later that he started seeing Jacqui as a friend and confidant; he found that he could share with her his inner-most secrets, knowing that she wouldn't betray him. The fondness he felt for her gradually turned to love. Jason tells me that it wasn't until he was older that he was able to recognize the Star Child within her, but he says he would have fallen in love with her even if she were "ordinary." She is a sweet, gentle person, and Paul and I are happy that she is now part of our family.

She too, enjoys the strange atmosphere, which still pervades his room confirming that she also sleeps in similar circumstances. Like him, she takes all the paranormal strangeness of our home in stride, mentioning things casually in conversation, as if she were describing a fancy dress she has seen. Only recently, she told me about her early-morning visitor.

They had both been staying in our mobile home, which is situated at the rear of our house. They felt that it afforded them both a little more privacy than his bedroom in the house. Just as the sun was rising one morning, Jacqui told me that she could hear a child talking. She said that she couldn't make out what the child was saying, but she could definitely hear a voice outside. Wondering what was going on, she got up and went to the door. Jason was still sound asleep. She opened the door and stared into the misty morning and there, just a few feet in front of her, was a small girl. The girl looked to be about eight or nine, had long blonde hair and was dressed in a checkered pale lemon dress. The girl smiled at Jacqui and then began fading away until she could no longer be seen.

Jacqui wasn't distressed about what had just happened, and, when telling me about it, she did so in a matter-of-fact way.

Although Paul, Jason and I had all seen this child before, none of us had mentioned it to Jacqui, as not to alarm her. We weren't sure how she would take to something like that, but obviously, we needn't have worried.

Paul was the first one to see her several weeks earlier when she was standing beside the barn entrance. Thinking she was visiting a neighbor down the lane and had wandered onto our property, he approached her, but was shocked to see her fade away.

Paul has spotted her three times since then in various places around the property. He seems to have accepted her presence without question, and just mentions to me that he has seen her again. For me, too, she has appeared and faded to nothing, the first time as I was feeding the chickens. She was standing at the end of the chicken run just watching the birds and smiling. She doesn't feel threatening in any way, in fact, she is always smiling and so pretty that she seems to lift our spirits. I have spoken to Jason about her and he tells me that he has spoken to her on several occasions. He says that she is not held here but comes by choice. She talks to him about her mother and little brother, and she says that she misses them both tremendously. She explained to Jason that she is, quite happy where she is describing the place as "a pretty fairy land" where she can easily "push" herself back into "normal land" whenever she wants to. He has asked her why she has chosen not to move on, and she tells him that she would miss her mother and brother too much, but this way she can still see them. She said that she could "feel" Jason when she was "pushing through" and came to see him out of curiosity, but she likes it here, so she comes back to visit. She told him that she likes to see the animals and feels that we are all "nice people," who aren't alarmed by her presence. Her name, we believe, is Sally, and I suspect that she will visit us now and then for a long time to come.

Jason and Jacqui had set the date for their wedding as August 13, 2003, however, they still hadn't yet decided on a venue. As neither of them hold fast to any religion, they both felt that a church wedding would be hypocritical of them both, which didn't leave them with many options other than a registry office. Jacqui had her heart set on wearing the traditional white gown with all the trimmings, and the thought of being married in a registry office seemed too bland, too oficious, and without true depth or meaning. They could ill afford hiring out even a small hotel for the service and reception. Then Paul had a suggestion - one which they both immediately jumped at. A few years earlier, Jason had accompanied Paul and me and several of our spiritual friends to a wonderful, old mansion house well hidden in the encroaching greenery of an almost forgotten part of Norfolk known as the Mangreen Crystal Healing and Light Centre. Although Jacqui had never been there, Jason's enthusiastic description of the place had her convinced that this would be the site of their wedding. They swiftly made plans to visit a few days later.

After arriving at the centre (it was open to the general public at certain times throughout the year), they took their time to acquaint themselves with its beauty - the manicured flower gardens, the various species of trees, which adorn the extensive grounds, the surrounding fields where cows and sheep grazed peacefully, the ancient stone circle surrounding an enormous and aged oak tree, and the crystal centre itself. They both knew that this was the place.

Having booked their wedding date over the telephone with Mangreen's proprietors, they both had to attend a meeting in April to discuss the arrangements they wanted. The pastor, Maureen, told them both that as the centre embraced no religion, she would not allow hymns to be sung. This suited our young lovers, and they both opted for the music of Jon Bon Jovi; their wedding ceremony was going to be exactly how they wanted it to be!

A further meeting was called in June to finalize everything and make sure that nothing had been forgotten. Jason and Jacqui found themselves sitting in the vast living room at the Edwardian manor house waiting for one of Maureen's assistants. They both told me later that it felt like waiting for the headmaster to arrive at his office after you had been sent there for doing something bad at school! Jean, the wedding co-ordinator, arrived and sat down opposite the pair. Apparently, while they were all talking however, the pages of Jean's book began to turn gently of their own accord. At the same moment, the lights began to dim, and Jean quietly announced that she felt that someone had entered the room. Jason and Jacqui became aware of the same thing, but continued with their discussion, ignoring the unseen intrusion. After all, what seems like strange behavior to anyone else, is perfectly "normal" to this pair! Jean continued, only stopping momentarily to announce that their unseen visitor was not of human origin, but was well known to both of her charges. The young couple smiled at each other, and Jason answered that he knew who was there, and that he didn't mind. Their discussion continued. At the end of the meeting, it was mutually agreed that if this intrusion was anything to go by, then the couple shouldn't be surprised if other strange things occurred at the actual ceremony!

# THIRTY ONE
# THE WEDDING

On August 13, 2003, Jason married Jacqueline Borden at the Crystal Healing and Light Centre in Norfolk.

Both of Jason's grandmothers had arrived three days earlier and were busy fussing around the pair of them. The house was in absolute turmoil from then on, and the arrival of my brother, Stephen, and his wife Anita, the day before the wedding, added to the turmoil and excitement of what was to come.

The only traditional thing about the big day was that Jacqui wore a beautiful white bridal gown with all the trimmings. She arrived at the Light Centre with her father in the back of one of Paul's prestige cars, his beloved Bentley. Jason and his best man - his brother Daniel - had been waiting nervously for what seemed like an age. Just as the wedding march began to play, an ashen-faced Daniel announced to his brother that he couldn't find the rings! As Jason started to panic, Daniel revealed his little joke, although Jason didn't seem amused by it!

The centre was beautifully decked out with dozens of white flowers. The foundations of the centre were formed from tons of quartz crystal which had been specially acquired and had the effect of energizing the whole place. Even guests at the wedding who had no knowledge of such things commented on just how wonderful the room felt.

There were enormous pieces of crystal - clear quartz, amethyst and rose quartz mainly - placed on window ledges all around the circular room. In the middle of the room was the altar which itself was constructed of milky quartz with other large crystal stones set around it. A beautiful archway - full of white flowers - had been erected around the altar and, just to the front of the altar and suspended by a chain from the high ceiling, was a huge glass dome housing yet another but larger piece of quartz crystal. The weight of the dome made sure that it didn't move.

Maureen, registrar and proprietor of the centre, conducted the ceremony. The words were a mixture of conventional ceremony, spiritual and personal comments, all culminating in the words from a traditional Apache wedding. Maureen then announced that they had been joined together by the Universal Light, and, after the official registration details, the wedding march was played again as the wedding party made their way out to the grounds followed by family and guests.

However, during the wedding itself, two strange things happened which I feel are worth mentioning. The first was that my brother, Stephen, had momentarily turned his head and stared into space to the right of Maureen. I had noticed this because he was sitting beside me, and, as he stared, his face seemed to drain of all color. I leaned behind my Mother and whispered to him asking if he was all right, but he didn't answer and didn't move - he just sat rigidly staring at the same space. I followed his gaze but saw nothing. By now, his wife, Anita, was also asking if he was okay. At the same moment, although Jason was looking the other way and hadn't seen his uncle's strange behavior, he too turned his head around and stared at the same spot. For a few seconds, Jason too seemed mesmerized by whatever he was seeing, then he smiled and nodded, as if acknowledging whoever was standing there. Maureen, sensing that she had lost his attention momentarily, had paused in the proceedings, carrying on only when Jason turned his head back around. I looked over at my brother who had also been released from the spell, and he seemed to be wiping his face with his hand. Again, I looked but could still see nothing.

When we were all assembled outside, mingling and talking while the photographer staged his next picture, I asked my brother, Stephen, why he had been intently staring into that particular space. He hadn't been his usual jovial self since the ceremony finished. He looked into my eyes and whispered, "It was Dad. I saw Dad standing there. He was dressed in his suit and was taking pictures with his camera. He looked straight at me and smiled." Stephen shuffled his feet nervously as he continued, "It was the strangest feeling I've ever had. I wanted to get out of my chair and run over to him, yet I found that all the time he was there, I couldn't move. Just couldn't move."

Photographs were taken in the grounds of the centre and more were taken inside of the huge stone circle. When enough photographs were taken, the wedding party set off on the journey to Lincolnshire for the reception in the back hall of the public house. It wasn't until much later that night that I finally got a chance to talk to Jason, and I asked him about what he had seen. Smiling, he answered that he had seen his beloved Grandad and added that he had known that his Grandad would be there. He said that he knew that he wouldn't let him down.

The other strange thing that happened was that while the newlyweds were taking their vows, they were standing beneath the huge dome suspended on a

**Jason & Jacqui at their Wedding.**

heavy chain. As they both uttered their words, the dome began to swing, gently at first, then gathering momentum until it was swinging quite fiercely in a circular motion around their heads. As all this was going on, I was not the only one who felt a sudden surge of energy that manifested as a brisk breeze in the room! A lot of our friends who had been invited to the wedding were very spiritually aware and most of them noticed this sudden change and mentioned it to me afterwards. This action lasted for about five minutes and then disappeared completely, leaving the dome to slow down and stop. Some "normal" guests suggested that it might have been a sudden sharp breeze, and, even though the heavy doors were closed as were the windows, there must have been a draft coming from somewhere. Yet even with this explanation, there were puzzled expressions!

With the newlyweds safely stashed in a hotel for the night, the reception party carried on until midnight. Everyone had a great time, and the guests who were the worse for wear with too much partying, were driven home by their partners.

When Paul and I arrived home, we had to make sleeping arrangements again for Stephen and Anita. The two grandmothers shared the guest bedroom, and, although my brother and his wife had slept in Jason's old room the night before, Anita said that she didn't like the feel of it and asked to sleep outside in our touring caravan. We agreed and supplied the van with bedding and pillows and bade our guests good night.

Anita was the first to come into the house the following morning, but she looked quite unwell. She hadn't had much to drink at the party, so she wasn't suffering from a hangover. I asked her if she was okay, and, as she sat at the table, she nodded her head affirmatively.

However, later that day, when Paul and I were alone with her, Anita confided to us just what had happened when she and Stephen had finally got to bed. She said that he had had a bit too much to drink and was out like a light as soon as he lay down. She said that she had heard noises outside the caravan, and, though she put this down to normal night noises, she snuggled up to my brother for comfort and was soon asleep. She then told us that for some reason, she found that she woke up some time later and was wide awake - not tired at all. She said that she lay there for a while then, still being unable to sleep, got up and shone a torchlight on Stephen's wrist watch to discover that it was ten past three in the morning. She said that she went to the cupboard to get a drink and sat on the couch for a while. She had arranged the pillows on the couch to try to sleep there but still felt wide awake. Eventually, she went back to bed and just lay there staring at the ceiling and thinking back on the day's events.

Unexpectedly, she felt a breeze around her face, and she realized that the caravan no longer had a ceiling - she was staring up at the stars and feeling the crisp night air. She tried to rationalize all of this; it was after all, impossible for the ceiling to have disappeared; she knew that, yet her eyes confirmed the irrationality of it all. Terrified by the reality of all of this, she tried waking her husband but was unsuccessful. She said that she was too afraid to go out into the darkness and found herself watching the stars through the caravan roof. She then tried convincing herself that she was asleep and dreaming and kept closing her eyes tightly but always they would open to the same scene. As she lay there, heart pounding, she claims that the stars began moving around each other. Although still terrified, she was fascinated, too as the stars began to form some sort of mass together and then the activity stopped momentarily. Then the mass began to move in a downwards direction until the sparkling shape was directly above her head. With another downward plunge, the sparkling shape was now inside the caravan, at which point Anita sat upright in the bed watching in utter disbelief. She said that she remembers that the shape was beginning to form into something - she doesn't know what - but the next thing she remembered was being awakened by my brother, and it was a sunny morning. She is adamant that it happened and that it wasn't a dream, for the glass was where she left it and the pillows were still positioned on the couch where she tried to sleep. She knew that she didn't dream it - she was awake.

As time wore on, she seemed to become more accepting of her experience, even joking to my brother that he was a fat lot of use as he slept through the whole thing. Interestingly, she mentioned this incident in passing to our friend, Hayden, and was surprised when he finished her story for her. He too had experienced the stars falling through the hole in the ceiling of the spare bedroom in our house when he stayed one summer weekend, and he too slept soundly until morning light after the stars took form around him!

Although Jason couldn't afford a proper photographer, a good friend of the family, John, had offered to fill the position using his state-of-the-art digital camera which connects directly into a computer, and the offer was graciously accepted. Another friend of the family, James, took plenty of video footage and sent us a duplicate tape of the ceremony. John's photographs have come out brilliantly - as can be witnessed by the pictures of the happy couple within these pages. However, all photographs taken with a normal camera have produced black/green blanks - including the two rolls of film that I personally took. I was so upset. I'm not that great at using a "normal" camera; for whatever reason, I usually mess something up, so, when disposable cameras were invented, they were a godsend to someone like me. Paul calls them idiot-proof cameras, as you just point them and click, and he reckons they were made with me in mind! Anyway, I had purchased two of these cameras from two different retailers and, when they were full of my son's wedding pictures, they were duly placed with two different developers - I didn't want to take a chance on anything going wrong. When I got them back however, there were about half a dozen pictures of an afternoon out prior to the wedding and these had come out perfectly, but all those taken of the wedding were completely blank. I complained bitterly to both developing outlets and was told that it wasn't the fault of the film - that greenish black blanks were on each and every frame, as if that were what I had photographed! I was devastated but didn't consider that it could be linked to the strangeness of our situation until one of our friends telephoned to tell me that her developed pictures were exactly the same. Just two days later, another friend rang to say that he had picked up his set of 36 greenish-black blanks, too. Intrigued, I made enquiries of other guests, and the story was exactly the same. Yet, all the digital pictures were perfect - as was the video footage. I was later able to ask Jason if he knew why this should happen, but all he could suggest was that perhaps it was due to the various energies, which he tells me were very apparent on that day. I'm just grateful for John's digital camera and James's video camera - otherwise we would probably not have any photos of that wonderful day.

As I write, Christmas 2003 is approaching, and my son and his young wife are looking forward to spending Christmas Day with us. Although it has only been five months since they married, they seem to be settling in to married life well. It won't be easy for either of them, adjusting to each other and putting up with their respective habits, but most of us go through this. To suddenly find that you

211

don't only have yourself to look out for any longer can be quite disconcerting - and a little frightening. I once asked Jason what it is he hopes to get out of this marriage, and he answered "If we have just one tenth of what you and Dad have together, then I'll be the happiest man alive."

Children are definitely on the agenda - but not for quite a while, which is wise. Right now they are both saving up hard to buy their own flat.

Jason and Jacqui are typical "Indigos" in that they both live in the moment. Their concept of time is most unlike yours or mine, and they have no further plans for their future, saying only that children will come into their lives when the time is right for them to do so. Whenever the subject is mentioned, I always joke with them that their baby will surely be an unknown quantity. After all, Star Children having children of their own! Who knows where that will lead us - or rather, what would the repercussions be for humankind itself?

# THIRTY TWO
# THE ACCIDENT

Sometimes I envy other people; ordinary people doing ordinary things. I ask myself why we can't be like that; just enjoying mundane, everyday things and looking forward to the weekend; where our biggest worry would be having enough money to pay all the bills on time. However, that will never be us; our family; not after everything we have all been through - and are still going through. Our lives have been changed by all this and we can never go back to `ordinary'. That's not to say that I consider myself special in any way; of course I'm not. We're just all more aware of the real state this planet is in. We feel more of a connection with the Universe, with Spirit and have more of an understanding of all things paranormal (if that's the right word). Most of all, we, as a family, have more understanding of what our son, Jason, is all about and why he is here.

Jason is - in his own words - a `walk in'; an energy form, or spirit if you prefer, who has chosen to occupy a human body in order to accomplish certain work important to the furtherance of mankind. Huge statement I know but one that can be backed up by anyone who has sat and listened to him talk at conferences. Now 23 years `old' (at least in human terms; he insists that he has been around in one form or another for millennia - and I don't doubt him either), the last conference he spoke at was in Blackpool, England, and he affected a lot of people in the audience, as he usually does, but added to this was the fact that some people actually saw him physically change; shape shift into different entities. Other people present that day also witnessed three small grey beings; two on his right side and one which appeared to be dancing around on his left hand side. Also seen was a leonine being and finally what appeared to be an old man dressed in the classic cloak garment complete with hood. It was this being which seemed to move forward and backwards right beside Jason as if whispering to him.

During the break, a middle aged man approached Jason and asked if he remembered him. Jason smiled and confirmed that he did and asked the man if he was feeling any better. The man began explaining to me and to Jason that during the night, he was aware of a presence and had a strange feeling in his head - almost like it was being crushed. He said it was so intense although it only lasted a matter of seconds and then he was aware of Jason being in the room with him! Their conversation continued although I had been distracted by someone else and was no longer within earshot!

Later that same day, a pretty young woman was talking to me telling me that she remembers Jason being with her one particular night. I joked that I hoped his wife, Jacqui, didn't know about his night time liaisons when Jason came over and, obviously recognizing the woman, asked her how she was feeling. Like the man, she thanked him for coming to help her and then went on to describe to both of us how she had felt as if her head was being `squeezed' just prior to his appearance. These were two people who came from different places, different backgrounds; obviously unaware of each other. Yet they both related the same details about their encounters with my son. This is just one example of collaboration. The truth is that Jasons' visits to various people by astral means DOES happen.

I have included here some photographs of Jason taken at the talk by a dear friend of our family, Ellis Taylor. I've also produced his statement of events - with his permission - about Jasons' talk.

"Here are the photographs. Although skeptics would (quite rightly) suspect that the effects are due to camera shake, they were not there and so would not have seen what I could see.

Before I took the photos, I asked Jean, the organizer, for permission. I told her that I could see entities all around Jason, but gave her no detail about what I was witnessing (I was in a hurry). She said that Jason had warned her that if people took photos, he could not be held responsible for any subsequent damage that might arise. I told her that I was aware of previous damage to cameras and electronic equipment but that I felt that it wouldn't be a problem.

I could see 'them' behind him and coming up to him from the rear. They seemed to be whispering in his ear as the questions came from the audience and then moving away. Some seemed to melt into him. I saw his appearance change several times. Several of the beings were similar looking to ones I have been in contact with. One type was the grey type that I have never seen as grey. They are always white or a kind of biscuit colour. Another was leonine and another was like an old man with a white beard and the classic gown. The last one came forward a few times. I also saw a group of greys which seemed to be dancing behind him. They were keeping the energy high.

It was interesting that after Jasons' talk, Sam, husband of Jean, told me what he

Photo by Ann Andrews

**Strange craft.**

Photo by Ellis Taylor

**Alien behind Jason.**

had seen. Jean had told Sam that I was witnessing strange phenomena around Jason and he had moved to a position where he could see what was going on too. Sam reported virtually the same things as I could see.

I hoped to pick some of this up on camera but it was obviously beyond the cameras' abilities. Mind you - the apparent shape shifting is what I could see too. One frame though does appear, on closer inspection, to show the face of one of the greys to Jasons' right. It is the same colour as the ones I see."

As usual, at the end of his talk, Jason became surrounded by people all clamouring to speak to him. However, it was on the way home that this strange situation took a sinister turn.

Whilst traveling along the main highway in torrential rain, I hit the brake to slow down for traffic - and nothing happened! Fortunately, we were able to use an escape lane and eventually slowed to a stop. We tried the brakes again - and they were useless, yet our car had recently been serviced. We contacted a breakdown service who confirmed that the braking system had failed and they transported us and the car home. The next day, the car was checked over yet the brakes were found to be in perfect working order.

This wasn't the first time that brakes had failed on one of our vehicles. A few months prior to this, the same thing happened whilst driving along a riverside road. Again, I was able to use the grass verge to finally stop. However, on that occasion, when the car was checked, it was found that the brake pipe had been deliberately cut. We reported this to the local police station who duly noted it down. They didn't seem too worried explaining that as our vehicle was a four wheel drive vehicle, it sat high off the ground thus making it easy for anyone to wriggle beneath it and damage it. The police concluded that it COULD be the work of mischievous teenagers. We let the matter rest on this occasion. However, the car we were driving to Blackpool rides low to the floor; there is absolutely no way that anyone could 'wriggle underneath it' to cause damage to the braking system; no way.

Around 10:30 p.m. on Monday, June, 5th in 2006, Jason and his wife, Jacqui, were involved in a horrendous car crash just a few miles from their home. Another vehicle had hit theirs side on at around 100 mph. and had flipped Jasons' car high into the air forcing it to roll over several times before veering down a bank. Convinced that there would be fatalities, people were reluctant to go down to the wreckage and it was left to an off duty police officer to venture down. Yet even she was amazed when Jason and Jacqui were pulled from the wreck with nothing more than minor cuts and bruises. Although the other driver responsible gave a false address to the police, he has since been apprehended and appeared in court where he was sentenced to three years imprisonment.

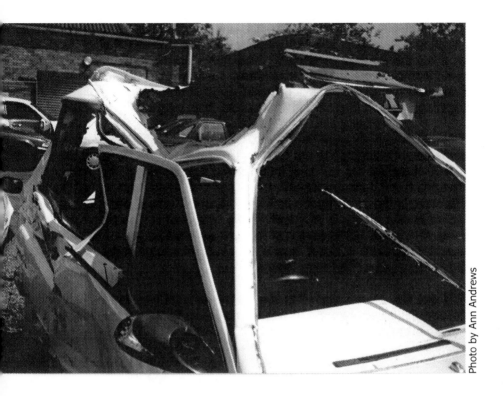

**Car wreckage that Jason and Jacqui walked away from.**

We received a phone call early that morning from a very calm Jacqui who explained that there had been a crash but she insisted that they were both okay. She asked if we would collect them from the hospital where they had both been taken so that they could be checked over by a doctor. Satisfied that neither of them had serious injuries, the hospital had released them.

When we arrived, we were surprised at how calm the pair of them were. Apart from a pounding headache for Jason and a slight wrist sprain for Jacqui - plus assorted small cuts and bruises on both of them - they looked well and insisted they were well when we dropped them off at their home.

The following morning we picked them both up and took them along to the salvage yard where the wreckage of the car had been taken. There were some personal effects that they wanted to collect. The four of us went into the office and asked the guy in the office where we could find Jasons' car. He looked surprised asking if indeed they were the young couple who had got out of the wreckage. Jacqui said they were. The look on the mans' face was one of utter disbelief as he asked them if they were joking; were they really the occupants of that car when it crashed in the early hours? Jason confirmed this and asked again where they could find the car. The man looked down at his desk and shuffled some paperwork and, finding the right form, told them where their car could be found.

Twice the four of us went to the place the man had said and twice none of us could see the wreckage of the car. Eventually the man had to come out with us and point out the car. It was at that moment that we all realized just why the man had found it so unbelievable that Jason and Jacqui were indeed the couple who were in the car when the accident happened. Jasons' prized car was not recognizable as a car at all; all the wheels had come off in the collision and so had some of the roof. What was left of the bodywork looked like it had had a great weight dropped on it. It was hard to imagine that anyone had survived such an impact let alone walked away from it.

This was also the moment when the severity of what happened actually hit Jacqui and she burst into tears. It was unimaginable to her too that they had walked away from this compressed remnant of a vehicle.

They've since got themselves another car bought with the money from the insurance payout and, yes, it's another sports coupe which is the new apple of Jasons' eye. However, neither of them are really comfortable with driving again but considering where we have all chosen to live, it is a means to an end and something they will have to accept and get on with.

Perhaps our family isn't just involved with the 'alien agenda'; perhaps we're also extremely unlucky when driving the roads in England where we live. Or perhaps someone, somewhere, doesn't want Jason talking to people, helping people with his healing abilities and - more importantly - helping people to understand their part in the Universal scheme of things and to become "all that they can be". Perhaps the conspiracy theorists concerning the illuminati controlling the World are right. After all, if the human race start to realize their real potential in that they can be so much more and in being all that, they realize their connection to Spirit, the Universe, then what hold would this illuminati have? People thinking for themselves? That is unimaginable!! What then would happen to the few controlling the many?

I'm just a Mother who's proud of her family and loves them all very much - especially my boys, Daniel and Jason - yet I feel blessed to have been 'chosen' to be part of Jasons' life and the work he has come here - to this little blue planet of ours - to do.

# THIRTY THREE
## CONFERENCES

Over the years, I have been asked to speak at a few UFO conferences and, from a very nervous and shaky start, my confidence in speaking at such events has grown. Jason, however, was entirely new to all this and I was really worried about how he would handle himself when he was first asked to give a talk at the World UFO Congress held in 2005 in Laughlin, Nevada, in America. This prestigious event is perhaps the largest gathering of like minded people in the world as both speakers and audience come from so many different countries so for Jason, this was a real 'baptism of fire' so to speak. However, I shouldn't have worried; he gave a very factual and balanced account of himself and what happens in his life and even left himself time to open the floor to questions. He was never hesitant with his answers either and at the end of our allotted time, he had the audience up on their feet clapping - a standing ovation.

We both spoke at Laughlin; me first as I needed to lay the groundwork so to speak and give the audience a little background to our family and the strange events which follow us. I then moved on to Jasons' part in events and went on to mention how he now knows exactly who he is; that he has been "awoken" by 'them' - the ET's - to realize why he is here. My part completed, I then took great pride in introducing my youngest son - and then I sat back and listened - and learnt!

Question after question was fired at him and his answers came back instantly. Most questions were intelligent coupled with prior knowledge of the subject people sought further information on but, even so, there were a couple of questions which did perhaps air on the side of levity. One such question - asked by a lady - was "Jason, are you really a grey?" (a standard term for the now recognized small grey extra terrestrial beings with the large almond eyes). I thought this would throw him or he would just grin and say no but he immediately held his hand up in front of his face, studied it for a few seconds and then answered, "well no, I'm a bit pinkish actually". There was quite a loud trickle of applause for this answer and a lot of laughter in appreciation. From then on, he left everyone in no doubt that this young, virtually unknown young man needed to be listened to; he had answers - real answers - that people had sought for years.

After our presentation, we couldn't move for the throng of people who were all eager to speak to us - well, more him than me actually - and he took it all in his stride. His only complaint was that he could no longer get across the hotel floor to get his food at Burger King inconspicuously - as he had done before our talk. He was now known to everyone - and everyone wanted to speak with him. All credit to Jason, he was very gracious and spoke to everyone who had something to ask him, but the number of times his beloved cheese burgers went cold before he could devour them was really starting to add up!!

Through the efforts of our publishers, Jason and I also attended the Bay Area UFO conference in 2005. As we had done in Laughlin, I spoke first and he followed on - again, to great applause when he had finished his question and answer slot.

During our presentation however, there was a very strange occurrence. I was sitting in the audience watching Jason give his talk when I noticed - as had everyone else - that he paused for a moment then seemingly acknowledged someone who had obviously just entered as we all heard the doors whine as they closed again. I turned around to see who it was but other than the sight of a small boy who had just sat down in one of the aisle seats, there was no-one. Jason continued with his talk.

At the end of our presentation, the doorman approached me and asked if I had seen a small child aged about seven. He was dressed in a stripey tee shirt with dark coloured shorts and open sandals. The boy was quite small in stature with dark hair and a well tanned complexion. The doorman went on to say that he had allowed him into the hall assuming that the child was meeting up with his parents. However, the boy then went and sat quietly on his own and remained there throughout Jasons' presentation. When it was over, he got up and walked towards the doors. Naturally, the doorman was concerned that a child of that age should be wandering around on his own and he chose to challenge him. He asked if the boy was staying at the hotel with his parents; the boy replied no. The next question was were his parents attending the conference for the day. Again, no was the reply. The guy on the door was obviously concerned for the child's safety and suggested he stay with him until he could summon someone from the hotel to take charge of him and find his parents. However, the boy ignored the well meaning doorman and strode quickly onwards in the direction of the pool area. Still concerned, the doorman followed. He told me that the boy walked through one of the big glass doors that led only to the pool. The pool area was surrounded by a myriad of glass doors leading from and to the foyer of the hotel on one side but on the other three sides, there was a high wall. The doorman followed - but there was no sign of the small boy. Of course, it's always possible that the child could have doubled back through the doors and gone either to the reception or into one of the lifts - but the doorman said he was right behind him.

I asked Jason if he had seen the boy enter but then it dawned on me that it was the child that Jason had paused to acknowledge. I asked him who the child was. Was he really a child at all and was he there to observe? But a huge grin and the words, "don't worry about it Mum," were the only answers I ever got.

It was good connecting with people however, the only down side was that this was a trip we had to make on our own; we couldn't afford for either Paul or Jacqui to accompany us. For me, this meant long nights sitting alone in my hotel room watching the television or ringing Paul back here in England. For Jason though, he was allowed to borrow a car and he made sure he saw as much of California as he could.

Whilst on one of his voyages of discovery, he found his way to a backstreet pool house and bar and naively entered the premises. Not realizing that large gangs of youths frequent these establishments, he strode boldly over to the bar and ordered himself a tall glass of coca cola! He then asked the barman if it was okay for him to play on the pool table. The barman snuffled his answer that it was perfectly fine with him but that the table was always hi-jacked by a large group of loud youths. Jason was further advised by the barman that, if he had any sense, he wouldn't intrude on their territory. However, grabbing his glass of coke, Jason strolled over to the pool table and asked a very portly young man if he was interested in a game. The young man stood up - and at around six feet six inches tall, he was almost as wide as he was tall - and through the silence which had now descended on the whole bar, he grabbed a pool cue and threw another to Jason. Announcing confidentially that he would make the first break, Jason began the game. The young man, Miguel, won the game and as he went to walk away, Jason remarked that it was probably a fluke and they should play another game. Again, the hush descended on the place and what began as a disbelieving glare from Miguel, turned to a wry smile as he asked Jason why he wasn't afraid of him. "Why should I be?" was Jasons' reply. Other members of the group began sniggering as Miguel motioned for a gangly leather clad youth to come forward. He stood in front of Jason and reached into his leather coat and produced a large pistol saying to Jason, "I'm packing this". "Cool" was my sons' comment, then, turning his attention again to Miguel - "well, you playing or not?"

Miguel laughed out loud and the rest of the group followed his lead. He grabbed his pool cue and began another game. From then on, Jason and Miguel became firm friends and it transpired that Miguel was the leader of the youths in the pool hall and obviously hadn't led a blameless lifestyle. They both had their love of fast cars - and Miguel took Jason to see a lot of these - and playing pool, but would spend other times just talking. It was during one of these times that Miguel asked Jason what an English guy was doing in Santa Clara. Jason had no hesitation in replying that he had been invited as a speaker to the UFO confer-ence being held there. Miguel was interested and questioned him more and then - after a few minutes of silence - opened up to him and told him about his experiences which had gone on since his childhood. He asked if Jason could help him understand what was happening. Jason did.

When my son was relating all of this information to me, I was quite alarmed at first - especially when he mentioned the gun that had been produced - but Jason said that he had been guided to this young man. He said that he had no fear about going into such a place as the pool hall bar on that first night because he knew he was protected; besides, he had a job to do!

I only met Miguel once - but I could totally understand how his presence and his manner could easily intimidate other youngsters into following him!

We didn't have much time for a social life whilst in California but one particular night, we were driving to a restaurant with Eileen and Pam - lovely ladies from our publishers and very spiritual too - when Jason called out for Eileen to stop the car. We all asked what was wrong but without a word, he got out of the car and walked towards a darkened alleyway. He paused long enough to order us not to follow him but to wait and even though we all wondered what on earth was going on, we waited for what seemed an age. The three of us were starting to grow really concerned for his safety and I was just about to go after him when he appeared under the street light - with a suitcase. Another figure followed him and both of them approached the car. "This is Karen," Jason told us, "we've had a talk and I said that we could drop her off at her Dads' house about three blocks from here. Is that okay with everyone?" Still not understanding what was going on, we all found ourselves in agreement and moved up as much as we could to make room for Karen.

She had been crying, that much was clear - but Jason sitting with her, holding her hand and smiling seemed to placate her. Karen was young; probably late teens and very ordinary in the sense that she was like most teenagers. Using Karen's directions - and Jason's at times - which seemed rather odd for someone who didn't know the area at all - we soon pulled up outside a small house. It was evening and the lights in the house were on when we noticed someone looking through the curtains to see who had arrived.

Karen got out of the car with Jason right behind her. They went to the back of the car to fetch the suitcase; spent a few minutes huddled in conversation but when the front door of the house opened, Jason got back into the car saying to

Karen "Everything will be fine now. Trust me - and trust yourself." She was crying again but smiled at him as a middle aged man put his arm around her and ushered her gently into the house. She appeared at the door one last time to say thank you to us for dropping her home and she thanked Jason telling him she wouldn't forget him. Then the door closed.

I think this time it wasn't me but Eileen who asked excitedly what that was all about and Jason explained: "As we were driving, I could feel Karen's pain. I simply homed in on it and knew she was crying in that alleyway. I can't go into it entirely but she had left home some months ago - against her farnily's advice - to live with a guy she thought loved her but he used her and then kicked her out. She had no-where to go other than home but was afraid to because of what her family would say so we had a chat and I know that everything will work out for her. Her family do love her and want her home. She'll be fine." Eileen was quite happy with his explanation and questioned him no more but, as usual, I tried asking him to go into more detail - which he politely refused to do - ending up with him saying, "Give it up Mum. You know I won't tell you."

# THIRTY FOUR
# DOGGED DAYS

This is our story so far - but it will never be completed. The 'book' is finally finished; the manuscript has been sent to the publishers and the printers have produced the copy that you are reading now: this is the final chapter of our book; this story is finished in that sense.

However, our lives are still interspersed with super natural and alien occurrences which will often test our very being in many different ways.

We're not unique; many people endure and accept similar situations to ours which is why I have decided to give the final say to two very good friends of the family who have witnessed an abundance of strangeness within their own lives as well as bearing witness to strange incidents which still occur here at our home in the flat but beautiful part of England known as Lincolnshire.

Dogged Days - by Ellis Taylor.

I was driving towards Long Sutton in Lincolnshire en route to stay with my friends Paul and Ann Andrews. Even for a seasoned otherworld traveller like me the months prior to this journey had been very strange. Orbs and coloured lights increasingly flashed around my country cottage, midnight telephone calls on landline and mobile that when answered only gave out odd sounds or sometimes nothing at all. After one international conversation, as we said our goodbyes, an American voice sinisterly cut in with his own 'bye now!' *

Emails, scores of them, failed to arrive. Someone had been in my home; I noticed things missing, significant things mostly. My mobile phone went walkabout for nearly 3 months (and then turned up in a place that I regularly searched through - the door pocket of my car), a piece of palisander wood that Peruvian shaman, Inti Caesar had given me and safely stored documents are other examples. Then there were the shadow people, who sometimes walked past my windows in both daylight and night time. I would hear knocking on my windows

**Orbs in field.**

at night but there was never anybody there. Sometimes flashlights would shine through my rear windows. I frequently heard garbled voices inside my home; two visitors heard them too. My neighbours told me that they would hear unusual sounds coming from my house when I was away and joked that there must be a noisy ghost. I began to arrange things inside when I left so that I would be able to tell if there had been intruders - and these confirmed there had been at first. Later these devices remained undisturbed but my neighbours continued to hear things being moved around and no one saw anyone entering or leaving my house. My home is very secure and the only entry point without making one hell of a noise is through the front door, which is open to view and easy to see from other properties. Vehicles would pull up outside my house and stay there for a while. Now and again, there would be a car sitting outside, with either one or two occupants, when I left for work. A couple of times an old man would be sitting on the park bench across the green and watch me intently as I drove away. One night I arrived home just after midnight and saw the silhouette of a man walk past my front window, inside the house. When I got inside there was no one there. As I write this I know I'm forgetting some things.

It was getting on for 2 o'clock in the afternoon and I think it was on the A43 road somewhere near Towcester that I suddenly had the thought that I ought to stop at a service station to visit the loo just in case I encountered traffic hold-ups. Everything is a bit of a blur before and after what happened next.

As I drove up the slope into the service station it struck me that it seemed unusually empty for such a busy time and main road. Way up the parking area near the motel was a couple of cars but there were no people. Anyway, I didn't think too much about it. I parked my car and looked for signs to the toilets. I didn't see any but in front of me were some double doors leading to the restaurants. Walking through I was again surprised to notice that there was no one there. At this point, a man appeared from out of view with a tray full of food and drink. Never taking his eyes off me, he sat down at a table facing me and continued to stare. I couldn't help thinking how unusual he looked and it made me feel a little uneasy. I looked away and tried to find signs for the toilets but there were none so I started to walk around the building and still the place was empty except for this peculiar man and me. I began to think that perhaps the toilets were outside so I walked back to the front door. Now, as I am writing this I'm wondering whether the man was still there at this point because I don't think he was, anyway...as I reached the front doors I noticed two uniformed youths standing by a fast food counter, a boy and a girl. I approached the lad and asked him where the toilets were. "This way," he said and led me around the back of the fast food counter; still I could see no signs saying that the toilets were this way. When I came out the boy and girl were still there, the man with the tray of food had certainly gone and still there was no other person there. I got back in my car drove down the slope and back on to the main road. I can recall thinking how very strange this experience was. I have never, ever, visited a service area on a busy road, not even at night (and this was lunchtime on a Friday) that is empty of people. I also realised that I didn't feel right and this brought to mind a previous journey I had made to Long Sutton, where I had experienced two hours of missing time. Immediately I looked at the car's clock but all seemed in order in that regard, and I didn't feel any where near as dislocated as I had on that occasion. I estimated that the visit to the service station had taken about 8 to 10 minutes.

As it transpired, I did meet some very heavy congestion on the journey and it was a good job that I had stopped. After one particular traffic jam, I was following another vehicle along a brand new and straight bypass when a couple of cops flashed a speed gun at us but I never received a ticket. Other than these incidents, the drive was uneventful and did not seem out of the ordinary in any way; except that I cannot remember much about the last stretch of the journey, the long, flat, straight as a die, road to Ann's house. There are anomalies that I cannot account for, at least, at the moment. One is to do with the time I arrived.

My recollection is that I drove straight to Sutton Bridge post office to pay my road tax. This, according to my receipt, was at 4.46 pm. Sutton Bridge is 5 minutes away from Paul and Ann's home by car. I remember the journey all the way from the post office to the crossroads near their house but after that is a mystery until I get out of my car, in the dark, at their house. I fumbled in the darkness to find the bolt on the iron gates, lifted it and cautiously inched my way across the lawn to the front door. I knocked and was relieved to see Ann's smiling face as she welcomed me in. Ann showed me into their newly built conservatory to the side of their spacious lounge where sat authors Mike Oram and his partner Fran with Paola Harris engaged in conversation. After greeting each other and being introduced to Paola, I was told that Jason and Jacqui, his wife, were expected shortly and that they were picking Sacha Christie up from the train station. The reason for my visit, other than to catch up with my friends the Andrews and Mike and Fran, was to attend a talk that Paola, a renowned Italian/American journalist and UFO researcher, was to give on the Saturday night for the Norfolk UFO Society in a place called Bergh Apton. Sacha was coming to interview Paola and to report on the event for UFO Data magazine.

I didn't question the circumstances at the time but it puzzled me during the next week how I had come to arrive in darkness. It was the 29th September and the night doesn't fall until between 7 and 8 pm at this time of year. It should have been no later than 5pm and still light. I telephoned Ann to see whether she could remember what time I arrived and she said that she thought it was between 7 and 8 pm and that it was dark because she had to put the light on. Paul, both he and Ann told me, had asked why I hadn't parked in the drive and I had answered that it was because it was dark and that I had found it difficult to open the gates. Ann, Paul and Fran, when I asked them later, said that I seemed very tired, and slightly dishevelled upon arrival. I had also complained of feeling out of sorts and having a bad headache. Ann had made me a sandwich and a cup of tea and remembered that she had to switch on the table lamp. Paul and Ann had assumed that I had driven down straight after finishing work and had had nothing to eat. (This seems to corroborate the late hour that it seems I arrived.)

According to the AA, the journey time should take 2 hours 33 minutes from my home to Long Sutton. I had left home at 12.30 pm so there are about 1 1/2 hours to be accounted for. There had, as I said before, been traffic jams along the route, two of them, and they were both quite long and tedious. I had stopped, once to visit a cash point in Wheatley (5 minutes max.) and then at the service station, but at that point, as I mentioned before, there was no time anomaly according to the car's clock. Another 10 minutes, say? So I must have been in the traffic delays for about 1 1/2 hours, or was I? And then how come there appears to be another 2 1/4 to 3 1/4 period of missing time if in fact I arrived at the Andrews at 7 or 8 pm rather than 5 o'clock?

There is another twist. Still perplexed by my arriving at the Andrew's home in darkness and the illogicalness of it I telephoned Fran. She said that she was pretty sure that I had turned up somewhere between 7 and 8pm, but that she would check with Mike, which she did. Mike said that he wanted to say between 7 and 8pm but seemed to remember it was 5pm, because Paola had mentioned that a car had just arrived - me. Fran said that she had deliberately not prompted Mike regarding the timing so why did Mike want to say between 7 and 8pm? I wrote to Paola and she emailed back:

About your arrival, It was at 5:00...but not dark...Not at all...and you saw a man in the rain..It was raining buckets.

I'd forgotten about the rain and I really don't think that I would have crept across the lawn if it had been light and raining buckets. Ann doesn't remember it raining when she opened the door to me either. Something is amiss and puzzling here; it suggests to me that time was somehow being manipulated or distorting. Someone (Paola) sitting in one part of the room was experiencing a radically different time and space perspective to other people (Ann and Fran) sitting just a few yards away, while someone else (Mike) who was sitting in between was unsure which reality he was experiencing. Of course this is all conjecture and the possibility exists that I did arrive at 5pm, that it was hissing down and that I was just tired from driving; but before you make up your mind read on... Before you do though...the man I saw, I'd forgotten about him too, but I remember now. It was a little while after I had arrived and I was looking out the window when I spotted a figure bolt across my view and through the gate into the chicken run. It was tipping with rain, chucking it down. I alerted the others and thought it was probably Paul going to lock the chickens up but Ann said they haven't got chickens anymore and the run isn't there now. In the morning, I went to take a look but there weren't any footprints in the now muddy ground either. (I do remember from a previous visit that I had discovered an energy stream flowing along this particular location, which may well be connected to this sighting.)

Paola had been staying with Ann and Paul for the previous two nights but had decided to book a hotel room for the next two. She had slept in Jason's old bedroom. Mike and Fran were staying too after a last minute decision to attend Paola's talk as well as the daytime Mind, Body and Spirit Fair that was to precede the evening event. I had been expecting to sleep in Jason's room but arrangements had been altered because Mike and Fran were there. They took Ann and Paul's elder son, Daniel's old room, which meant that Paola was accommodated in Jason's.

[For readers that are not aware of this Jason Andrews, now 23-years-old, has conscious recall of all his previous lives and has had continuous experiences with otherworldly beings since before he was born (this time). Every member of his family has witnessed supernatural events, mostly to do with Jason; although previous to this it was Daniel alone who was attracting these entities, or so they thought. It has subsequently been discovered that Ann herself has a long, and sometimes very emotional, history too. It seems to be incredibly difficult for some people to accept until they meet them that the Andrews are just a very ordinary family, much like most others, as Ann would insist.

I've known them for quite a few years now and I'll tell you what, if you didn't know that their lives were filled with such bizarre experiences you would never guess. Even after all the media attention they have had, there is not one iota of ego and no airy-fairy airs; down-to-earth is what they are. They are good, honest, hard-working people with the same bills and everyday concerns as everyone else but on top of this they've had to cope with always perplexing, sometimes frightening incidents from otherworldly intruders as well as our own military and government agencies. As well, like me and many others who live with similar experiences, they have to somehow synthesise what their experiences show them is reality with what ordained convention says is true; it isn't easy. They, like I do, find that the very best way to deal with these experiences and the inane and ignorant pronouncements of resolute sceptics and Moloch's mouthpieces is to see the funny side. To banish this dis-ease of the Darkness we laugh. I thoroughly recommend the two books that Ann has written about their interrupted lives; Abducted, The True Story of Alien Abduction (with Jean Ritchie) and Walking Between Worlds - Belonging to None[1]).

Paola, who has interviewed some of the most influential people in ufology, conspiracy, remote viewing and secret technologies, did not want to spend one more night in the farmhouse. "I want to get some sleep! I have to give a presentation tomorrow." she admitted. During both nights she had been woken frequently by doors creaking open and by footsteps walking up and down the stairs and along the landing; footsteps that belonged to no incarnate person! It was like Piccadilly Circus! Mike and Fran had heard them too and Mike had ventured out to investigate. He found nobody but the footsteps continued. At one point, their bedroom door opened and someone or something sat on the end of Fran's bed. Paola's no scaredy-cat, the nature of her work means that she just cannot think that way. She just needed some sleep! Paola and I swapped books and I recommend her book, Connecting the Dots to everyone who is interested in what is really going on in our world. It is crammed full of fascinating interviews with such people as Col. Philip Corso, Zecharia Sitchin, Dr. Michael Wolf, Dr. Steven Greer, Sgt. Clifford Stone, Sgt. Major Robert O. Dean, Richard Hoagland, Padre Corrado Balducci (Vatican), David Icke, Dr. Richard Sigismond, R. Leo Sprinkle, Clark McClelland

---

1. Ann Andrews and Jean Ritchie, Abducted, The True Story of Alien Abduction, Headline Book Publishing Ltd, 1998, ISBN 0747221219

(NASA), Alex Collier, Uri Geller, Ingo Swann, Paul Smith, Dr. Courtney Brown, Dr. Russell Targ, and more, I loved it. [2]

Anyway, back in the conservatory, as we chatted and listened to Paola's absorbing stories of her friendships and meetings with so many intriguing characters, I realised that I felt extremely tired and hungry and that my head was pounding. At this time, I had not realised how long my journey had been; I had no idea it was so late. Ann, bless her, hurried off and brought me a plate of cheese sandwiches and a cup of tea and soon I was feeling much better. I still had a banging headache though, but I hoped the food would put paid to that. Shortly after this, we all moved to the lounge and continued our chat when Jason, Jacqui and Sacha arrived. We had a really entertaining evening discussing all the interesting stuff we all experience and then, I think about midnight, we decided it was time for bed. I think it was Paul who drove Paola to her hotel. Mike and Fran retired to Dan's old bedroom, Sacha to Jason's and me (what a gentlemen!) got the sofa. I remember whilst Ann was sorting out blankets for me she asked whether I would prefer to sleep on the sofa in the conservatory "as it is much more comfortable". Something urged me not to.

I lay down to sleep on the sofa and was just drifting off when the clock chimed loudly. 'I hope that it doesn't keep me awake all night,' I thought. Then immediately, I heard this loud scratching noise coming either from the patio doors or the back window. 'Oh, go away,' I thought, I'm not up for this tonight, I'm too tired.' The next thing, directly behind me, I could hear several objects moving about on the coffee table, scraping along the surface and through my closed eyelids I saw bright lights flashing around the room. Then came some garbled voices, what they were saying I could not comprehend. Then quick as a flash, something came right into my head. It felt like my brain was being squeezed, and it bloody well hurt! By this time, I was paralysed and could not move and I had the sense that whatever this was it was trying to read my mind. I saw visions... a great long bridge that spanned a bay, which could have been the Golden Gate Bridge in San Francisco, although after looking at photos of this, it was much longer. I think it was symbolic. Right now I cannot remember what the other visions were but what came next left me with proof that what was happening was very real. Somehow I got to be standing at Ann's back door. I was looking out towards the sheds but it was pitch black, darker than hell. Then I noticed something moving around my feet; and it rose up. It was a large black dog, with flecks of white on it, and it began to chew on the tips of the fingers on my right hand; not biting: chewing, and hard. I felt the dampness and the breath and I couldn't move or call out. From behind this dog came another big black dog which also rose up.

2. Paola Harris, Connecting the Dots, Wild Flower Press, 2003, ISBN 0926524577

The first dog nudged the second away and then resumed its chewing... and then the clock chimed, and there was daylight. It seemed to me as if I had only just gone to bed. I got up and climbed the stairs to the bathroom. As I did so I passed Jason's bedroom and saw that the door was open. Sacha was awake and dressed sorting the bedclothes out. "I've had the most terrible night!" she trembled. Not wanting to awaken anyone else, I suggested that we go down stairs, have a cup of tea, and then she could tell me about it.

"I heard these voices talking to each other," she said shaking, "And I couldn't move, but I could see that I was wrapped in something like cling-film, and I was hot and sweating." "I brought this tape recorder along with me and I left it on. It starts recording when it hears something and listen to this..." She switched it on and peculiar sounds emanated from the device. There were more things that happened but I'll leave that for Sacha to relate.

I then told her what had happened to me. 'And then there was this dog...' I said... "The dogs, oh no, the dogs!" she cried. "They were biting the top of my hand...look they've left bruises on it." Then she paused, seeming to be confused, "they were biting my other hand, this one! How can that happen?" On Sacha's left hand were several small dark reddish-brown bruises. Several weeks later they were still there.

I had no bruises on my own fingertips that could be seen but they felt very tender, and still did for weeks afterwards. The skin was very sore to touch - as if they were severely sunburnt. My hair fell out in clumps and my facial hair did not grow for nearly a week. For a long time, weeks, I did not feel myself. It was as if my mind had been split and hadn't been put together again properly. Things I could easily do with my eyes shut I found difficult. I was forgetting simple things and more concerning, I seemed to be a different person in some ways. I found myself saying things that I didn't agree with. My friends started to notice these discrepancies. I think this has been much the same for Sacha.

Before I had arrived at Ann's house, I think it was on the Wednesday, Paola had taken some photographs of Jason's bedroom and also the landing, two of which she has very kindly allowed me to reproduce in this article. On the Thursday, Ann took a video of Jason's room and a bedside light seems to be fading in and out of our reality. On the Saturday morning, I was standing in the garden chatting with Mike and spotted a seagull flying over. As it reached a point maybe 70 yards be-hind the house, it suddenly crashed into something invisible, seemed to reverse, rallied itself, and then flew around whatever the unseen barrier was.

Paola gave an excellent presentation, which everyone enjoyed, and the Saturday night went off without any more incidents. I drove home on the Sunday after-noon and made much better time arriving home in just 2 1/2 hours!

Ellis Taylor
16th November 2006.

(Ellis is also the author of the most excellent book "In These Signs Conquer").

Another good friend of ours is Sacha Christie. She is a talented journalist/researcher working for the UFO Data Magazine here in England. She's a bright, vibrant and bubbly young woman who has had many experiences throughout her life. We first met Sacha at a conference in Leeds, England. After the event, Sacha approached us to tell us some of her intricate story and our friendship grew from that meeting. I'm sure she won't mind me saying that she can talk - a lot - although she makes it clear that she won't suffer fools gladly. She resides in the North of England - `born and bred' she tells us - but crack the happy go lucky exterior and you'll find a sweet but somewhat vulnerable person inside who sometimes struggles to cope with her own strange alien experiences. This is Sachas' account in her own words of the same weekend:

In September, 2006, I went to stay with some friends in Lincolnshire, Ann and Paul Andrews. They were putting on an event and invited me to stay for a few days along with some other people. On the night of the 29th, I went to bed and slept in a particularly notorious bedroom. I set up my voice activated analogue recorder and settled down to sleep. For some reason, I also decided to turn out the light - which I never do - not even at home!

I was fast asleep when I suddenly became aware. I had woken up but could not move nor open my eyes. I felt my covers being pulled back away from me down towards the bottom of the bed. The next thing I recall is being absolutely ice cold....) mean freezing....like I'd been inside a freezer naked. This lasted for a few seconds. Then I was aware of lying on a surface and I felt like I had been shrink wrapped from the waist upwards. I couldn't breathe or move my arms but my legs were thrashing around. I was in a total state of panic. I know my legs were really thrashing around because I have a serious problem with my left knee if I do anything sudden or dramatic, I can be out of action for a few weeks. I could feel real pain as my legs were kicking. Then I could breathe; whatever had been covering my face was gone but I still couldn't move. I was trying to speak but my voice wasn't loud. I can remember saying "someone help me. Please help me" but I knew I was too quiet so I concentrated on making my voice louder. There were plenty of people staying in the house and I was sure one of them would hear me. Eventually, I said something loudly but no one came.

I could hear two male voices and I feel so sure that they were discussing me but I couldn't make out what they were saying. Besides, I was still asking for help. I then became aware of something pinching my fingers on my left hand and, for some reason, even though I can't remember seeing anything else at all, I saw a black dog chewing my fingers!

When I awoke the next day, I sat in bed worrying until I heard someone go to the bathroom. I ventured out of the bedroom as Ellis came out of the bathroom. I know I must have looked like the 'wild eyed woman of wonga' as I told him what had happened and he interrupted my story with his own very similar account of his night (over to Ellis if he wants to tell you).

Later that day, I was sat outside in the sun with Jason and Jacqui when I noticed a set of marks on the back of my right hand. There were bruises and needle marks: six in total: five on the back of my hand and one further up above the wrist on my arm. All over, veins were prominent apart from one which had the biggest bruise and I could not touch this one for a month it was so painful. I couldn't believe what I was seeing. There is no way that I could have accidentally done that to myself without knowing! I swear like a para trooper and have the occasional tendency to be a bit of a drama queen - but I would have remembered inflicting bruises which were so painful that I couldn't touch them for a month. The air would have been all shades of blue, I'm telling you!! Then I got a phone call from my Mum "Sacha? Are you alright? I had the most awful dream about you on Friday night. You were lying flat on your back in just your panties on a sofa. You were sweating from the waist up and mumbling incoherently. I was livid because I thought you'd started taking drugs. Your legs were kicking about and you were sweaty. LXXX (my son) was there and he was sitting on a steel table looking at you but blankly. He then hopped off the table and he was gone. I could see two men dressed in black and one of them had a hat on. His face was blue but his skin was so wrinkly it looked knitted! They were talking about you but I couldn't hear what they were saying. Then you were gone too."

I got back to Leeds and went to the office and told everyone what had gone on. While I was there, someone put on a DVD called 'The Journey' and whilst I was sat with Russ, on the screen appeared this alien face....with skin so wrinkly it looked knitted!! (I'm pointing out synchronicities with this bit, that's all). I mentioned it to Russ and he said "Isn't it funny how these things `knit' together?" ...ha ha, very funny - but, yes it is!!

After the weekend in Lincoln, I became very distressed and confused. My memory - which is normally fairly good - was shot to pieces and I had to write everything down that I had to do right to the minute because I could not retain any information whatsoever - which was a real bummer. I spoke to Ellis and to the person whose house it was - and her son - but the damage was done. I couldn't sleep or think and that was that.

Just a few days after I returned home, I went to bed one night and settled down o sleep. I woke up and was aware of someone in the room with me (bearing in mind that I live on my own....this is more than unusual!). I then realised that I couldn't move although my eyes were open. My head was tilted to the right and I could see my right leg in the air. I tried to pull it down but it wouldn't budge. I then saw that my right arm was in the air. I don't recall straps or anything - but I do recall a very bright green light in the crook of my elbow, like a dot but about two millimetres in circumference. I can remember thinking that my hand was cold and tried to pull it back down but to no avail. I then said to the person in the room "put the light on". I was very relaxed and spoke as if to a friend. Nothing happened so I said it again... and again. I remember thinking, "I'll be able to move if they put the light on". No one switched on the light but suddenly my arm dropped and I flexed my fingers a good few times to get the blood flowing back into my hand. I then had pins and needles.

When I woke up the next morning, I thought about what had happened and then I realised that I couldn't have been in my room because there's a street light directly outside my bedroom window so the light in my room is always orange. The light in the room I was in was grey. It also struck me that my legs had been in the air. The only other time that has happened to me was when I had a gynecological procedure at the hospital.

This second time I was not afraid in the slightest but the first one in Lincoln, I was terrified. My gut feeling is that both experiences were not the same beings. I know how mad it sounds, but I think the second time was to counteract whatever had gone on the first time!

I have witnesses and photographs; I did not make any of this up and have been talking to certain individuals along the way as each event has happened. I just haven't discussed this openly because I wasn't the only person involved. This is another reason why I have not ventured out or had anything to do with ufology for a couple of months; I seriously needed time out to collect myself.

Believe it or don't believe it; it doesn't matter. I have someone in my life who shared this experience with me so I know I'm not alone with it which is the biggest relief. Anyway, that's it as it happened.

I don't know how this fits in but I did see a little girl in a white dress and pigtails. She looked very sweet and innocent. I felt drawn to her but when she smiled, her face was demonic. Ellis saw her too**. Screen memory perhaps?

P.S. The voice activated recorder picked up a click and a whirr...then some very strange 'wowowowowo' kind of electronic noise...then nothing. Not even me getting up in the morning. When I got back, I couldn't find the tape so that I could play it to Russ and when I did eventually find it, it had melted and warped like it had been exposed to a heat source. I'm not lying and I have no idea how it happened but I do accept that it isn't necessarily paranormal. I just can't explain how it would warp. I have no fires in my house; only central heating and I never left it anywhere near a radiator. Besides, even if I did, they wouldn't possibly get hot enough to do that to plastic.

I did play the tape to those at the house in Lincoln and they agreed that it sounded very unusual.

** As Ellis hadn't mentioned seeing this little girl in his account, I phoned him and asked him about it. He told me that he had indeed seen the same child as Sacha mentioned but he had decided not to mention this as he wasn't certain in his own mind whether or not he had seen her in his mind in a sort of 'dream state' or in a physical reality. He explained that the more he thinks about it, the more he feels it was indeed in a physical reality. He confirmed that as she drew near, she smiled, but then her features - which had been of a sweet child - transformed and she appeared to him as a demonic being. As it is with most of us who have had to endure alien/paranormal experiences for much of our lives, we become very sceptical and we question and investigate every strange situation thoroughly in our own minds before we even talk about it. We have to be so sure of ourselves and judge ourselves harshly because we know that there are enough people out there who will judge us just as harshly - if not more so.

Thanks Ellis and Sacha; and thanks too to everyone who has participated in some way to the making of this book.

In conclusion, I would just add that whatever your beliefs, I hope you have enjoyed reading this book and to all...

May you find what you are looking for in this life and I hope that leads you to - (in Jason's words) - BE ALL THAT YOU CAN POSSIBLY BE.

WITH LOVE AND LIGHT,
ANN ANDREWS.

# THIRTY FIVE
# JASON'S INTERVIEW

To give the reader a better insight into what Jason is all about, I thought it may help to include the transcript of an interview that he agreed to do some time ago for the Discovery television channel.

Questioner: It has been well documented now that you possess certain abilities, which are unusual to say the least! You claim that you have endured abductions by alien beings for most of your life, but you are now at a point in your life where you both welcome their intrusion and actually learn from them. You even go as far as to state that `they' have awakened you to the reality that you yourself are of alien origins. As `they' have taught you so much, could you explain perhaps, how you are able to travel astrally and astrally project yourself?

Jason: These two are not the same thing - they are different. To astrally project myself to another place - I simply concentrate and think hard that I want to see that place - all of that place - I want to be there in the same reality in which I exist here. To be able to see and be seen. Part of me-myself-my energy then goes to that place and sends images to my brain. I can even communicate with people whilst there, and again my brain is able to store the conversation as if I had physically been present. Obviously, as most of my energies are still here within the physical, I suppose I must seem like an apparition - a ghost or something whilst I'm there, but I can still walk around and talk in this reality. It's a bit like watching a television program whilst doing loads of other stuff at the same time.

Astral travel is much easier, and most people can do it - whether conscious of being able to do this or not. It happens when you are out of body. You are able to move easily and freely through objects, through walls, etc., and just wander around in that state. The more you are able to master this, the faster you are able to move, and you can take yourself anywhere. As you don't have to worry about breathing or drowning or anything, you can go anywhere - even space.

Questioner: When you visited Australia though, Isabelle de Beaumont, the lady you stayed with had never met you before - nor you she - and yet you were able to `visit' her a week before you left England. If you had never been to her home before, how could you project yourself there - you wouldn't have known where it was and yet you described the house - and Isabelle - perfectly. Isabelle was also able to relate the conversation that she had with you, yet how is this possible to travel to an unknown destination?

Jason: The first thing that you have to understand is that there is no such thing as time, but in order to explain myself to you, I shall have to revert back to your beliefs about time in linear form. In a way, I was able to see into the future - just enough to know where we would be staying the following week. I saw how we arrived there and met Isabelle and in this way, I was able to recognize her and her home. I shouldn't have gone really, but I was so excited about going to Australia - oh, and I also wanted to check her out to make sure that she would be able to handle all of this stuff. She could and did. It was a pleasure to spend time with such an enlightened person.

Questioner: You say that you can see into the future? Can you see impending disasters? For instance, the recent tragedy in America with the bombing of the twin towers? Did you see that before it happened?

Jason: Of course I did.

Questioner: Why did you not try and warn the authorities or tell someone or the press?

Jason: One of the most important lessons that I have learnt from 'them' is that we do not have the right to interfere. Every person has his own destiny- a time to live- a time to die. The events which unfolded on September 11th were horrendous but destined to happen. In your terms, it was meant to be. I know this seems harsh, but families of the victims will learn to move on, find new meaning in their lives, take new partners eventually. It all fits into the scheme of things, and remember that it is you, the human race, who orchestrate your own destinies ultimately. A few times I have `seen' accidents waiting to happen to a member of my family or friends, and then I will intervene to warn them and stop it from happening. Remember, the future is never set in stone and as time doesn't exist, events can be changed. However, stopping someone close to me from being in a car accident or something is hardly world shattering and will not change future events too much - not like a national disaster. To put it another way, September 11th sparked other stuff into being- countries coming together- armies mobilizing- journalists reporting events, etc., as science would say, 'cause and effect.' Humankind as a collective was responsible for making September 11th possible in the first place with the introduction of aircraft and bombs. You still don't understand just how powerful you all are without all this rubbish do you?

Questioner: Explain please?

Jason: Understand that everything- absolutely everything on this planet - including the planet - is energy. You can be taught to use this energy, manipulate it - as I do - and respect it. Look at the grain of a table under a microscope- tiny, tiny molecules all huddling together to give the table its density to make it firm enough to hold things - other harnessed energies. What happens when you burn the table- smoke rises from the fire. All you have done is turn that dense energy into a new type of energy. It's the same with everything- nothing ever dies or ceases to be. It just becomes a different type of energy - or vibration. This goes for people too when they die. The physical body ceases to be- it goes back into the ground or becomes smoke. Yet the soul - or the energy - goes on. It may take another physical form eventually, or it may even explore the Universe. Whilst I don't entirely agree with reincarnation in the 'former lives' sense, I do know that energies that you perceive as souls are able to choose to take up form anywhere in the Universe - and beyond.

Questioner: Then how do you explain Mediums who get messages from people for living relatives?

Jason: That's easy. These people, these mediums, are already one step ahead of you in that they are able to use their energies - you would call it a gift probably- in order to 'see' with their inner sight. Some energies leave an imprint behind, like a letter almost, and these `gifted' people are able to read these letters. All forms of energy have memory, even water, and this has been tested by science. [Take] a river which is dammed up every year and then released down the same route of gullies. Had that route deliberately changed one year and a gully which was usually dammed up was left free whilst the usual route of the water was blocked. However, the surge of water ignored the open route and kept crashing against the blockade on its usual route until it gave way. So, in other words, the river remembered which way it had flowed for centuries and was determined to keep to this route. Anyway, you could all do it if you would only let go of your own fears and misgivings. Humans were able to do all this - and then some - thousands of years ago: telepathy, projection, predictions, all the things which you ostracize anyone for now. The only reason you are interviewing me is because to your standards, I'm strange- different- and that makes me interesting to the general public.

Questioner: Jason, you are a wonderful, young man who is very knowledgeable. Is this your secret? Have `they' given you so much knowledge that you are able to do what you do?

Jason: Let me first say that no one ever knows everything. That is for the Source- the One. And you're wrong because it isn't a case of knowing - of having immense knowledge - but the art is in knowing how to use that knowledge; having the key to it if you like. Know how to use the knowledge that you have, and you will go far.

Questioner: You mention the Source, the One. I assume that you are referring to God?

Jason: I suppose so if that is what you want to call it.

Questioner: How do you understand this to be?

Jason: My understanding is that eons ago there was the void and out of the void some sort of energy began to be. As this energy grew, it became powerful and, over time, the 'Source' split itself into other energies much like itself. There were twelve forms of energy to be exact. This is where your Bible gets confused. When the scribes write about twelve disciples, twelve tribes of Israel, etc., they are really referring to the twelve entities, if you like, produced by the Source. These new forms dispersed throughout the void and gradually created the Universe. As the decades passed, their knowledge increased. So, technically, your 'big bang' theory would be correct in a way if you perceive that everything is energy and it reacts against itself. Of course, the more intelligent the twelve became, the more independent they were and, to my knowledge, three of them committed the ultimate sin, and went against the Source by interfering with the creations they had helped to mold. As I said earlier, we can only advise and help whenever possible, but we can never interfere directly. The consequences of their actions were that they were cast out from the Source (you know like your Bible says that God cast out the Devil). It doesn't mean that they were evil as such, but you can't ignore the ultimate and only rule. The nine remaining have visited you from time to time throughout your history, and you have known them as great men like Jesus Christ, the Buddha, Mohammed, etc., but they've been to other places too throughout the Universe and have been acclaimed in much the same way.

Questioner: I would love to go into this subject further, Jason, but we only have a limited amount of time here so I do need to go on and ask you about other things. Can you tell me about your method of healing?

Jason: Fine. Basically, this happens mainly when I sleep. I feel where and when to go to a specific place - like a major accident - and I do this by travelling astrally. I am usually at the place before events have transpired but I wait and help out wherever I can. Some victims are supposed to recover, and that's where I help to heal them and keep them alive until they are recovering in the hospital out other people are meant to end their physical time at that moment, and again it is my job to help them to move on to their next stage. Some people are very confused, as they don't realize that they are dead, and some are angry because they have unfinished business and stuff, but I and others like me, have to gently assist them and help them deal with and accept the situation. You mentioned the twin towers tragedy, but I was there doing all I could to help - as were many others.

Sometimes though, those of you who know how to project for yourselves, come to me, to my home, and ask me for help with illness and stuff for them and their families, so I travel with them to do what I can.

I do some healing in the physical sense when my parents allow visitors to come to the house and, as with all healing, it is all about moving the energies around in people's bodies and unblocking them. There are no guarantees, but if the damage isn't long term, then I can usually help. In these circumstances, I like to try to teach the people who come for healing how to sort themselves out in the future, and for most of them, this has been very successful.

Questioner: That's intriguing, people - ordinary people - 'projecting' to your home. Are they easily visible to you?

Jason: Of course they are. It's quite funny sometimes, because certain people turn up who, whilst projecting correctly, are so out of place. Remember that I said that all energies can be read much like a letter? Well, the government or army or something keeps sending these people to me - to spy or something - but I can pick them out in an instant. Did you not know that during the Gulf War, everyone thought that Saddam Hussein was quite mad when he claimed that the Americans were spying on him by using psychics who transported their spiritual bodies? All they were doing was remote viewing and then projecting themselves to the given co-ordinates in order to report the layout of any strategic points. I told you, there are a lot of your people who are easily able to do this.

Questioner: To go on to something else now very quickly, you also state that you have knowledge of the `Star Children'. For those of us who don't know, who or what are these children, and why are they here now at this moment in time?

Jason: The `Star Kids' are mostly born to parents where one of them is an alien abductee - whether they are aware of this or not - but most parents do know. These children are incredibly bright even at a very young age, and they know from the beginning that, whilst they love their parents, they understand that their real home is elsewhere - out there somewhere amongst the stars. This feeling often fills them with sadnessa longing to explore and discover just who they really are. Although they know that when they are ready, this information will be revealed to them - just as it was to me. They will find for the most part that they don't fit in with conventional society and its demands. As they grow, they feel almost limited in their physical bodies, as they know that they are so cumbersome and that they themselves are capable of so much more - but this has to be confirmed to them. I use the word confirmed as, like I said, these kids know exactly who they are - and more to the point, just why they are here at this precise moment in time. Ultimately, they are your salvation. They are the new race of humanity who, if allowed, will lead the world on it's pathway to peace and understanding. These kids are now being recognized the world over. Dr. Richard Boylan in America is working with many of them. This is happening, too, in Australia and, to a lesser extent, in the United Kingdom. A lot of these so-called `experts' are skeptical about their abilities - and their motives - whilst still other `experts' put them under the supervision of psychiatrists `for their own good.'

Questioner: That's staggering Jason. Just how many of these kids are there?

Jason: That's not for me to say. I don't feel that it's right for me to come up with figures and facts without their permission. All I will say is that there are enough of them growing up to make a difference. Whether they will be allowed to or not will be up to the rest of you.

Questioner: Jason, I want to thank you for taking the time to talk to us, and I know that you said at the very beginning that you would not give us any demonstration of your abilities as you don't do party tricks, but is there just a little thing that you could do - just for the viewers?

Jason: I really don't like being put in these situations. I have been very honest and up front with you about everything that I do, but you still require proof. No wonder your planet is in such a sorry state- no one has faith or belief in anything or anyone anymore - unless they prove it. Well, as this interview is over, you will have no more need for your camera to work - or the lighting - will you?

At this point, the bulb in the main light over Jason blew, and the cameraman was amazed to find that though the film he took was okay, the camera refused to work further, although there appeared to be nothing wrong with it. These facts were later added to the interview tape.

# THIRTY SIX
# THE 2004 TSUNAMI

[Note: Jason was asked several questions about his work as a healer during the late 2004 events in the Indian Ocean. The following is the conversation between him and his mother.]

I asked Jason if the tsunami was the beginning of the Earth changes, and he replied,

"No. That all started several months ago. If you have been having trouble with electrical equipment or problems tuning the radio, or poor television reception, etc., then that is an indirect result of the changes occurring in the energy field. Basically, the energy is changing in order to prepare all of you for the next stage. When will that be? That, again, will be up to all of you. There is no time limit in force here because time does not exist. Again, time is merely something that humankind invented to make them feel in control. When - and only when - the world is ready for the next stage will it occur, but the energies are already changing in preparation. I've already stated that the Earth herself is beginning to grow tired of the abuse by humans so the next stage is inevitable.

"Besides, the tsunami didn't begin as a natural disaster. I 'felt' this. A bomb was detonated below the floor of the Indian Ocean which resulted in movement in the tectonic plates. This then caused the massive underwater earthquake that led to the devastating tidal wave."

"Jason, we talked earlier in the book about your fear of disincarnate beings. Do you now work regularly with these beings?"

"Some souls are drawn to me or, more correctly, to my energy, and I have had to learn how to help them to move on. It's not much unlike my work when I am present at accidents or tragedies, only at those times, I do my best to help the living, too, by doing healing work until physical help arrives."

Just out of interest, I asked Jason to reiterate just what he does on the occasions when he is present at such accidents or tragedies. He answered,

"I am drawn to a human's energy field if they are still alive, and then I am seen by them to be very real. Just like when I attended the 9/11 tragedy, I was seen as a fireman.[1] As I said, I do what I can in the healing department and help to keep people alive until physical help arrives. Some people are really badly hurt, and, although they could recover in hospital, I always take into account their wishes. If they tell me to let them go as they have endured enough and no longer wish to carry on, then I take a step back until they have expired."

I cut him off at this point and said that he should automatically do all he can to save lives but he replied,

"No way. It's not my choice to make - it is theirs and I will always abide by their wishes."

Again, I said that perhaps he should go against their wishes - if they are able to recover - and show more compassion. After a few seconds of silently staring at me, he replied,

"If I had compassion in dealing with these situations, then I couldn't do my job. Compassion is an emotion, and emotions will always get in the way with this work. I have been very tired of late because, like many, many others, I have been helping out at the tsunami tragedy. There are hundreds of 'normal' people there who are able to travel - like me - and do all they can. However, so many 'helpers' can't handle what they see - which is understandable - and they just break down and become very emotional. So what possible use are they to anyone? Then someone else will have to come away from their work in order to help these emotional helpers, and this creates even more problems.

"Do you understand what I'm saying here? If I were ruled by emotion, then I simply could not do what I do. Apart from the mental strain, there would be the guilt of knowing that I would probably have been able to talk someone round and 'force' them to 'decide' to live. You consider that all life is precious - and it is, don't get me wrong - but you are all more than that, which is why you make choices in the first place. It is this about the human race which makes you what you are - you each have free will - the power to choose for yourselves, and that's what makes you worthwhile."

---

1. With regard to the 9/11 tragedy, it has since been confirmed to the author by two separate people (who are able to travel as he does) - who don't know each other - that they saw Jason going up a staircase as they were coming down. He was "dressed" as a fireman.

I then asked Jason about the several miraculous stories of survivors after the tsunami - some were found five to fourteen days later, and they didn't look that bad. One of these was a baby found floating on a mattress, who wasn't even sunburned. Could there be a "walk-ins" involved here? His reply was enlightening.

"Very possibly. I didn't see any news coverage about this particular event, but having said that, with so many bodies being vacated, then, yes, there would have been so many entities who would have thought it was their birthday - literally speaking as well! And as for the baby having hardly a scratch and not even being sunburned, that is easy to explain. You see, when an entity 'walks in' to a body, it doesn't matter what state the 'shell' is in, as long as it's intact, so it's very possible that the child could have been badly hurt and very sunburned. It's also possible that the child could have been dead for quite a while. As an entity prepares to use a body, that entity also has the power to repair damage, but only before said entity takes charge of the 'shell'. It cannot be done from within, as then the 'walk-in' has no power, as it would be inhibited by the human form and subject to the same laws of physics as the rest of you. This is why you read about these miraculous people who are thrown clear of major disasters and survive without a scratch on them, but that's after they have been 'repaired' by the new tenant! Also, many times you will find that these miraculous survivors suffer from amnesia. This is because the longer the body is left after the original inhabitant has vacated i.e. the person is dead, then the harder it is to access their memories. When the soul moves on, usually, so do all the memories of that incarnation."

I interrupted Jason here and asked if the "walk-ins" would have all been extraterrestrial. He replied,

"Define extraterrestrial, Mum."

"You know - beings not from here."

He sat staring at me for a moment then gave me a wry smile as he said, "But none of you are from 'here'."

At my insistence, he further explained:

"You have to remember that all creation of everything began with the One and spread out from that. Your souls are not indigenous to this world - they just inhabit the vehicles which are prepared for them, e.g. the mother having a baby as a result of both parents creating that baby. As the soul is indestructible, it is also an energy form - an entity if you prefer - and becomes human only when it 'takes up residence' in a human body.

"So, technically, you are all extraterrestrials in that sense, because there is no one amongst you who 'comes from here.' As everything began with the One, you must realize that no matter where you happen to reside - or what you reside as - we are all the same - energy from the One. This is true of all the solar systems, the planets, the many suns, this galaxy and other galaxies beyond and into infinity: They are all energy and all created from the One.

"This is what you humans have to aspire to - you must realize that you are all part of each other - a true collective, so to speak; but only when you can learn to stop judging each other and accept this, the ultimate truth, only then will .you be ready to ascend to join the many higher beings and develop your true potential. Whilst it is true that we each create our own destiny through the choices we make, on a bigger scale, this then is your ultimate destiny - to understand and accept your part in the creations of the One."

# Thirty Seven
# Jason's Thoughts

**Jason Andrews**

Photo by Paola Harris

I don't expect you to believe every word I say; I don't even ask you to believe every word I say; all I do ask is for you to try to keep an open mind about everything I tell you.

It was my choice to come here to this little blue planet in her hour of need in a desperate attempt to try to awaken people to:

> • their true potential; i.e. that they are all part of the Universe and, indeed, connected to Mother Earth herself, in that they are all able to use their psychic abilities for the good of humankind.

To help:

> • prevent people from following others blindly - like sheep; to make them think for themselves.

And,

  • to help people to be all that they can be, in any way that I can.

Having said all this - and everything that I have told Mum to add to the book - I still stress that I am very normal. To quote the Bard, "If you cut me, do I not bleed?" (literally, I might add! I hate the sight of blood - especially when it's mine!) My biggest problem on the human scale at the moment is getting my car to run properly, and to find a nicer area to live in for me and Jacqui!

I don't think I'm better than any one else - just different - and it's my job to try to help. I totally believe in the physical and mental potential of all humans, and I can see into their hearts. I'm just trying to do my bit as best I can.

Out of all the abilities I have, the one I appreciate most is being able to help others and being able to see the true being inside each of us. Whether I am doing healing work on this physical plane or on an astral plane, I am here to help.

People who know the real me always ask me those big questions: "Why am I here?" "Where am I from?" "What is my mission?" and even - "What is the point?" Other people ask me stuff on a more 'down-to-earth' basis like "How long have you been around?", "Did you know the Atlanteans? Were you around then?" "Does magic really exist?" "What's with all these so-called `Star Kids'?" However, no one's yet asked me if I know Elvis! I'm quite upset by that really, but in case you're wondering, the answer is `No, I don't know Elvis!'

Anyway, back to the serious stuff: I've been around in one form or another for millennia. I've known the Earth to destroy herself hundreds of times and I've no doubt that she will do so again. See, you have to start thinking outside the box in order to understand just where I'm truly coming from. Once you grasp the concept of time not existing, you'll see the entire Universe as being on a sort of constant loop - the same stuff happens again and again. This is why you will always find unexplained mysteries on this world - remnants of buildings which were built with such advanced technology yet in your estimation, they are thousands of years old. Now try taking away the age thing and look at them again - ancient texts and pictures depicting air ships and such - maybe you, too, will start to understand. Mind you, it's not all done by humankind; some of it was done by other travellers who visit from time to time, in the case of the Pyramids, for instance. You get so excited by it all, yet it's all a product of the loop.

The Atlanteans: now they were truly a race to be proud of. With them, it was like watching your kid win at the school sports day and being so proud you could burst. When they became all that they could be, we thought "Yes. Finally, we've cracked it." They were the result of all our hard work. They were what we had intended humankind to be all along. We did it. Their culture touched every remote part of the planet - they were spiritual people who lived in harmony - they were so intelligent. Your own Bible talks about "the garden of paradise." Think about it! This is why you now find so many things attributed to them.

The Atlanteans weren't just another race - like the Aztecs or Sumerians - they were humankind who had finally evolved. This is the part that you're not understanding: The Atlanteans encompassed all human kind throughout the globe. They were your predecessors - then they blew it. All that work, all that pride we had for them, our children, and they threw it away. Though spiritual, their intelligence kept their minds active - creating, and they soon put all this activity into technology. At first, it was harmless; just for fun, but then came the technological weapons, then the jealousy of others who had more or better - then, finally, the wars. They were responsible for wiping out not only themselves but the Earth, which had nurtured them so lovingly.

Think about it - where did such geniuses as Albert Einstein, Leonardo da Vinci, Wolfgang Mozart come from? It wasn't just luck of the draw. No, these guys had bypassed a few generations when they were born here, and they had conscious recall of their time in the paradise of Atlantis. I believe in the Buddhist religion, which says you are judged by what you do during this lifetime on the Earth, and, if you were one of the good guys, then you are given a better life in the next incarnation. But, if you did badly, then you'll be born again but descending the ladder, as it were. Finally, each of you should progress enough to be able to reach ascension - like crossing dimensions. So, hence, the genius gene - Einstein and company were just calling up the supreme intelligence they had once upon a lifetime.

Unfortunately though, this process also works in reverse, like this Illuminati lot, or, as some of you say, the New World Order. They have managed to manipulate their situation - again, thanks to their supreme intelligence - and they don't play by the same rules as the Buddhists do. You'll find that the guys at the very top of the tree, the highest echelons of power, are all direct descendants of Atlanteans. Hence the total recall of supreme intellect. Yet these were the guys who were directly responsible for the demise of Atlantis - and they'll do it all again. They will use every means at their disposal, including magic and the services of certain reptilian races who have their own agenda. They already have total control over world leaders - their puppets who think that money and power is the ultimate prize. But even the puppets are in for a real shock. Their masters use money and power merely as tools in the bigger game. No, they seek dominion over the very souls of others - of people who, like sheep, will blindly follow, tempted by the promise of whatever makes their shambles of a life on this Earth worthwhile.

No power, supreme being or other force, can ever take from you what you will always have - your soul - the essence that is everything you are. You wear the earthly bodies much as you wear your clothes, and that is in order to enjoy the physical aspects of the Great Mother - to see the colors of nature, feel the touch of another, to smell the flowers, to interact with other like-minded souls, to touch another's life, to care for and appreciate the beautiful animal kingdom. Your bodies are nothing more than a technological tool to facilitate appreciation of the physical. Your soul energy is the indestructible force of all humans, and this can never be controlled by another force - unless you allow it to be by giving your consent. So, be warned. This is what the Illuminati are all about. It is you - all of you - they want. They're trying to set themselves up as rivals to 'The One' - to `All That Is' as the Native Americans say. With regard to their control of this planet - they've already won that round. You'll never stop them. It's too late. Since technology improved so drastically in the last decade or so, it gave them the edge they needed. Their control is complete. It's the puppets I feel a little bit sorry for. They still don't understand that money and power soon won't mean a thing. Still, as they say, shit happens.

Magic. Does it exist? Of course it does, and just like everything on this planet, it is there to be used by all of you. So, what is it? Magic is purely the manipulation of the energies all around you. It can be used to control electrical things as well as the party tricks of moving objects `with the mind.' Levitation can be achieved for not only yourselves but also for heavy objects. The ones that came before you - human as well as other beings - knew all this; how else do you think the Great Pyramids and other such monumental buildings were built? Just think for a moment that the whole planet relies on electro-magnetic pulses to keep it spinning, and all electrical equipment is tuned in to these pulses in order to make them work. You can't see it; it's like the very air you breathe; yet you know it's there.

Remember too that everything in existence can be reduced to energy in one form or another. Think just a little further then and understand that magic is no more than the ability to manipulate such energy. However, to be able to do this, you have to be able to become as one with that energy in order to read it, to understand it, and, finally, to be able to bend it to your will. It is said that the force of your thought is very powerful, and mark my words, it is. It's hard to describe the prowess of magic in words but, as an example, think about this: You stand at one end of a large room whilst your friend stands at the far end of the same room. Now, if you whisper to your friend, they will not hear you, but if you shout, they will. So, in effect, what you are doing then is projecting your voice on a higher frequency. You are raising the tone of your voice. This frequency catches the energy pulses emanating around you and carries your voice to your friend. This is a very simplistic example of energy manipulation, but I hope you can understand the concept of magic a little more. And there's another thing which is grossly misunderstood, and I, personally, hate it when I hear people talk about 'black magic.' There is no such thing. Magic is magic, and it's the people who use it - whether for good or bad - who are themselves, good or bad.

Star Kids or Indigos. They are here at this time to teach and not to save. All throughout this work, I have maintained that I am not here to change the course of your history but purely to help, and only if that help is asked for. The Star Kids are doing exactly the same thing. We cannot interfere with you as a species, but we can try to teach you to help you head down the right road to becoming all that you truly are. The Star Kids are a reality - get used to it. Yet you still judge them by your standards. You don't understand yet that just because some of them are extremely young - like three or four of your years - and have no schooling and can't read or write, they can still teach you. You still believe that a three-year-old would have nothing to teach you. How arrogant you are. They are not coming from the standpoint of a mere child; they are much more. Their abilities should not ever be judged by your standards: Reading, writing, mathematics, etc., are all things by which you judge intelligence, yet these kids are so far advanced - that they don't necessarily need any of it. They can 'read' books if they want to - simply by running their hands over the pages and ` reading' or picking up the energy signature of the writer. They will know the gist of the story as well as how the writer felt when creating the words. They don't get the same picture of the book at the end of it as you do, but they can understand it in their way, and it makes sense to them. So, don't be fooled by their years, but rather connect with them; allow your life force to merge with theirs to learn, to become one - to become all that you are and can be.

Earth Changes. When the inevitable happens to your world - and this will happen - the Star Kids will be safe. Like me, they will continue; albeit in another form, but, no matter what happens - even if the planet is gone - we will ALL continue. However, the form in which you continue is maybe something that you should be thinking about! Have you done enough to warrant a new incarnation on a new planet? I've heard that scientists reckon that the Earth had a sister planet at one time, but take it from me, she has more than one - and all capable of sustaining life. Do you see what I'm getting at here?

Anyway, destruction of this planet may be a direct result of the power of the Illuminati, or, perhaps it will be that your Sun - which is nothing more than a giant hydrogen ball of gas - will finally penetrate the planet's protective barriers, or perhaps the Sun itself will explode, wiping out everything in the Solar System. There again, maybe Mother Earth herself has had enough of the desecration and outrageous rape of everything she has given you, and she will decide that enough's enough and will allow her core - her very life force - to cease rotation and will slowly allow herself to die whilst she still has some dignity. Maybe she will become angry - angrier than you could ever imagine - and will throw all sorts of "natural disasters" at you all, culminating in the great oceans rising and taking back the land. Maybe the dolphins and whales can then take back their rightful place - as the intelligence and guardians of this planet, as it was before the human race experiment was begun.

Do I know what is going to happen? Maybe. But then again - nothing is ever written in stone. Your destiny can be changed, but only you can decide if you've left it too long. I suggest that you all give it some serious thought.

I was recently asked what is my view of reality? My perception of reality is that there is no reality. As I, personally, consider all life forms and inanimate objects to be easily reduced to energy forms of one sort or another, then reality in such a context, has no meaning for me.

However, I consider that the one constant in all of this would be the energy of emotion; it is the love vibration in all of physical creation which could, ultimately, be perceived as my view of reality.

This view would be different of course for every human. Reality to someone would be to work for five days a week and then go to the pub at the weekend. That is their reality. Still others live for their families so their children would be their reality. A good career and ambition would be yet someone else's view - and that's fine; whatever works for you. For me though, I have the good fortune (or misfortune), to see beyond what is real and tangible so my view of reality encompasses the whole and goes beyond that which is known and taken for granted. As the spiritual energy of unconditional love nurtures the entire Universe that, then, is my reality - belief in the continuance of such a force.

Try to live in peace and harmony, or, as Mum always signs her letters:

With Much Love and Light,
Jason Simon Andrews

# THIRTY EIGHT
# FINAL THOUGHTS

Well, this is our story. Believe it or don't believe it - the choice is yours. I have shared with you the details of Jason's journey from infancy into young adulthood and beyond. I feel that much more awaits him in the future, including his responsibility to help the people of this planet in the way that only he knows.

Personally, I have always maintained that I am not on a crusade to change people's beliefs. We are not all sheep - most of us think for ourselves and have to make up our own minds as to what the truth really is.

Coming back to my own personal overview of our situation, we have many witnesses to things which go on here at our home - manifestations in and around the property, strange healings, channellings of entities, and strange lights in the sky which are drawn to this house.

Researchers have visited us in order to write about the strange phenomena, and those who have stayed overnight have gone away amazed by their own experiences.

We have, and do, interact with many different entities among which are the now much-talked-of greys, although apparently, size and different colorings make it clear that there is more than one type. Then there are the beautiful beings I refer to as Lion People, who are perhaps the designers and builders of great monuments here on Earth, such as the Great Pyramid at Cheops. I have also included my drawing of one such "cosmic warrior of wisdom."

There are the Pleiadians - light beings - who radiate love and compassion. Some people, on seeing them, have mistaken them for angels because of the love vibration that they carry and their appearance.

Daniel's soldier man, Junus, is one of the so-called "Nordics" - very human-looking entities.

Perhaps the most ancient of our visitors would have to be the "Guardians," who resemble giant preying mantis' (or grasshoppers as Jason first saw them) in appearance, but whose knowledge and wisdom is without equal. Jason tells me that even the young of these beings, are born with the same knowledge of their peers, as this information is passed on to them genetically.

All of these entities are here now, not just with us, but with many others around the world. All of these events, experiences, sightings, contacts, etc. are gathering momentum. There is a need - now - for people to be aware of what is happening to their world and around it and accept the fact that we don't - and never have - stood alone in the Universe.

The Native Americans have known about "them" for centuries and refer to "them" as the "Star Nations." Make no mistake, these "Star Nations" really do exist and are offering us, the people of the Earth, a helping hand - if we want to accept it.

# ABOUT THE AUTHOR

Photo by Paola Harris

**Ann Andrews**

Ann Andrews was born in South London and had a poor, but very happy upbringing. Her mother was a middle-class housewife, and she received her great love of nature and animals from her Romany father. At age 12, they moved to the country, where she subsequently met her husband, Paul of 29 years. They have two sons, Daniel, 27, and Jason, 23. It was after Jason was born that another well-hidden part of their lives came to light - that Jason and Ann are alien abductees. From that time the whole family was plagued by strange paranormal experiences. It took nearly 12 years to finally accept the possibility of alien interaction in their lives, after searching for any other explanation.

Ann is also the author of Abducted: The True Story of Alien Abduction in Rural England (1998), which documented the truth of their situation, and their fear, anger and confusion. Walking Between Worlds Belonging to None is written from a place of calm knowing of who they are. The entire family now feels able to deal with the alien agenda and all the paranormal things that continue to occur in their home, albeit it can still be disconcerting at times. Ann states that they now feel thankful - in a strange sort of way.

LaVergne, TN USA
12 August 2010
193089LV00005B/83/A